In case you want to be welcomed there.

We're here to see that you're always welcomed at establishments everywhere. That's why millions of people carry the American Express® Card — for peace of mind, confidence, and security, around the world or just around the corner.

do more **AMERICAN EXPRESS**

Cards

In case you're running low.

We're here to help with more than 190,000 Express Cash locations around the world. In order to enroll, just call American Express at 1 800 CASH-NOW before you start your vacation.

do more AMERICAN EXPRESS ®

Express Cash

And in case you'd rather be safe than sorry.

We're here with American Express® Travelers Cheques. They're the safe way to carry money on your vacation, because if they're ever lost or stolen you can get a refund, practically anywhere or anytime. To find the nearest place to buy Travelers Cheques, call 1 800 495-1153. Another way we help you do more.

do more

Travelers Cheques

Take a good look at the diners and notice that the menu appeals equally to body-builders and hedonists. Favorites include the vegetarian or eggplant lasagna, oven-roasted chicken Dijon, and Cajun-style ahi—and there are new specials every month. Future plans call for expansion into the space next door.

Kakaako Kitchen. 1216 Waimanu St. ☎ **808/596-7488.** Main courses $5.75–$8.50. Mon–Fri 6:30–10:15am and 10:30am–2pm; Sat 7–10:15am and 10:30am–2pm. No credit cards. GOURMET PLATE LUNCHES.

Island-style chicken linguine, homestyle pot roast, and "Kakaako burger" on a taro bun are among the many headliners in this industrial-style kitchen (decorated with art by local artists) near Ala Moana Center. The owners of 3660 On the Rise, a popular Kaimuki restaurant (see below), have turned their attentions here to elevating the local tradition called a plate lunch. Vegetarian specials, gourmet plate lunches, grilled lemon-miso salmon, homestyle mashed potatoes, homemade tofu burgers, fresh catch, ahi steak, and "mixed plate" with two entrees are becoming the lunches of choice among office workers in the area. The bread puddings, brownies, and lemon bars are among the award-winning desserts. At breakfast, omelets, scones, and fried rice fly out of the open kitchen. Although much of the business is takeout, there are tables for casual dining in a high-ceilinged, warehouse-like room.

Kua Aina. 1116 Auahi St. ☎ **808/591-9133.** Sandwiches $3.50–$5.70. No credit cards. Daily 10:30am–9pm. AMERICAN.

A North Shore fixture for years, the ultimate sandwich shop has come to the Ward Center area (near Borders and Starbucks), and the result is dizzying. Phone in your order if you can. During lunch and dinner hours, long lines of the faithful wait patiently for Kua Aina's famous burgers and sandwiches: mahi-mahi with ortega and cheese (a legend); grilled eggplant and peppers; roast turkey; tuna-avocado; roast beef and avocado; and about a dozen other selections on Kaiser rolls, multigrain wheat, or rye breads. Because there are more diners than space (only a few tables and a small counter), takeout is a good idea.

Mocha Java. At Ward Centre, 1200 Ala Moana Blvd. ☎ **808/591-9023.** Most items under $7.95. MC, V. Mon–Sat 8am–9pm; Sun 8am–4pm. COFFEEHOUSE/CRÉPERIE.

This tiny cafe is a Honolulu staple; loyal followers love the spinach-lemon crêpes and the eight types of veggie burgers, as well as the Java Jolt double espresso and light-and-tasty tofu scramble. Light, wholesome fare is the order of the day: breakfast crêpes and omelets; sandwiches, salads, burritos, and crêpe specials for lunch and dinner; fresh fruit smoothies; homemade soups; and many other choices. The eclectic menu includes stir-fries, Mexican salads and burritos, curried crêpes—nothing fancy, but satisfying.

Siam Orchid. 1517 Kapiolani Blvd. ☎ **808/955-6161.** Reservations recommended. Main courses $6.95–$12.95. AE, DC, DISC, JCB, MC, V. Mon–Sat 11am–2pm and 5:30–9:30pm; Sun 5:30–9:30pm. THAI.

Just around the corner from its previous location and still a stone's throw from Ala Moana Center, this restaurant serves its tasty-beyond-belief Tom Yum spicy shrimp soup; fiery Thai garlic shrimp; and a panang vegetable curry with tofu, one of a dozen great offerings for vegetarians. Noodle lovers may consider the pad Thai fried noodles with shrimp, and curry lovers will be pleased with the extensive selection of chicken, beef, pork, shrimp, and vegetables in the rich, nutty panang sauce or in traditional red, green, and yellow versions. For $11.95, the buffet lunch offers a generous sampling of this popular cuisine.

ALOHA TOWER MARKETPLACE
MODERATE

✪ **Chai's Island Bistro.** 1 Aloha Tower Drive. ☎ **808/585-0011.** Reservations recommended. Main courses $14–$20. AE, DC, JCB, MC, V. Mon–Fri 11am–4pm; daily 4–10pm. PACIFIC RIM/ASIAN.

Owner-chef Chai Chaowasaree, also owner of Singha Thai Restaurant in Waikiki, has done a fine job of creating a tasteful tropical fantasy in the Aloha Tower Marketplace, where visually arid interiors are the norm. His 200-seat restaurant has high ceilings, a good location (although not on the waterfront), indoor-outdoor seating, a discreetly placed (not in-your-face) open kitchen, gleaming bar, mirrored walls with arches, and attractive dinnerware on white linens. This is not your typical good-food-but-ambience-be-damned ethnic restaurant. Large windows wrap around the dining room, offering good people-watching views that are transformed in the evening when the trees outside, entwined with fairy lights, light up. And the food is equal to the ambience. The appetizer sampler ($19.95 for two) appears in a boat-sized platter, a visual and gustatory feast of ahi katsu with yellow curry sauce and wasabi; crisp duck lumpia, tasty and not at all oily; macadamia-nut crusted tiger prawns; and Alaskan king crab cakes. These delights are gorgeously presented on perky lettuces that reach skyward from a wedge of pineapple and slices of cucumber. The menu is much more ambitious than Singha (and pricier too), with fusion dishes such as Japanese eggplant and zucchini souffle, escargots, steamed onaga, Asian osso bucco with kabocha pumpkin, and an ample selection of vegetarian dishes. Highly recommended are the mahi-mahi with Thai red curry sauce and the grilled chicken sate with Thai peanut sauce, the latter fork-tender and perfect. Fresh warm focaccia appears in a rattan steamer with Thai peanut dipping sauce—a nice touch.

Don Ho's Island Grill. 1 Aloha Tower Drive. ☎ **808/528-0807.** Reservations recommended. Main courses $6.95–$15.95. AE, DC, JCB, MC, V. Daily 11am–2am. HAWAIIAN/CONTEMPORARY ISLAND.

The frequent appearances of the Brothers Cazimero at this new harborfront site signal a vigorous new direction for the Aloha Tower Marketplace. A welcome sight, the Brothers have been packing in the dinner and after-hour crowds despite so-so food quality. Let's hope that changes. Don Ho's shrine to Don Ho is a mix of nostalgic interior elements: koa paneling, thatched roof, split-bamboo ceilings, old pictures of Ho with celebrities, faux palm trees, and open sides looking out into the harbor. Down to the vinyl pareu-printed tablecloths and the flower behind the server's ear, it's kitschy and charming. But the food, despite consultant Mark Ellman's (of the erstwhile Avalon) involvement, gets lower marks than the atmosphere and service. Too much grease, too little sizzle. A safe bet: the "surf pie" pizza.

Gordon Biersch Brewery Restaurant. In Aloha Tower Marketplace, 1 Aloha Tower Dr. ☎ **808/599-4877.** Reservations recommended. Main courses $8–$20. AE, CB, DC, DISC, JCB, MC, V. Sun–Wed 10:30am–10pm; Thurs–Sat 10:30am–12pm. NEW AMERICAN/PACIFIC RIM.

German-style lagers brewed on the premises would be enough of a draw, but the food is an equal attraction at Gordon Biersch, one of Honolulu's liveliest after-work destinations. The lanai bar and the brewery bar—open until 1am—are the brightest spots in the marketplace, always teeming with downtown types who nosh on pot stickers, grilled steaks, baby-back ribs, chicken pizza, garlic fries, and any number of American classics with deft cross-cultural touches. Live music is a popular weekend feature.

DOWNTOWN

Downtowners love the informal walk-in cafes lining one side of attractive **Bishop Square**, at 1001 Bishop St. (at King Street), in the middle of the business district, where free entertainment is offered every Friday during lunch hour. The popular **Che Pasta** is a stalwart of the square, chic enough for business meetings and not too formal (or expensive) for a spontaneous rendezvous over pasta and minestrone soup. With its sandwiches, salads, and pasta and sprinkling of tables outdoors, **Heidi's Bread Basket** is another Bishop Square staple. Nearby, **Yummy's BBQ** serves Korean plate lunches; **Harpo's** caters to the pizza set, and **Kyotaru** to lovers of Japanese bento lunches. Some establishments open for breakfast and lunch, others open for lunch only, but most of them close when the business offices empty. Watch for **On the Juice** to open soon.

MODERATE

Café VIII. 1067 Alakea St. ☎ **808/524-4064.** Main courses $5.50–$11. AE, DC, MC, V. Mon–Fri 11:30–2:30; dinner by special arrangement for 8 or more. ITALIAN.

The downtown crowd can barely get enough of this indoor-outdoor cafe and its great Italian fare: kiawe-wood grilled panini (steak, vegetarian, and chicken) and a select menu of soup (puréed red pepper with roasted vegetables), kiawe-grilled steak on zucchini pesto pasta, and pasta dishes. Lasagne, puttanesca, carbonara, Bolognese—the pastas are the draw here, but we like the polenta and mashed potatoes, too. Forty can sit indoors, but there is a garden terrace for the overflow crowd.

Honolulu Coffee Co. In Grosvenor Center, 741 Bishop St. ☎ **808/533-1500.** Sandwiches $6.45–$7.75. JCB, MC, V. Mon–Fri 6am–5pm. COFFEEHOUSE/SANDWICHES.

Formerly Café Vienna, this gleaming coffeehouse/sandwich bar is the saving grace of busy downtown working folks and travelers in the mood for a quality, fresh-brewed coffee drink and sandwich. This isn't the kind of place in which you'd linger over a power lunch, but the sandwiches have gained a reputation: Tuscan salami, smoked turkey breast, Reuben on rye, vegetarian panini, roast chicken with havarti cheese and lemon basil aïoli. The salads—mixed greens fresh from Waimanalo, sesame chicken, white bean, herbed potato, grilled vegetables—go perfectly with all of it, including the creamy Seattle clam chowder. Espresso, cappuccino, gelato, and pastries round out the small but well-executed menu.

Indigo Eurasian Cuisine. 1121 Nuuanu Ave. ☎ **808/521-2900.** Reservations recommended. Lunch $5.50–$16.50; main dishes $12–$20 at dinner. CB, DC, DISC, JCB, MC, V. Tues–Fri 11:30am–2pm and 5:30–9:30pm; Sat 5:30–9:30pm. EURASIAN.

Hardwood floors, red brick, wicker, high ceilings, and an overall feeling of informal luxe give Indigo a stylish look. Dine indoors or in a garden setting on choices that include pot stickers, Buddhist bao buns, brochettes, tandoori chicken breast, miso grilled salmon, Asian-style noodles, dumplings with Far-East fillings, lilikoi-glazed baby-back ribs, and a host of offerings from east and west.

✪ **Legend Seafood Restaurant.** In Chinese Cultural Plaza, 100 N. Beretania St. ☎ **808/532-1868.** Reservations recommended. Most items under $15. AE, DC, JCB, MC, V. Mon–Fri 10:30am–2pm and 5:30–10pm; Sat–Sun 8am–2pm and 5:30–10pm. DIM SUM/SEAFOOD.

It's like dining in Hong Kong here, with a Chinese-speaking clientele poring over Chinese newspapers and the clatter of chopsticks punctuating conversations. Superb dim sum comes in bamboo steamers that beckon seductively from carts. Although dining here is a form of assertiveness training (you must wave madly to catch the server's eye and then point to what you want), the system doesn't deter fans from returning. Among our favorites: deep-fried taro puffs and prawn dumplings; shrimp dim sum;

vegetable dumplings; and the rolled seafood with shiitake, scallops, and a tofu product called *aburage*. Dim sum is served only at lunch, but at dinner, the seafood comforts sufficiently.

Palomino. In Harbor Court Building, 66 Queen St. ☎ **808/528-2400.** Reservations recommended. Main dishes $5.95–$26.95. AE, DC, DISC, MC, V. Mon–Fri 11am–2:30pm; Sun–Thurs 5–10pm; Fri–Sat 5–11pm. MEDITERRANEAN.

Palomino came galloping in and took Honolulu by storm. Now *the* downtown hot spot, it offers splendid harbor views, stunning architecture, conscientious service, and good food that's also affordable. It's huge but always full (including the separate bar and lounge, Honolulu's liveliest spot), with a cheerful open kitchen festooned with strands of peppers and garlic. From the kitchen stream kiawe-grilled fish and meats; spit-roasted pork loin and garlic chicken; pastas and salads; and pizzas with savory embellishments, such as caramelized onion and spinach. We adore the grilled wild mushrooms (a meal in itself), the Basque chicken with polenta mashed potatoes, and the cedar-plank roasted salmon with garlic vermouth butter. Roasted garlic, zesty dips for the focaccia, and a devastating pear bread pudding offer heaps of dining enjoyment.

✪ **Sunset Grill.** Restaurant Row, 500 Ala Moana Blvd. ☎ **808/521-4409.** Reservations recommended for dinner. Main courses $8–$26. AE, DC, DISC, MC, V. Mon–Thurs 11am–11pm; Fri 11am–midnight; Sat 5pm–midnight; Sun 5–10pm. SAN FRANCISCO–STYLE BISTRO CUISINE.

When *Wine Spectator* granted its "Award of Excellence" to Sunset Grill recently, it highlighted the extensive wine list. Rare vintages, a strong selection of wines by the glass (including one of Hawaii's best selections of hard-to-find Turley), a 400-bottle wine list, and an impressive menu of homemade pastas, fish, meats, appetizers, and homemade desserts are among the offerings. Standouts include smoke-infused salmon with warm shiitake mushroom salsa on seasonal vegetables, and the seared crab cakes with shoyu vinaigrette, a nice touch. Count on crisp, straightforward, elegant, ungimmicky cuisine: pasta with fresh ahi and tomato-basil sauce; a changing roster of risottos; kiawe-grilled ribs; and special touches such as Tuscan mashed potatoes, housemade Cajun-style potato chips, and oven-roasted garlic with goat cheese. A good bet, all the way around.

✪ **Yanagi Sushi.** 762 Kapiolani Blvd. ☎ **808/597-1525.** Reservations recommended. Main courses $8–$33; complete dinners $11.50–$18.50. AE, CB, DC, DISC, JCB, MC, V. Daily 11am–2pm; Mon–Sat 5:30pm–2am; Sun 5:30–10pm. JAPANESE.

We love the late-night hours, the sushi bar with its fresh ingredients and well-trained chefs, and the extensive choices of combination lunches and dinners. But we also love the à la carte Japanese menu, which covers everything from *chazuke* (rice with tea, salmon, seaweed, and other condiments—a comfort food) to shabu-shabu and other steaming earthenware-pot dishes. Nosh on noodles or complete dinners with choices of sashimi, shrimp tempura, broiled salmon, New York steak, and many other possibilities. Dine affordably or extravagantly, on $6 noodles or a $30 lobster nabe, or on nearly 20 different types of sashimi. Consistently crisp tempura, affordable combination lunches, and one of the town's finer spicy ahi hand-rolled sushi also make Yanagi worth remembering.

INEXPENSIVE

Kengo's. 500 Ala Moana Blvd., Restaurant Row. ☎ **808/533-0039.** Lunch buffet, adults $11.95, children $7.95; dinner buffet adults $23.95, children $10.95. AE, DC, DISC, MC, V. Daily 11am–2pm and 5:30–9:30pm. LOCAL BUFFET.

Kengo's is the place that pleases parents, kids, and grandparents, who line up for the prime rib and seafood buffet, the salad and fresh fruit bar, the sushi bar with sashimi and poke, and the dessert bar with soft-frozen yogurt and surprises. The dinner buffet isn't cheap, but for crab legs and sashimi, it's a value for those with unabashed appetites. Kengo's is known for its salad bar of local favorites, everything from kimchee to seaweed salads and local fruit in season.

Ocean Club. In Restaurant Row, 500 Ala Moana Blvd. ☎ **808/526-9888.** Reservations recommended. No T-shirts or beachwear allowed, and the minimum age is 23. All items $5–$9 ($2–$5 at happy hour). AE, DISC, MC, V. Tues–Thurs 4:30pm–2am; Fri 4:30pm–3am; Sat 6pm–3am. SEAFOOD.

Ocean Club could be listed as a restaurant or a night club, but we list it here because it's so much more than a drinks-only joint. Brilliant and masterfully executed, Ocean Club is a sleek, chic magnet that has redefined happy hour with its extended hours of slashed prices, excellent appetizers-only seafood menu, and ultra-cool ambience of fake mahi-mahi and frosted glass dangling from the ceiling in a quasi-fifties-retro mood. Galvanized steel counters, mahogany bars lined with shoyu bottles, linoleum tile floors, and oddly attractive pillars resembling pahu (Hawaiian drums) are a wonderfully eclectic mix. Add deejays in bowling shirts and cat-eyed eyeglasses playing the Kingston Trio, and you get the picture. The menu of appetizers lives up to its "ultimate cocktail hour" claim, especially from 4:30 to 8pm nightly, when great seafood is slashed to half-price and the upbeat mood starts spiraling. A happy-hour sampling: huge lobster claws; a toothsome spinach and artichoke dip served with tortilla chips, salsa, and sour cream; Pacific crab dip; ahi tacos; fresh ahi poke; fresh, good-quality sashimi; and oyster, shrimp, or crab shooters.

Payao. In Restaurant Row, 500 Ala Moana Blvd. ☎ **808/521-3511.** Lunch special $8; dinner main courses $7.95–$12.95. AE, CB, DC, DISC, JCB, MC, V. Mon–Sat 11am–2pm; daily 5–10pm. THAI.

With its few tables indoors and 30 seats in open-air terrace-style dining, Payao brings a pleasing presence to Restaurant Row. The owners of Chiang Mai restaurant (see below) opened their uptown version with their familiar Thai specialties, among them the best-selling green fish curry, hot spicy seafood combo, spicy Tom Yum soup, and Thai vegetarian broccoli noodles. Payao's Thai noodle dishes (curried, in black-bean sauce, and with vegetables) are a good bet, as is the popular lemongrass chicken and eggplant with basil and tofu.

KALIHI/SAND ISLAND
MODERATE

La Mariana Restaurant & Bar. 50 Sand Island Rd. ☎ **808/848-2800.** Reservations recommended, especially on weekends. Main courses $11.95–$17.95. AE, MC, V. Daily 11:30am–11:30pm; lunch 11:30am–2pm; pupus 3–5pm; dinner Sun–Thurs 5–9pm, Fri–Sat 5–10pm. AMERICAN.

To find it, turn makai (toward the ocean) on Sand Island Road from Nimitz Highway; immediately after the first stoplight on Sand Island, take a right and drive to the ocean—it's not far from the airport. Try to find a spot more evocative, more nostalgic than this South Seas oasis at water's edge in the bowels of industrial Honolulu, with carved tikis, glass balls suspended in fishing nets, 1950s shell chandeliers, and tables made from koa trees before they became scarce. Owner Annette La Mariana Nahinu, who also runs the La Mariana Sailing Club, is the most sprightly octogenarian you could hope to meet, a bon vivant who crossed the South Pacific in a 36-foot sailboat before settling in Hawaii, where she wound up converting a Honolulu junkyard into a lush marina. Enveloped in greenery at water's edge, and furnished with furniture from the old Trader Vic's and South Seas restaurants, this unique 45-year-old establishment is popular for lunch, sunset appetizers, and impromptu Friday and Saturday night sing-alongs at the piano bar. Seared Cajun-style ahi is your best bet as appetizer or entree.

Sam Choy's Breakfast, Lunch, Crab & Big Aloha Brewery. 580 Nimitz Hwy., Iwilei (in the Iwilei industrial area near Honolulu Harbor, across the street from Gentry Pacific Center). ☎ **808/545-7979.** Reservations recommended for lunch and dinner. Main courses $5–$10 at breakfast; $6–$27 at lunch; $19–$35 at dinner. AE, DC, DISC, JCB, MC, V. Mon–Fri 6:30–10am, 10:30am–4pm, 5–10pm; Sat–Sun 6:30–11:30am, 11:30am–4pm, 5–10pm. ISLAND CUISINE/SEAFOOD.

Until Sam Choy's opened in this industrial part of Honolulu, Hawaii diners had long lamented the absence of an informal, roll-up-your-sleeves-and-get-messy kind of restaurant where you could crack crab with mallets and wear plastic bibs with abandon. Voilà! This is a happy, carefree eatery, elegance and cholesterol be damned. Chef-restaurateur Sam Choy's long-awaited crab house, open since May 1997, features great fun and fabulous food (big meals are, after all, the Choy trademark). Imagine dining in an all-wood sampan (it's the centerpiece of the 11,000-square-foot restaurant) and washing your hands in an oversized wok in the center of the room, under a faucet activated by an automatic sensor (the kind that wreaks havoc in airport bathrooms). That giant wok comes in handy, as the menu ensures delightfully messy dining—if not on beef stew, omelets, and fried rice at breakfast, or the Hawaiian plate and fresh fish at lunch, then decidedly at dinner, when all thoughts turn to the featured attraction: crab.

A 2,000-gallon live crab tank lines the open kitchen, serving as temporary shelter for the assortment of crabs in season: Kona, Maryland, Samoan, Dungeness, and Florida stone crabs. Clam chowder, seafood gumbos, assorted poke, and an oyster bar and brew pub are also offered at dinner, which, in Choy fashion, comes complete with soup, salad, and entree. The priciest items are the surf-and-turf combinations of lobster or crab with ribs or New York steak—heroic, for sure. Children's menus—needed more than ever at Choy's restaurants—are an additional family feature. The eight varieties of "Big Aloha Beer," brewed on-site, go well with the crab and poke.

✪ **Yohei Sushi.** 1111 Dillingham Blvd., across from Honolulu Community College. ☎ **808/ 841-3773.** Reservations recommended. Lunch entrees $6–$15; complete dinners $15–$24. DC, JCB, V, MC. Mon–Sat 11am–1:45pm and 5–9:30pm.

Yohei is difficult to find, tucked away in a small, nondescript complex just before Dillingham crosses the bridge into Kalihi, Honolulu's industrial area. But it's well worth the hunt, especially for lovers of authentic Tokyo-style sushi. Duck into the tiny room, find a seat at the sushi bar, and partake of the sweet shrimp (amaebi), surf clam (akagai), yellowtail tuna (hamachi), butterfly tuna (negi toro temaki), bluefish (kohada gari chiso temaki), and wonderful assortment of seafood, fresh as can be. A friend from Tokyo discovered this restaurant for us and gave it her highest approval for authenticity, freshness, quality, and—surprise!—price. An evening at Yohei is like a trip to a Tokyo sushi bar, where regulars know the chef and even familiar gastronomic territory can be a grand adventure. A must for the sushi aficionado.

MANOA VALLEY/MOILIILI/MAKIKI
EXPENSIVE

✪ **Alan Wong's Restaurant.** 1857 S. King St., 3rd floor. ☎ **808/949-2526.** Reservations recommended. Main courses $15–$30; chef's tasting menu $45–$85. AE, DC, JCB, MC, V. Daily 5–10pm. HAWAII REGIONAL.

A brilliant chef with staying power, Alan Wong has influenced the direction of regional cuisine, and owns what is arguably Honolulu's busiest restaurant: a 90-seat room with a glassed-in terrace and open kitchen, accented with stylish and imposing floral arrangements, minimalist avant-garde lighting, and curly-koa wall panels. Superb food offerings come in creative architectural presentations—high-rise towers of multiple layers and colors, such as the famous ahi cake with layers of grilled eggplant, Maui onion, seared ahi, and Big Island goat cheese with Puna goat cheese–lemongrass dressing. Wong's offerings are always at the cutting edge, with flavors that sizzle with Asian lemongrass, sweet-sour, garlic, wasabi, and other assertive ingredients that he deftly melds with the fresh seafood and produce of the islands. The California roll is a triumph, made with salmon roe, wasabi, and Kona lobster, served warm—and without rice. We love the imaginative opihi shooter, the kalua pig lumpia with luau leaves and butterfish, and the ginger-crusted onaga with miso-sesame vinaigrette. But don't get attached, because the menu changes daily.

✪ **Chef Mavro Restaurant.** 1969 S. King St. ☎ 808/944-4714. Reservations required. Main courses $27–$34. AE, DC, MC, V. Daily 6–9:30pm. MEDITERRANEAN/FRENCH.

Chef-owner George Mavrothalassitis, a native of Provence, has fans all over the world. At La Mer in the Halekulani and Seasons in Four Seasons Resort Wailea, he master-minded many of Hawaii's most memorable culinary experiences. People talked about his dinners for days. Finally, in a conveniently accessible, un-touristy neighborhood in McCully, not far from Alan Wong's, he has opened his own restaurant, a warm and elegant place of pampering. You can choose from an à la carte menu or three prix-fixe selections ($48 for three courses, $57 for four courses, $72 for six courses, more with paired wines). Underscoring Mavro's allegiance to the total dining experience, even the à la carte menu has suggested wine pairings. To his list of signature items (ahi tartare with caviar, award-winning onaga baked in Hawaiian salt crust), he's added new taste sensations: gingered Hudson Valley foie gras (using hard-to-find Hawaiian salt from Hanapepe, Kauai), charboiled Keahole lobster with Molokai sweet potato purée, roasted Sonoma squab with wild mushrooms and truffle sauce, and goat cheese from the Loire Valley. Hints of Tahitian vanilla, lemongrass, ogo, rosemary, and Madras curry add exotic flavors to the French-inspired cooking and fresh island ingredients. The room is quiet and cordial, seating 68, and the menu changes monthly to high-light seasonal ingredients at their peak. This is Mavro magic at its best.

MODERATE

Chiang Mai. 2239 S. King St. ☎ **808/941-1151.** Reservations suggested for dinner. Main courses $8–$13. AE, DC, DISC, MC, V. Mon–Fri 11am–2pm; daily 5:30–10pm. THAI.

This was one of Honolulu's early Thai restaurants and it has retained a stalwart following despite fierce competition. Recently expanded to accommodate 100, Chiang Mai made sticky rice famous, serving it in bamboo steamers to accompany excellent red, green, and yellow curries. Chiang Mai makes great noodles, from vegetarian broccoli to curry rice noodles, and tasty green papaya salad and hot spicy clams. Spicy shrimp soup, eggplant with basil and tofu, and the vegetarian green curry are some time-honored favorites. The vegetarian menu is superb, and new fresh-fish dishes are a welcome addition.

Contemporary Museum Cafe. In The Contemporary Museum, 2411 Makiki Heights Dr. ☎ 808/523-3362. Reservations recommended. Main courses $8–$11. MC, V. Tues–Sat 10am–2pm; Sun noon–2pm lunch, until 3pm dessert. PACIFIC RIM/MEDITERRANEAN.

The surroundings play an integral part of the dining experience at this tiny lunchtime cafe, which is located in an art museum nestled on the slopes of Tantalus. Set amid carefully cultivated Oriental gardens, the cafe also has a breathtaking view of Diamond Head and priceless contemporary art displayed indoors and outdoors. The menu is limited to sandwiches, soups, salads, and appetizers, but you won't leave disappointed: They are the perfect lunchtime fare, especially in this environment. Before crowning the meal with flourless chocolate cake, consider the grilled eggplant sandwich, excellent bruschetta, portabello or Greek salad, or the fresh fish specials.

Diem. 2633 S. King St. ☎ **808/941-8657.** Reservations recommended for dinner. Main courses $6–$10. AE, DISC, JCB, MC, V. Mon–Sat 11am–3pm; 5–9:30pm. VIETNAMESE.

We love Diem for its Royal Seafood noodle soup; its roll-up appetizers (fish, shrimp, beef, seafood); its spicy fried rice, vegetarian or with shrimp or chicken; its eggplant with tofu and basil; and its lemongrass fish, chicken, seafood, and vegetarian dishes. Crisp fish and energetic curries also score high on this menu of simple delights, which caters as much to tofu-loving vegetarians as to beef and pork enthusiasts. The tiny eatery in the university area has earned its following by word of mouth and spreads the taste treats with a thriving catering business.

Fook Yuen Seafood Restaurant. 1960 Kapiolani Blvd., Suite 200. ☎ **808/973-0168.** Reservations recommended. Daily lunch buffet $6.95; main courses $8.99–$14.50. AE, DC, DISC, JCB, MC, V. Daily 11am–2pm and 5:30pm–3am. CANTONESE.

Tables fill up quickly at this popular Hong Kong–style Cantonese restaurant, where the happy clicking of chopsticks resounds over platters heaped with Dungeness crab, sizzling king prawns, and urns of exotic soups (shark's fin, bird's nest, dried scallop, fish maw with crabmeat). There are nearly 140 items on this extensive menu, most of them seafood (live Maine lobster, live Dungeness crab, steamed fresh fish, shrimp Szechuan-style, sautéed king clam, sautéed sea bass). Some of these items are market priced by season and can be expensive, but the menu choices are vast enough to make Fook Yuen a strong recommendation for all but the tightest budgets. The "sizzling platters" come crackling with king prawns, oysters, scallops, beef, and chicken, served with tasty accompaniments (satay, Szechuan, black-bean sauces). The house specialty, sautéed king prawns with honey-glazed walnuts, is a major attraction.

Maple Garden. 909 Isenberg St. ☎ **808/941-6641.** Main courses $5–$29.50. AE, JCB, MC, V. Daily 11am–2pm and 5:30–10pm. SZECHUAN.

In addition to the Peking duck—which has earned its noble reputation and must be ordered a day in advance—Maple Garden is known for many specialties. The Chinaman's Hat, a version of mu shui pork, is reliably good, and you can order it vegetarian as well. *Hot tip:* The crisp green beans are out of this world, vegetarian or not. Other hits are braised scallops with Chinese mushrooms, spicy garlic eggplant, diced chicken with chili, prawns in chili sauce, and chicken in five spices. The more subdued can try the vegetarian selections (sautéed spinach is a good bet) or any of the dozens of seafood entrees—everything from sea cucumbers to lobster with black-bean sauce and braised salmon. An ever-expanding visual feast adorns the dining-room walls, covered with noted artist John Young's original drawings, sketches, and murals.

Shipley's Alehouse and Grill. 2756 Woodlawn Drive. ☎ **808/988-5555.** Reservations recommended. Main courses $11.50–$20.50. AE, DC, DISC, MC, V. Tues–Fri 11:30am–10pm; Sat–Sun 4–10pm; bar open until midnight, 2am on weekends. AMERICAN.

If you're curious about Kona Lilikoi, Wild Irish Rogue, Taddy Porter, Black Butte Porter, Spaten Optimator, Oatmeal Stout, and nearly 100 other beers from the breweries of the world, ship off to Shipley's. Sunday night jam sessions with top Hawaiian performers add to the convivial atmosphere in the split-level, high-beamed room, and the food is hearty—gregarious American stuff, friendly all the way. Best loved are the beer-battered fish (fresh mahi-mahi) and chips, the fresh beer-battered onion rings, and the clam chowder. Top of the line are the wonderful cedar-roasted salmon entree ($18.50) and fresh farm-raised salmon roasted by the Shipleys themselves, served with an oven-baked apple half, spinach mashed potatoes, and a lemon-sherry butter sauce.

Live Hawaiian music from 9:30pm Saturdays and 7:30pm Sundays keeps new diners coming and fans returning.

Sushi King. 2700 S. King St. ☎ **808/947-2836.** Reservations recommended. Main courses $11.50–$25. AE, CB, DC, DISC, JCB, MC, V. Wed–Mon 11:30am–2pm and 5:30pm–2am; Tues 5:30–10pm. JAPANESE.

Brusque service sure doesn't deter diners from arriving in throngs for the lunch specials here, and they're highly recommended. This is the king of excellent jumbo platters, with soup, pickles, California roll, and your choice of chicken teriyaki, beef teriyaki, shrimp and vegetable tempura, and calamari and vegetable tempura—all for an unbelievable $6.95. Other combination lunches offer generous choices: sashimi, tempura, butterfish, fried oysters, soba noodles, udon noodles, and more than a dozen other selections. The à la carte menu is equally appealing, with noodles, *donburi* (steamed rice with tempura and other toppings), grilled fish, sushi-sashimi combinations, and sushi from the always-full sushi bar. The robata bar offers a wide selection of grilled shellfish, fish, meats, and vegetables, from $3.50 to $9.95 an order. The specials are continued as early-bird specials daily from 5:30 to 6:30pm. This is a top value for lovers of Japanese food.

INEXPENSIVE

Andy's Sandwiches & Smoothies. 2904 E. Manoa Rd., opposite Manoa Marketplace. ☎ **808/988-6161.** Also at 745 Keeaumoku St. near Ala Moana Center, ☎ 808/946-6161. Most items less than $5. MC, V. Mon–Thurs 7am–6pm; Fri 7am–5pm; Sat 7am–2:30pm; Sun 7am–2:30pm. GOURMET HEALTH FOOD.

It started as a health-food restaurant, expanded into a juice bar, and today is a neighborhood fixture for fresh-baked bread, healthy breakfasts and lunches (its mango muffins are famous), and vegetarian fare. Andy's is a roadside stop that always carries fresh papayas, sandwiches, and healthy snacks for folks on the run. The ahi deluxe sandwich is tops, but the fresh-roasted turkey sandwiches are the acclaimed favorite.

India Bazaar. Old Stadium Square, 2320 S. King St. ☎ **808/949-4840.** Main courses $6–$7. No credit cards. Daily 11am–9pm. INDIAN.

Spicy curries, crispy papadams, moist chapatis, and the full range of Indian delicacies are served from a counter where you point and choose. The vegetables are overcooked in the Indian fashion, but the flavors bring redemption. A few tables are scattered about a room filled with the scent of spices; one wall is lined with exotic chutneys and Indian condiments for home-cooking. The vegetarian thalli is a favorite: The spiced Indian rice comes with your choice of three vegetable curries and other choices, such as lentil, cauliflower, eggplant, tofu/peas, potato, spinach/lentil, garbanzo beans, and okra. Chicken tandoori (with two vegetable curries) and shrimp thalli appeal to non-vegetarians.

✪ **Jimbo's Restaurant.** 1936 S. King St. ☎ **808/947-2211.** Reservations not accepted. Main courses $5–$10.75. MC, V. Daily 11am–3pm; Sun–Thurs 5–10pm; Fri–Sat 5–11pm. JAPANESE.

Jimbo's could have been featured in *Tampopo,* the movie about the quest for the perfect bowl of noodles. It's tiny (fewer than a dozen tables), and there's such a demand for its sublime fare that you may have to wait for a seating. It's worth it. A must for any noodle lover, Jimbo's serves homemade udon noodles in a flawless homemade broth with a subtly smoky flavor, and then tops the works with shrimp tempura, chicken, eggs and vegetables, seaweed, roasted mochi, and a variety of accompaniments of your choice. The Zouni, with chicken, vegetables, and mochi rice roasted to a toasty flavor, is one of life's great pleasures. Cold noodles, stir-fried noodles, donburi steamed-rice dishes with assorted toppings, Japanese-style curries, and combination dinners served on trays are among the many delights that keep diners returning. The earthenware pot of noodles, with shiitake mushrooms, vegetables, and udon, and a platter of tempura on the side, is the top-of-the-line combo, a designer dish at an affordable price. Our fave is the nabeyaki (an earthenware pot of udon with tempura on top), but the curries are also popular. Owner Jimbo Motojima, a perfectionist, uses only the finest ingredients from Japan.

Mary Catherine's Bakery & Café. 2820 S. King St. ☎ **808/946-4333.** Breakfast $3.50–$5.95; lunch main courses $5.50–$6.95. AE, MC, V. Bakery Mon–Sat 7am–7pm; cafe daily 7am–2pm. BAKERY/ECLECTIC.

The popular Mary Catherine's Bakery has taken over the Old Waialae Road Café's breakfast and lunch service, and although some may bemoan the loss of kal bi and local-style plate lunches, there is plenty here to satisfy. This is one of the best breakfast spots in Honolulu: eggs fluffed and cooked in an espresso machine; eggs Benedict on Mary Catherine's home-baked cheese scones; a scrumptious breakfast quesadilla (black beans, eggs, rice and cheese in flour tortillas, with guacamole and tomato salsa and excellent home fries); spiced-up "paniolo eggs" with onions, peppers, and hot sauce. The pastries (including the cornbread accompanying the homemade Portuguese bean soup) are baked fresh here, the salads are fresh gourmet baby greens, the roasted veggie sandwich a bounty of vegetables with melted provolone, and the vegetarian made-from-scratch lasagne a memorable gourmet feast. Grilled mahi-mahi sandwiches and stir-fry, tuna sandwiches, garlic shrimp pasta, and open-faced roast beef sandwiches round out a menu that uses fresh ingredients and made-to-order service. Order at the counter, and then dine at the casual, shaded tables outdoors surrounded by trellises with grapevines. Inside, a top-notch European-style bakery sells everything from lavishly tiered wedding cakes to chocolate decadence cake.

KAIMUKI/KAPAHULU
EXPENSIVE

3660 On the Rise. 3660 Waialae Ave. ☎ **808/737-1177.** Reservations suggested. Main courses $18–$25. AE, DC, DISC, JCB, MC, V. Tues–Thurs 5:30–9pm; Fri–Sat 5:30–10pm; Sun 5:30–9pm. EURO-ISLAND.

This is a busy, noisy restaurant with a menu that has retained only tried-and-true favorites. Chef Russell Siu adds an Asian or local touch to the basics: Australian rack of lamb in Asian barbecue sauce; seared breast of chicken with shiitake mushrooms and shiso, in soy-citrus-butter sauce; and grilled salmon in a scallion sauce. Our favorites: the ahi katsu, wrapped in nori and deep-fried rare, an excellent appetizer; Caesar salad; and the fresh catch simmered in a Chinese black-bean broth. The new New York Steak Alaea (Hawaiian red rock salt) and the award-winning desserts keep 3660 on the rise.

✪ **Ninniku-Ya Garlic Restaurant.** 3196 Waialae Ave. ☎ **808/735-0784.** Reservations recommended. Main dishes $11–$28. DISC, MC, V. Tues–Sat 5:30–10pm; Sun 5:30–9pm. EURO-ASIAN.

Plain and simple, this is a great garlic restaurant, a paean to the stinking rose. Cozy, in an old home with tables in a split-level dining room and under old trees outdoors, Ninniku-Ya titillates the palate with garlic surprises galore. Seasonal specialties (winter pumpkin in garlic potatoes, opah during winter, beet-colored sauces for Valentine's Day) are fine, but not necessary, because the staples are entirely satisfying. Garlic bread comes with a mound of garlic, the three-mushroom pasta is sublime, the hot-stone filet mignon is tender and tasty, and the garlic rice is a meal in itself. Everything contains garlic, but it doesn't overpower, even in the homemade garlic gelato. Yes, that's *garlic* gelato, and it's good.

✪ **Sam Choy's Diamond Head Restaurant.** 449 Kapahulu Ave. ☎ **808/732-8645.**
Reservations required. Main courses $19–$30; Sun brunch $24.95 adults, $14.95 children.
AE, DISC, DC, JCB, MC, V. Mon–Thurs 5:30–9:30pm; Fri–Sun 5–10pm; Sun brunch buffet
9:30am–2pm. HAWAII REGIONAL.

You'll know you're in the right place if you see a parade of exiting diners clutching their
Styrofoam bundles, for leftovers are de rigueur at any Sam Choy's operation. In the
tradition of someone whose motto is "Never trust a skinny chef," the servings are
gargantuan. But the food is as big-bodied and big-hearted as the servings. Choy has
won over a sizable chunk of Hawaii's dining population with his noisy, informal, and
gourmet-cum-local style of cooking. The master of poke, Choy serves several of the
best versions ever invented, among them a whitefish (ono and opakapaka) drizzled
with hot oil and topped with chopped herbs and condiments. Heartily recommended
are the Brie wontons, the teriyaki-style rib eye steak, and the no-fat steamed fish with
ginger and shiitake mushrooms.

MODERATE

Genki Sushi. 900 Kapahulu Ave. ☎ **808/735-8889.** Individual sushi $1.20 and up per
order; combination platters $7.40–$38.65. AE, DC, DISC, MC, V. Sun–Thurs 11am–9pm;
Fri–Sat 11am–10pm; takeout available daily 11am–9pm. SUSHI.

Fun! Crowded! Entertaining! Take your place in line for a seat at one of the U-shaped
counters at which conveyor belts parade by with freshly made sushi, usually two pieces
per color-coded plate, priced inexpensively. The dizzying variety is full of possibilities:
spicy tuna topped with scallions, ahi, scallops with mayonnaise, Canadian roll (like California roll, except with salmon), tako poke, sea urchin, flavored octopus, sweet shrimp,
surf clam, corn, tuna salad, and so on. Genki starts with a Japanese culinary tradition
and takes liberties with it, so purists miss out on some fun. By the end of the meal, the
piled-high plates are tallied up by color, and presto—your bill appears, much smaller
than the pleasure. Brilliant combination platters stream across the take-out counter.

INEXPENSIVE

Bueno Nalo. 3045 Monsarrat Ave. ☎ **808/735-8818.** Most items less than $9.95. AE, MC,
V. Mon–Sat 11am–9pm; Sun 11am–8pm. MEXICAN.

Olé for Bueno Nalo and its sizzling fajitas, hearty combination platters, and famous
chimichangas. There are two tables outside, six tables indoors, and a brisk take-out
business among those who like its straightforward Mexican fare and adjoining juice
bar. The juice bar is smoothie central, and for good reason.

Cafe Laufer. 3565 Waialae Ave. ☎ **808/735-7717.** Menu items 65¢–$8.25. AE, CB, DC,
DISC, JCB, MC, V. Sun–Mon and Wed–Thurs 8am–10pm; Fri–Sat 8am–11pm. COFFEE AND
PASTRY SHOP.

This small, airy, and cheerful cafe features frilly decor and sublime European-style pastries, from apple scones and Linzer tortes to fruit flans, decadent chocolate mousses,
and carrot cakes to accompany the latte and espresso. Fans drop in for hearty soups
and deli sandwiches on fresh-baked breads; biscotti for their coffee break; or a hearty
loaf of seven-grain, rye, pumpernickel, or French for breaking bread the next day. It's
a solid hit for lunch: soup-salad-sandwich specials for a song, Chinese chicken salad
for $6.75, a superb spinach salad for $7.25, gourmet greens with mango-infused
honey-mustard dressing—a small but satisfying menu. The smoked Atlantic salmon
with fresh pumpernickel bread and cream cheese, Maui onions, and capers is a solid
hit. The special Saturday-night desserts such as the made-to-order souffles—fresh
lemon or strawberry, chocolate, Grand Marnier, and other fantasy flavors—draw a
brisk after-movie business.

Hale Vietnam. 1140 12th Ave. ☎ **808/735-7581.** Reservations recommended for groups. Main courses $4.50–$16. DISC, MC, V. Daily 11am–10pm. VIETNAMESE.

Duck into this house of *pho* and brave the no-frills service for the steaming noodle soups, the house specialty. The stock is simmered and skimmed for many hours and is accompanied with noodles, beef, chicken, and a platter of bean sprouts and fresh herbs. Approach the green chiles with caution; it's hard to know if they're the ones with the astronomical scoville units. We love the chicken soup and shrimp vermicelli, as well as the seafood pho and imperial rolls. All in all, a great house of pho; but be advised that, like most other Vietnamese eateries, there's MSG in the soup.

3 East of Honolulu & Waikiki

VERY EXPENSIVE

✪ **Hoku's.** In Kahala Mandarin Oriental Hotel, 5000 Kahala Ave. ☎ **808/739-8779.** Reservations recommended. Main courses $18–$32.50; prix-fixe dinner $65. AE, CB, DC, DISC, JCB, MC, V. Daily 11:30am–2:30pm and 5:30–10:30pm. PACIFIC/EUROPEAN.

Elegant without being stuffy, creative without being overwrought, the fine dining room of the Kahala Mandarin has gained a loyal following with its elegant lunches and dinners, combining European finesse with island ingredients and flavors. The ocean view, open kitchen, and astonishing bamboo floor are stellar features. Reflecting its cross-cultural influences, the kitchen is equipped with a kiawe grill; an Indian tandoor oven for its chicken and naan bread; and Szechwan woks for the prawn, lobster, tofu, and other stir-fry specialties. The steamed Hong Kong–style whole fresh fish is an occasion, but traditionalists can also choose rack of lamb, grilled chicken, pan-seared mahi-mahi, or peppered ahi steak. At lunch, the baked Caesar salad with tiger prawns is smashing.

MODERATE

The Patisserie. 4211 Waialae Ave., Kahala Mall. ☎ **808/735-4402.** Deli sandwiches $3.75–$4.75; complete dinners $13.50–$17. MC, V. Dinner service Tues–Sat 5:30–8:30pm; deli service Mon–Sat 7am–9pm and Sun 7am–5pm. GERMAN/AUSTRIAN.

The complete dinners are a pleasant surprise, more elegant than the casual mall surroundings would indicate and surprisingly kind to the pocketbook, too. In its bakery setting with eight tables and a gleaming deli counter, The Patisserie sells everything from deluxe wedding cakes and European breads to inexpensive deli sandwiches (tuna, egg salad, pastrami, Black Forest ham), and nearly a dozen types of complete dinners. The Tuesday-through-Saturday dinners include sauerbraten, osso buco, veal ribs, baked pork tenderloin, braised lamb shank, and a particularly memorable sautéed chicken breast in a Marsala mushroom sauce and linguine. A fish dinner is offered every Friday, and the German dinners are popular among those longing for Wiener schnitzel, pepper schnitzel, and potato pancakes with sour cream and applesauce. Served with garden salad and rolls, the dinners are a good value. The Patisserie also has deli/bakeries at Outrigger West Hotel (2330 Kuhio Ave., Waikiki) and Outrigger Edgewater Hotel (2168 Kalia Rd., Waikiki).

INEXPENSIVE

✪ **Olive Tree Cafe.** 4614 Kilauea Ave., next to Kahala Mall. ☎ **808/737-0303.** Reservations not accepted. Main courses $5–$10. No credit cards; checks accepted. Mon–Thurs 5–10pm; Fri–Sat 11am–10pm. GREEK/EASTERN MEDITERRANEAN.

Olive Tree fans are continually amazed at the delectables streaming out of the tiny open kitchen at bargain prices. Recently voted "best restaurant in Hawaii under $20" by a local survey, Olive Tree is every neighborhood's dream: a totally hip restaurant with divine Greek fare and friendly prices—one of the top values in town. There are umbrellas over tables on the sidewalk and a few seats indoors—no pretenses, a real cafe. The tabouleh salad, perfectly balanced in flavor and texture, is generously greened with herbs and mint, and the falafel, eggplant salad, ceviche, mussels, and taramasalata—a pink caviar—have a huge following as well. We love the souvlakis (kebabs in pita bread), ranging from fresh fish to chicken and lamb and spruced up with the chef's signature yogurt-dill sauce. You'll order at the counter from a blackboard menu that includes the daily specials: lamb shank in tomato and herbs, lemon chicken, and spanakopita. Located next door to Kahala Mall (where you can buy your own libations), Olive Tree is BYOB, which means a large group can dine like sultans, for a song, and take in a movie next door, too.

4 East Oahu

NIU VALLEY
EXPENSIVE

✪ **Cliquo.** 5730 Niu Valley Shopping Center, Kalanianaole Hwy. ☎ **808/377-8854.** Reservations recommended. Main courses $16–$29; prix-fixe $27. AE, DC, DISC, JCB, MC, V. Mon–Sat 5:30–9pm. FRENCH.

Chef Yves Menoret has a glowing reputation in Honolulu as the man who established the erstwhile Bagwell's and the still-popular Bali By the Sea before opening his own 50-seat dining room 4 years ago. His French fare is prepared with care and Old World meticulousness, particularly the flaky opakapaka with watercress and ginger beurre blanc; seared foie gras with leek and Yukon potato; and vol-au-vent, buttery escargots in clouds of leeks and garlic. It is a spare, elegant menu with attractive prix-fixe selections.

Swiss Inn. Niu Valley Shopping Center, 5730 Kalanianaole Hwy. ☎ **808/377-5447.** Reservations recommended. Complete dinners $14.50–$22. AE, CB, DC, DISC, JCB, MC, V. Wed–Sun 6pm–closing; Sunday brunch 10:30am–1pm. CONTINENTAL.

Martin and Jeanie Wyss have been welcoming families for more than 15 years to their cordial "chalet" in suburban Honolulu. The quintessential neighborhood restaurant, Swiss Inn is known for its Wiener schnitzel ($16.50), New York steak ($22), and baked chicken ($14.50). The complete dinners include soup, salad, vegetables, and coffee or tea; light dinners range from $5.75 to $7.75. Families have always been welcome at Swiss Inn, and when the kids grow up, they bring their friends and families, too. Specialties include the veal dishes and the fresh fish, usually mahi-mahi or onaga in a lemon-butter-caper sauce, and at Thanksgiving and holidays, the home-cooked turkey dinner is just the way mom made it.

HAWAII KAI
EXPENSIVE

✪ **Roy's Restaurant.** 6600 Kalanianaole Hwy. ☎ **808/396-7697.** Reservations recommended. Main courses $9–$25. AE, JCB, MC, V. Daily 5:30–9:15pm. EUROPEAN/ASIAN.

He built in Hawaii Kai, and diners came—in droves. Roy Yamaguchi's flagship Hawaii restaurant was the first of more than a dozen throughout Hawaii, Asia, and the Pacific—but don't count on that figure, because his dining empire grows faster than we can count. A prolific winner of culinary awards, Yamaguchi devised a winning formula: open kitchen, fresh ingredients, ethnic touches, and a good dose of nostalgia to go with the European techniques. The menu changes nightly, but you can generally count on a varied appetizer menu (summer rolls, blackened ahi, hibachi-style salmon); a small pasta selection; and entrees such as lemongrass roasted chicken, garlic-mustard short ribs, mustard-crusted lamb shanks, hibachi-style salmon in ponzu sauce, and several types of fresh catch prepared at least five different ways. Roy's is also renowned for its high-decibel style of dining—always full and noisy.

5 The Windward Coast

MODERATE

Assaggio Italian Restaurant. In the Kailua Business Center, 354 Ulunui St., Kailua. ☎ **808/261-2772.** Reservations recommended. Main courses $9–$18. AE, DC, DISC, MC, V. Mon–Fri 11:30am–2:30pm; daily 5–10pm. ITALIAN.

You may not want to make the half-hour trip over the Pali for dinner here, but surprisingly, many people do. Affordable prices, attentive service, and some winning items have won Assaggio loyal fans throughout the years. The bestselling hot antipasto has jumbo shrimp, fresh clams, mussels, and calamari in a sauce of cayenne pepper, white wine, and garlic. You can choose linguine, fettuccine, or ziti with ten different sauces in small or regular portions, or any of nine chicken pastas (the chicken Assaggio, with garlic, peppers, and mushrooms, is especially flavorful). The extensive list of seafood pastas is impressive.

Baci Bistro. 30 Aulike St., Kailua. ☎ **808/262-7555.** Reservations recommended for dinner. Main courses $12.95–$19.95. AE, JCB, MC, V. Mon–Fri 11:30am–2pm; daily 5:30–10pm. ITALIAN.

Baci fans come here for the casual indoor-outdoor dining room in which hip Kailuans can nosh on homemade gnocchi, fresh-made raviolis (ravioli of the day, a Baci specialty, is something to look forward to), and squid-ink fettuccine with scallops and saffron cream sauce. Baci fans also tout the charcoaled shrimp with lime and feta cheese ($9.95), veal Baci (the signature scaloppine with artichoke hearts, sun-dried tomatoes, capers, and wine, for $18.95), and the fresh raviolis with lamb, lobster, or combinations of fresh seafood. The lunch and dinner menus include salads, hot and cold appetizers (they're famous for their bruschetta), risottos, homemade pastas, and veal, seafood, and chicken entrees. The lighter lunch fare includes inexpensive sandwiches.

Casablanca. 19 Hoolai St., Kailua. ☎ **808/262-8196.** Reservations recommended. Main courses $10.95–$16.75. MC, V. Mon–Sat 6–9:30pm. MOROCCAN/MEDITERRANEAN.

You can't miss the striking blue-and-yellow entrance with a Moorish arch over a tiny concrete pathway painted in brilliant primary colors. This gets our vote for the most cheerful ambience in Kailua. One section features traditional Moroccan dining on the floor, without utensils, while there are tables in the front section. Couscous with vegetables, chicken, and lamb in brochettes, braised, with eggplant, and with prunes, are among the savory offerings of this charming eatery. Large shrimp sautéed with Pernod and finished with sweet anise are a taste treat, while some swear by the Cornish hen in Moroccan spices, cinnamon prunes, and honey.

INEXPENSIVE

Ahi's Restaurant. 53–146 Kamehameha Hwy., Punaluu. ☎ **808/293-5650.** Reservations for 8 or more. Main courses $6.50–$12.95. No credit cards. Mon–Sat 11am–9pm. AMERICAN/ LOCAL.

There is no place like Ahi's in Hawaii—in a beautiful rural setting, with tasty local fare, and the generous aloha of Ahi Logan and his three-generation family business. Ahi's is a lush roadside oasis with split-level indoor dining and an airy, screened-in room (for larger parties), a charming throwback to preresort, premarble, preplastic Hawaii. A rolling green lawn and shade-giving trees surround the wooden structure; it's informal and comfortably rural. The shrimp—the menu highlight—comes plump and served four ways: cocktail, scampi, tempura, and deep fried. The mahi-mahi and fresh-fish specials are straightforward and good. On Saturdays, the generous Hawaiian lunch plate offers lau-lau, grilled fish, shrimp, and pipikaula (dried, salted beef). Come here when you're hungry for the taste of the real Hawaii that resorts long ago abandoned.

Brent's Restaurant & Delicatessen. 629-A Kailua Rd. ☎ **808/262-8588.** Menu items $5–$12.95. MC, V. Tues–Thurs and Sun 7am–8pm; Fri–Sat 7am–9pm. KOSHER DELI.

Finally, a kosher deli with real cheese blintzes, cream-cheese and shrimp omelets, and some spirited cultural digressions, such as pesto poached eggs and an artichoke-laced frittata. And bagels galore, with baked salmon, sturgeon and cream cheese, or any number of accompaniments to compete with the New York–style pastrami and hot corned-beef sandwiches on Brent's abundant menu.

Bueno Nalo. 20 Kainehe St., Kailua. ☎ **808/263-1999.** Main courses $4–$10. AE, DC, DISC, MC, V. Daily 11am–10pm. MEXICAN.

Now in two locations (the other location is in the Kapahulu-Diamond Head area; see the listing under "Honolulu Beyond Waikiki"), this popular eatery, once a fixture in Waimanalo, has transplanted itself very successfully in suburban Kailua. Familiar south-of-the-border basics include chicken chimichangas, fajitas, Bueno burritos, fajitas, and sizzling combination platters.

Buzz's Original Steak House. 413 Kawailoa Road, Lanikai. ☎ **808/261-4661.** Reservations required. Shirt and shoes required. Lunch main courses $6.95–$12.95; dinner main courses $10.95–$24.95. No credit cards. Daily 11am–3pm and 5–10pm. STEAK/SEAFOOD.

A Lanikai fixture for 36 years, Buzz's is a few feet from Kailua Beach (windsurfing central), just past the bridge that leads into Lanikai. A small deck, varnished-koa bar, rattan furniture, and wood walls covered with snapshots and surf pictures will put you immediately at ease. Great burgers at lunch (including a $7.95 mushroom garden burger), fresh catch, superb artichoke appetizer, and steak-and-lobster combos are among the items much loved by fans. Steak and seafood—surf and turf—are appropriate fare for the salt-kissed locals who love this place night and day.

Kimoz. 41–1537 Kalanianaole Hwy., Waimanalo. ☎ **808/259-8800.** Plate lunches $5.25–$6.95; sandwiches $3.95 and up. AE, CB, DC, DISC, MC, V. Mon–Thurs 6:30am–9pm; Fri 6:30am–2am; Sat 8:30am–2am; Sun 8:30am–8pm. LOCAL/KOREAN.

Kimoz is doing a brisk business with its popular plates and generous *kal bi,* the spicy marinated Korean meat. Lovers of local food will find no stone unturned, from generous Portuguese sausage or seafood omelets to plate lunches, grilled mahi-mahi, made-from-scratch mandoo, saimin, and homestyle potatoes. Breakfast is served all day, but at lunch, the homestyle hamburgers, meat loaf, seafood, and Hawaiian plates are among the popular items on a diverse local menu. You'll sit at wooden picnictable–style booths with a view of the jukebox and the bubble-gum machines at the entrance. *Caveat:* karaoke in the evenings.

6 The North Shore

MODERATE

✪ **Jameson's by the Sea.** 62–540 Kamehameha Hwy., Haleiwa. ☎ **808/637-4336.** Reservations recommended. Downstairs lunch menu $7–$14; main courses $13–$$24.95 in upstairs dining room. AE, DC, DISC, JCB, MC, V. Downstairs, daily 11am–5pm; pub menu Mon–Tues 5–9pm; Sat–Sun brunch 9am–noon, dinner until 9pm. Upstairs, Wed–Sun 5–9pm. SEAFOOD.

The roadside watering hole across the street from the ocean is always full with fun-loving North Shore types or rubbernecking tourists agog with the beauty of the area. It's a happy place; duck in for cocktails, sashimi, and salmon pâté, or for other hot and cold appetizers, salads, and sandwiches throughout the day. Especially popular are the Thai shrimp rolls, chilled seafood platter, grilled crab and shrimp sandwich (pardon the mayonnaise) on sourdough bread, and the fresh-fish sandwich of the day, grilled plain and simple. Upstairs, the much pricier dining room opens 5 nights a week for the usual surf-and-turf choices: fresh opakapaka, ono or ahi, and mahi-mahi; scallops, lobster tail, scampi, New York steak, and filet mignon.

INEXPENSIVE

Cafe Haleiwa. 66–460 Kamehameha Hwy., Haleiwa. ☎ **808/637-5516.** Reservations not accepted. Main courses $5.50–$10.50. AE, MC, V. Daily 7am–2pm. MEXICAN/LOCAL.

This time-tested cafe is the breakfast joint of surfers, urban gentry with weekend country homes, reclusive artists, and anyone who loves mahi-mahi plate lunches and homemade Mexican food. It's a wake-up-and-hit-the-beach kind of place, serving generous burritos and omelets with names like Off the Wall, Off the Lip, and Breakfast in a Barrel. Surf pictures line the walls, and the ambience is Formica-style casual. You can order a mahi-mahi plate lunch with home fries, rice, or beans; spicy chicken tacos; fish tacos with grilled mahi, tomatoes, lime, and cilantro; and burritos, tostados, and combination plates. It also serves tuna salad, mahi-mahi, burgers, steak sandwiches—made with individual attention and grilled onions on request. Our favorite breakfast is the truly epic huevos rancheros, smothered with cheese and salsa. Service is brisk because everyone's dashing to the beach. Breakfast is served all day on weekends.

Coffee Gallery. In North Shore Marketplace, 66–250 Kamehameha Hwy., Haleiwa. ☎ **808/637-5355.** Reservations not accepted. Most items under $6. AE, DC, DISC, JCB, MC, V. Daily 7am–8pm. COFFEEHOUSE/VEGETARIAN.

On the other side of town from Kua Aina (see below) and its meat-lover's cuisine, this indoor-outdoor coffeehouse has carved a firm niche in the hearts of Haleiwa's health-conscious diners, vegetarians, and coffee lovers. The lemon squares here are famous (its recipe was printed, by popular request, in the local newspaper), and the granola is made with premium Big Island honey. There are tofu burritos with fresh spinach and roasted garlic tomato sauce, bagels, salads, pastas, vegan soup, spinach pesto, vegetarian enchiladas, and many other health-conscious choices.

Kua Aina. 66–214 Kamehameha Hwy., Haleiwa. ☎ **808/637-6067.** Most items under $6. No credit cards. Daily 11am–8pm. AMERICAN.

"What's the name of that famous sandwich shop on the North Shore?" We hear that often. Kua Aina is as much a part of the North Shore ritual as a Ke Iki Beach sunset. The lines are still long at this tiny North Shore beehive because demand still outpaces the kitchen for the renowned French fries and legendary grilled hamburgers and mahi-mahi sandwiches. Fat, moist, and homemade, the burgers can be ordered with avocado, bacon, and many other accompaniments in addition to their tower of sprouts and greens. Also recommended are the roast beef and fresh-fish sandwiches. Because the few tables on the streetside porch fill early, customers often pick up their burgers and head for the beach.

North Shore Pizza Company. In North Shore Marketplace, 66–250 Kamehameha Hwy., Haleiwa. ☎ **808/637-2782.** Main courses and pizzas $7–$21. AE, MC, V. Mon–Fri 4–9pm; Fri 4–10pm; Sat–Sun 11am–10pm. PIZZA.

Pizza delivery in Haleiwa is more than a convenience; it's a damn good idea. People like to stay put after they've driven an hour from town to get home, and who wants to hop in the car when there's a sunset to be ogled? North Shore Pizza isn't cheap, but it's reliable and delicious, and it won't cause arguments with the kids. The same people who opened trendy Portofino and who introduced Zorro's Pizza to Hawaii also make and deliver the pizzas, calzones, focaccia sandwiches, and pastas. The 16-inch New York–style pizzas are named after North Shore surf spots and topped with fresh island produce, such as Maui onions, North Shore basil, Portuguese sausage, and, for pizza heretics, Hawaiian pineapple.

Paradise Found Cafe. 66–443 Kamehameha Hwy., Haleiwa. ☎ **808/637-4540.** Most items under $6.75. No credit cards. Mon–Sat 9am–5pm; Sun 10am–5pm. VEGETARIAN.

This is one of the many reasons we love Haleiwa: non-deprivation vegetarian food! A tiny cafe behind the Celestial Natural Foods, Paradise Found takes looking for, but it's a charming way to begin a North Shore sojourn. Vegan Caesar salad, ginger-teriyaki tempeh burgers, tofu scramble, and a legendary vegetarian chili are some of the reasons to love Paradise. The menu features Mexican and Middle Eastern food (burritos to baba ganouj), organic coffee, smoothies, fresh organic juices, and tasty salads and sandwiches.

Portofino. In North Shore Marketplace, 66–250 Kamehameha Hwy., Haleiwa. ☎ **808/ 637-7678.** Reservations recommended. Main courses $6.25–$18. AE, DC, MC, V. Mon–Fri 8am–10pm; Sat 8am–11pm; Sun 10am–10pm. NORTHERN ITALIAN.

Terra-cotta tile floors, columns and arches, and hand-painted murals bring a splendid scene of Portofino into the airy room. Although the decibel level can get high, it's a cordial environment in which to enjoy the aromas and creations emanating from the wood-burning oven and open kitchen. Chefs from Italy have devised a menu of home-made pastas, focaccia, panini, calzones, sandwiches, oven-baked fish (grilled ahi with portabello) and wood-fired pizzas, as well as everyday comforts such as rosemary chicken, meat loaf, and roasted-garlic mashed potatoes.

7

Fun in the Surf & Sun

by Jeanette Foster

Pictures of hotels lining the shores of Waikiki Beach and canyons of tall buildings in downtown Honolulu have given Oahu a bad rap. The island is much more than an urban concrete jungle or a tropical Disneyland blighted by overdevelopment; it's also a haven for the nature lover and outdoor enthusiast. With year-round air temperatures in the upper 70s, ocean temperatures in the mid- to high 70s, and miles of verdant and unspoiled landscape, Oahu is perfect for outdoor activities of all kinds, including hiking, golf, tennis, biking, and horseback riding. The island's waters, though, are where the majority of both residents and visitors head for relaxation, rejuvenation, and recreation. Locals don't think of their island or state boundaries as ending at land's edge—rather, they extend beyond the reefs, well out into the ocean.

1 Beaches

Oahu has more than 130 beaches of every conceivable description, from legendary white-sand stretches to secluded rocky bays. Waikiki, of course, is the best known, but there are many others—some more beautiful, all less crowded. What follows is a selection of Oahu's finest beaches, carefully selected to suit every need, taste, and interest, from the sunbather in repose to the most ardent diver.

WAIKIKI BEACH

The name of the world-famous 2-mile stretch means "spouting water," and probably refers to the duck ponds that once occupied this former swampland. A crescent-shaped beach of imported sand on Oahu's south shore, Waikiki extends—interrupted periodically by seawalls, rock groins, and a yacht harbor—from the Ala Wai Canal to the foot of Mount Leahi (better known as Diamond Head). As Hawaii's most popular beach, Waikiki is always crowded with tourists. You can experience nearly every type of ocean activity here: It is one of the best places on Oahu for swimming, but you can also board- and bodysurf, paddle an outrigger canoe, dive, sail, snorkel, and pole fish. Every imaginable type of marine equipment and toy is available for rent. The many hotels that line the beach offer an array of food and drink. The best place to park your car is around Kapiolani Park. Facilities on the beach include showers, lifeguards, public rest rooms, and picnic pavilions at the Queen's Surf end of the beach (near the park).

Caution

Keep in mind—wherever you are on Oahu—that you're in an urban area. Never leave valuables in your car. Thefts do occur at Oahu's beaches, and locked cars are not a deterrent.

✪ HANAUMA BAY

Formerly a playground for Hawaiian royalty, this beautiful bay is now a Marine Life Conservation District and the most popular snorkeling spot on Oahu for visitors and residents alike. The enclosed 2,000-foot beach just east of Koko Head fronts a pristine bay, which is actually a volcanic crater open to the ocean on one side. Hanauma's shallow shoreline waters and bountiful marine life are both a blessing and a curse; the number of visitors to the bay is so overwhelming that some fear the ecology of the marine preserve is in danger. Because of the existing threat, both parking and access by commercial operators have been restricted. Since Hanauma Bay is a conservation district, taking anything from the ocean is prohibited. Facilities include parking, rest rooms, a picnic pavilion, grass volleyball court, lifeguard, barbecues, picnic tables, and a food concession. Expect to pay $1 per vehicle to park and a $3 per-person entrance fee.

If you're driving, take Kalanianaole Highway (going east) to Koko Head Regional Park. To avoid the crowds and ensure yourself a parking space, go early on a weekday morning. Or take TheBUS no. 22 to avoid the parking problem. The Hanauma Bay Shuttle runs from Waikiki to Hanauma Bay every half hour from 8:45am to 1pm; you can catch it at the Ala Moana Hotel, the Ilikai Hotel, or any city bus stop on the route. It returns every hour on the hour from noon to 4pm. The park is closed on Tuesdays, so the fish can have a day off; on all other days, it closes at 6pm.

SANDY BEACH

Also part of Koko Head Regional Park, Sandy Beach is one of the best bodysurfing beaches on Oahu. Unless you're experienced, though, you might be restricted to watching the expert bodysurfers and boogie boarders ride the waves. The chiseled bodies strutting up and down the shore aren't all that bad to look at either. This 1,200-foot-long beach is pounded by waves nearly all year long. The quick, steep drop-off underwater adds to the intensity of the waves and produces a strong, forceful backwash. The backwash is especially dangerous for children and weak swimmers. (The lifeguards here make more rescues in a year than those stationed at any other beach, except nearby Makapuu.) Visitors unfamiliar with the beach and its dangers—and fooled by the experienced bodysurfers who make wave-riding look so easy—all too often find themselves overwhelmed by the waves. As a result, the lifeguards have developed a flag system that warns you of the surf's danger level: Green means safe, yellow caution, and red indicates very dangerous water conditions. Be sure to check the flags before you dive in. Facilities include rest rooms and parking. The best times to avoid the crowds are weekdays; the best times to watch top bodysurfers are weekends. TheBUS no. 22 (Kuhio) will get you to Sandy Beach from Waikiki.

MAKAPUU BEACH PARK

At the base of the Koolau Mountains on Oahu's easternmost point is Makapuu Beach Park—Hawaii's most famous bodysurfing spot. Movie fans will recognize this classically beautiful, 1,000-foot-long white-sand beach, bordered by the stark black cliff of

Beaches & Outdoor Activities on Oahu

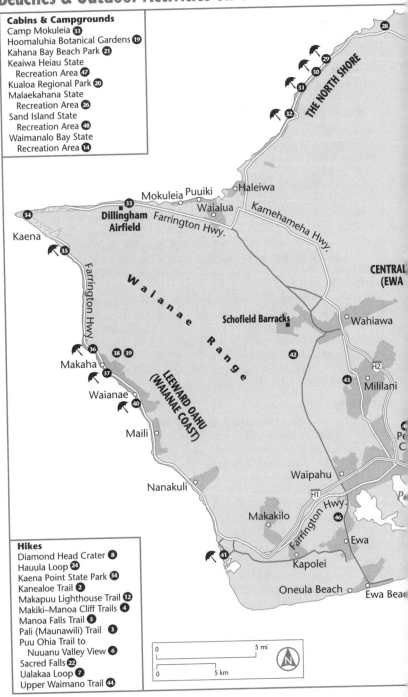

Cabins & Campgrounds
Camp Mokuleia ③③
Hoomaluhia Botanical Gardens ⑲
Kahana Bay Beach Park ㉑
Keaiwa Heiau State
   Recreation Area ㊼
Kualoa Regional Park ⑳
Malaekahana State
   Recreation Area ㉖
Sand Island State
   Recreation Area ㊽
Waimanalo Bay State
   Recreation Area ⑭

Hikes
Diamond Head Crater ⑧
Hauula Loop ㉔
Kaena Point State Park ㉞
Kanealoe Trail ②
Makapuu Lighthouse Trail ⑫
Makiki–Manoa Cliff Trails ④
Manoa Falls Trail ⑤
Pali (Maunawili) Trail ③
Puu Ohia Trail to
   Nuuanu Valley View ⑥
Sacred Falls ㉒
Ualakaa Loop ⑦
Upper Waimano Trail ㊹

THE NORTH SHORE

Mokuleia Puuiki
Haleiwa
Waialua
Kamehameha Hwy.
Dillingham
Airfield
Farrington Hwy.

Kaena

CENTRAL
(EWA

Wahiawa

W a i a n a e   R a n g e

Schofield Barracks

42

H2

Makaha

38 39

43   Mililani

36

37

Waianae

40

LEEWARD OAHU
(WAIANAE
COAST)

Maili

Waipahu

Nanakuli

H1

Makakilo

Farrington Hwy.

46

Ewa

41

Kapolei

Oneula Beach

Ewa Beac

0   5 mi

0   5 km

N

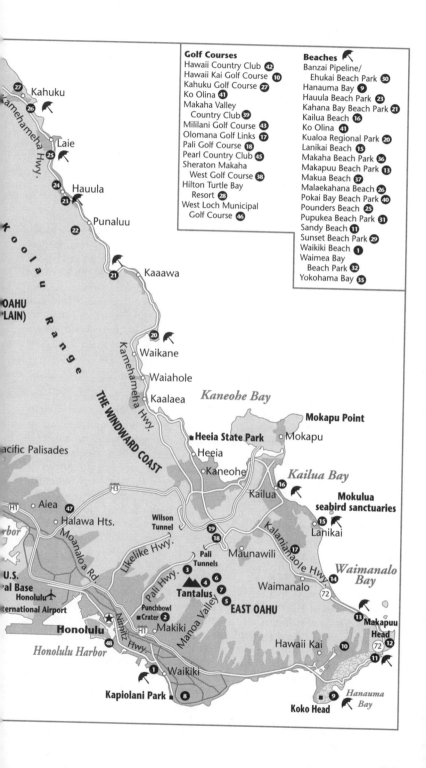

Golf Courses
Hawaii Country Club ④②
Hawaii Kai Golf Course ⑩
Kahuku Golf Course ㉗
Ko Olina ④①
Makaha Valley
  Country Club ㊴
Mililani Golf Course ④③
Olomana Golf Links ⑰
Pali Golf Course ⑱
Pearl Country Club ④⑤
Sheraton Makaha
  West Golf Course ㊳
Hilton Turtle Bay
  Resort ㉘
West Loch Municipal
  Golf Course ④⑥

Beaches
Banzai Pipeline/
  Ehukai Beach Park ㉚
Hanauma Bay ⑨
Hauula Beach Park ㉓
Kahana Bay Beach Park ㉑
Kailua Beach ⑯
Ko Olina ④①
Kualoa Regional Park ⑳
Lanikai Beach ⑮
Makaha Beach Park ㊱
Makapuu Beach Park ⑬
Makua Beach ㊲
Malaekahana Beach ㉖
Pokai Bay Beach Park ㊵
Pounders Beach ㉕
Pupukea Beach Park ㉛
Sandy Beach ⑪
Sunset Beach Park ㉙
Waikiki Beach ①
Waimea Bay
  Beach Park ㉜
Yokohama Bay ㉟

Kahuku
Laie
Hauula
Punaluu
Kaaawa
Waikane
Waiahole
Kaalaea
Mokapu Point
Kaneohe Bay
Heeia State Park
Mokapu
Heeia
Kaneohe
Kailua Bay
Kailua
Mokulua
seabird sanctuaries
Aiea
Halawa Hts.
Wilson Tunnel
Lanikai
Pali Tunnels
Maunawili
Waimanalo Bay
Waimanalo
Tantalus
EAST OAHU
Honolulu
Punchbowl Crater
Makiki
Hawaii Kai
Makapuu Head
International Airport
Waikiki
Kapiolani Park
Koko Head
Hanauma Bay
Honolulu Harbor
Koolau Range
THE WINDWARD COAST
Kamehameha Hwy.
Likelike Hwy.
Pali Hwy.
Moanaloa Rd.
Nimitz Hwy.
Manoa Valley
Kalanianaole Hwy.
acific Palisades
OAHU (PLAIN)

Makapuu Point, as a location for the famous Burt Lancaster–Deborah Kerr love scene in *From Here to Eternity*. Picturesque Rabbit Island lies just off the coast. During the summer months the ocean can be as calm as a backyard pool, making swimming and diving a breeze, but extremely dangerous currents and surf can be present from September through April, when the pounding waves erode the beach and expose rocks and boulders in the shorebreak area. Because these conditions are ideal for expert bodysurfers, board surfing is prohibited by state law. Only small boards, 3 feet or less with no skeg (bottom fin), are permitted. Facilities include rest rooms, lifeguard, barbecue grills, picnic tables, and parking. To get to Makapuu, follow Kalanianaole Highway toward Waimanalo. TheBUS no. 57 or 58 (Sea Life Park) will get you there from Waikiki.

✪ LANIKAI BEACH

Hidden by the residential area of Mokulua Drive on the windward side of the island, Lanikai is a beautiful mile-long beach that's safe for swimming and—with the prevailing trade winds—excellent for sailing and windsurfing. The fine, hard-packed sand along the shoreline is perfect for jogging. Offshore, the two tiny islands called the Mokuluas (which are seabird sanctuaries) are easily reached by kayak. Because Lanikai is off the main roads, undeveloped, without facilities, and surrounded by residential homes, it's less crowded than other beaches on the windward side. It's the perfect isolated spot for a morning of swimming and relaxation. Sun-worshipers should arrive in the morning, as the Koolaus' shadow blocks the sun's rays in the afternoon. From Waikiki, take TheBUS no. 56 or 57 (Kailua), and then transfer to the shuttle bus.

✪ KAILUA BEACH PARK

A 30-acre public park on the east end of Kailua Bay, Kailua Beach Park is a broad, grassy area with picnic tables, a public boat ramp, rest rooms, a pavilion, a volleyball court, and food stands. The wide, sandy beach area is popular for diving, swimming, sailing, snorkeling, and board- and windsurfing. In fact, the dependable winds make it one of the more popular windsurfing areas on Oahu. The water conditions are generally safe, but parents should keep an eye on young children, who are often attracted to the brackish water pond in the middle of the park. The seemingly shallow pond has deep holes and has been the site of several drownings. The park gets extremely crowded with local families on weekends; the best time to come is during the week. To get to Kailua Beach Park, take the Kalanianaole Highway or the Pali Highway to Kailua Road, which loops around to Kawailoa Road. Parking is available. From Waikiki, take TheBUS no. 56 or 57 (Kailua) into Kailua, and then take the no. 70 shuttle.

KUALOA REGIONAL PARK

In ancient Hawaii this was a very sacred spot, and today the park is listed on the National Register of Historic Places. Hawaiian chiefs brought their infant children here to be raised and trained as rulers. When canoes passed offshore, sails were lowered in recognition of Kualoa's sacredness. It is easy to see why this was considered a sacred place: The curtain of the Koolau Mountains provides a spectacular backdrop for this broad grassy park bordered by a white-sand beach, with the islet Mokolii (popularly known as Chinaman's Hat) in the distance. The offshore waters are shallow and safe for swimming year-round; they're also excellent for kayaking and fishing. Lifeguards are on duty, and picnic and camping areas are available. Since both residents and visitors frequent this huge beach park, it's better to go on a weekday. The park is located on Kamehameha Highway in Kauloa; you can take TheBUS no. 55 (Circle Island) to get here.

✪ KAHANA BAY BEACH PARK

This white-sand, crescent-shaped beach is backed by a huge, jungle-cloaked valley with dramatic, jagged cliffs, and is protected by ironwood and kamani trees. The bay's calm water and shallow, sandy bottom make it a safe swimming area for children. The bay is famous for the *akule* (big-eyed scad), which come in seasonally; papio and goatfish are also found here. The surrounding park has picnic areas, camping, and hiking trails. The wide sand-bottom channel that runs through the park and out to Kahana Bay is one of the largest on Oahu—it's perfect for kayakers. Visitors and residents come to this relaxing beach, so weekdays are best. The beach park is located on Kamehameha Highway in Kahana; take TheBUS no. 55 (Circle Island) to get here.

HAUULA BEACH PARK

The town of Hauula and nearby Hauula Beach Park were named after the *hau* trees that were once abundant. Although less plentiful now, hau blossoms into a bright yellow flower every morning during July and August. The yellow flowers change color as the day progresses, until they are a reddish gold by dusk and dark red by night, when they fall to the ground. The cycle is repeated the next day.

Hauula Beach Park fronts Kamehameha Highway, is straight and narrow (about 1,000 feet long), and is shaded by kamani and ironwood trees. An offshore reef protects the waters off the beach, but the shallow and rocky bottom make the area unsafe for swimming. Snorkeling is good along the edge of the coral reef, and fishing for papio and goatfish can be fruitful. There are picnic and camping facilities. Weekends tend to be more crowded here, too. TheBUS no. 55 (Circle Island) will get you to Hauula Beach.

POUNDERS BEACH

Because of its easy access and its great bodysurfing waves, Pounders is a popular weekend beach. The beach used to be called Pahumoa, after a local fisherman who arranged the local *hukilau* (the catching of fish in a net) and made sure that the elderly living in the area received a portion of the catch. The name change occurred in the 1950s, when a group of students at the Church College of the Pacific (now Brigham Young University—Hawaii) called the beach "Pounders" after the crushing shorebreak that provided brief but spectacular bodysurfing rides; the nickname stuck.

Pounders is a wide beach, extending a quarter mile between two points. At the west end of the beach, next to the old landing, the waters usually are calm and safe for swimming; at the opposite end, near the limestone cliffs, there's a shorebreak that can be dangerous for inexperienced bodysurfers. The bottom here drops off abruptly, causing strong rip currents. The weekends and after-school hours are the busiest time for this beach; weekday mornings are the quietest. Park on Kamehameha Highway in Kailua, or take TheBUS no. 55 (Circle Island) to get here.

✪ MALAEKAHANA STATE RECREATIONAL AREA

According to Hawaiian legend, a beautiful young princess, Laieikawai, was hidden here to guard her from mortal men. But word of her beauty got out, and many princes tried to woo her. Like the princess, public access to this beautiful, long (over a mile), curving, sandy beach was once restricted; wealthy families used the area for private beach homes. The state has since reclaimed the land, turning it into a recreational area with picnic spots and camping. TheBUS no. 55 (Circle Island) takes you right to the park. As you enter through the main gate off Kamehameha Highway, 2 miles north of the Polynesian Cultural Center, you'll come upon the wooded beach park area; it's excellent for picnicking, shore activities, and swimming. There's no lifeguard here, but the inshore waters are protected from the ocean swells most of the year, making the area safe for swimming.

Mokuauia (Goat) Island, which lies just offshore, is a state bird refuge. You can wade out to the island at low tide and visit secluded Mokuauia Beach, on the island's leeward shore. Surprisingly, very few visitors come to Malaekahana Beach—it's one of the best on Oahu and a true find.

✪ SUNSET BEACH PARK

Surfers around the world know this famous site for the spectacular winter surf—the waves can be huge thundering peaks reaching 15 to 20 feet. Oddly enough, this surfing site wasn't really "discovered" until the 1940s; before that, surfers preferred Makaha on the leeward side of the island. During the winter surf season, September to April, swimming is very dangerous here, due to the alongshore currents and powerful rip currents. The "Sunset rip" has been the site of many rescues and has carried numerous surfboards out to sea. The only safe time to swim at Sunset is during the calm summer months. Sunset also features a huge sandy beach adjacent to the street. This is a great place to people-watch, but don't go too near the water when the lifeguards have posted the red warning flags. One of the most popular beaches on the island, Sunset attracts local surfers, sunbathing beauties, and visitors wanting to get a glimpse of this world-famous surf spot. To avoid the crowds, go during midweek. On the other hand, if people-watching is what you want, try Saturdays and Sundays. Located right on Kamehameha Highway in Paumalu, TheBUS no. 52 (Circle Island) will get you there if you would rather not drive.

BANZAI PIPELINE/EHUKAI BEACH PARK

These are actually three separate areas, but since the sandy beach is continuous with only one sign, EHUKAI BEACH PARK, most people think of it as one beach park. Located near Pupukea, the actual Ehukai Beach Park is 1 acre of grass with a parking lot. The long, broad, white-sand beach is known for its winter surfing action. Swimming is good during the spring and summer months, but currents and waves prohibit safe swimming in the winter. The surf in front of Ehukai Beach Park is excellent for body and board surfers.

The park also provides access to Pipeline and Banzai. **Pipeline** is actually about 100 yards to the left of Ehukai Beach Park. When the winter surf rolls in and hits the shallow coral shelf, the waves that quickly form are steep—so steep, in fact, that the crest of the wave falls forward, forming a near-perfect tube, or "pipeline." Surfers have tried for years to master Pipeline; many have wiped out, suffering lacerations and broken bones on the shallow reef. The first surfer to ride Pipeline successfully was Phil Edwards in the early 1960s. Even today, Pipeline still causes injuries and a few fatalities.

Just west of Pipeline is the area surfers call **"Banzai Beach."** The Japanese word *banzai* means "10,000 years"; it's given as a toast or as a battle charge, meaning "go for it." In the late 1950s, filmmaker Bruce Brown was shooting one of the first surf movies ever made, *Surf Safari*, when he saw a bodysurfer ride a huge wave. Brown yelled: "Banzai!" and the name stuck. In the winter, this is a very popular beach with surfers, surf fans, curious residents, and visitors; it's less crowded in the summer months. Again, access is via Ehukai Beach Park, located off Kamehameha Highway on Ke Nui Road in Pupukea. TheBUS no. 52 (Circle Island) will drop you on the highway.

PUPUKEA BEACH PARK

This 80-acre beach park is a Marine Life Conservation District; as such, it has strict rules about taking marine life, sand, coral, shells, and rocks. There are two major swimming areas in the Marine Life Conservation District: **Shark's Cove** and **Three**

Tables. Don't worry: Shark's Cove, near the northern end, is *not* named for an abundance of sharks that call this home (in fact, it's relatively uncommon to see a shark here); rather, it's a popular snorkeling and dive site. Diving is best outside the cove, where caves promise interesting night diving. During the calm summer months, this is a popular dive site both day and night.

At the southern end of the Marine Life Conservation District is Three Tables, which is named for the three flat sections of reef visible at low tide. Snorkeling is good around the tables where the water is about 15 feet deep. Diving outside the tables, where the water is 30 to 45 feet deep, is excellent—there are many ledges, arches, lava tubes, and a variety of marine life. Swimming, diving, and snorkeling are best from May to October, when the water is calm; nevertheless, watch out for surges. In the winter, when currents form and waves roll in, this area is very dangerous, even in the tide pools; there is no lifeguard present. Summers find this Marine Life Conservation District brimming with visitors weekdays and weekends; it's a popular site for local dive operators to take their clients. In the winter, it's nearly empty during the week. It's right on Kamehameha Highway in Pupukea; there's a small parking lot. TheBUS no. 52 (Circle Island) stops at the park.

✪ WAIMEA BAY BEACH PARK

Despite what the Beach Boys croon in their hit song, (Why-a-*mee*-ah), the name of this famous surfing beach is pronounced Why-*may*-ah. Waimea Bay is known in the surfing circuit as the home of some of the biggest ridable surfing waves in the world. During the winter—October to April—huge, pounding waves come rolling in, creating strong rip currents. Even expert surfers think twice when confronted with these 30-foot waves. When the surf's up, it seems like everyone on Oahu drives out to Waimea to get a look at the monstrous waves and those who ride them. It's hard to believe that during the summer this same bay is glassy and calm, a great place for swimming, snorkeling, and diving. Since this beach is popular with local residents, weekdays are best. From Waikiki, take The BUS no. 52 (Circle Island) to get to Waimea Bay Beach Park.

MAKAHA BEACH PARK

Makaha means "fierce" or "savage," and many people think the name refers to the giant surf and dangerous rip currents, shorebreaks, and backwashes that occur from October through April. The word actually refers to a community of robbers who lived in the Makaha Valley and who threatened anyone who walked through. Today Makaha is still not the safest place for visitors to roam, but when the surf's up at Makaha Beach, it's spectacular. This is the original home of Hawaii's big-wave surfing championship: When the north or west swells run during the winter, monstrous waves pound the beach here. During the summer months, the waters are perfectly safe for swimming. To get to Makaha Beach from Waikiki, take TheBUS no. 51 (Makaha). You'll not find many visitors here; some in the community feel that there are plenty of beaches for visitors and Makaha should be reserved for the locals. Chances are good no one will bother you, but you might want to respect these feelings and stop at another beach for swimming.

MAKUA BEACH

Visitors rarely sojourn to this long, gently curving sandy beach, known for its diving, fishing, swimming, and limited bodysurfing. Makua was a movie star in the 1960s, when it was used in the movie *Hawaii.* Swimming is good here during the calm summer months, but when the big swells roll in, so do turbulent and dangerous currents. The eastern end of the beach is popular for catching moi. The area off Makua Cave has the best snorkeling. *Be warned:* There is no lifeguard here. Mostly local residents use this beach, which never gets really crowded. It's located on Farrington Highway past Makaha Beach; there is no bus service.

✪ POKAI BAY BEACH PARK

This wonderful beach, off the beaten path for most visitors, offers excellent swimming year-round, even when the rest of the Waianae shoreline is getting battered by heavy surf. A protected bay, the waters inside are calm enough for children and offer excellent snorkeling. The swimming area is marked by buoys. Waianae-area residents have a bit of a reputation for being xenophobic; however, they want the same things most people want. So go with respect for local customs, be a good steward of the land, and appreciate the local resources. Do what the locals do, pick up your garbage, don't play loud music, and be courteous and friendly. On weekdays, you can practically have the area to yourself. The beach park is located on Waianae Valley Road, off Farrington Highway. TheBUS no. 51 will drop you off on the highway, and you can walk the block to the park.

KO OLINA

The developer of the 640-acre Ko Olina Resort has created four white-sand lagoons to make the rocky shoreline more attractive and accessible. Only two of these man-made lagoons are currently open. The northernmost lagoon, next to the Ihilani Resort and Spa, is the best. The nearly circular lagoon, with calm, shallow waters and a powdery white-sand beach bordered by a broad, grassy lawn, is the most attractive of the four lagoons. Lifeguards and rest rooms are on the site, and the amenities and restaurants of the hotel are steps away. The other lagoon that's open right now is three lagoons away from the Ihilani Hotel. There's plenty of public parking, a lifeguard station, and rest rooms. This scenic, calm lagoon is used mainly by local residents, but it doesn't have quite the ambience of the lagoon next to the hotel (only part of which is used by hotel guests). Located off H-1 in Kapolei, there is no local bus service to Ko Olina; the closest bus stop is on Farrington Highway, more than 4 miles away.

2 Hitting the Water

Every type of water activity is pursued on Oahu, from professional surfers braving giant winter waves on the North Shore to recreational water-skiers enjoying the calm waters of Hawaii Kai. You can kayak from Lanikai Beach to the Mokulua Islands or float above Waikiki on a parasail as a speedboat tows you blissfully through the air. If you have something of an adventurous spirit, you might scuba dive the walls of the Kahuna Canyon, swim with clouds of *ta'ape* (butterfly fish), or view an occasional shark from the comfort of a passenger submarine. No matter what your water recreation interests are, whether you're a beginner or an expert, you can find it on Oahu.

AN AQUATIC PARK

For those who love the water, but are a bit intimidated by the ocean, the answer is a water park with everything from inner tube rides to mechanically generated waves for bodysurfing.

Hawaiian Waters Adventure Park. 400 Farrington Hwy., Kapolei. ☎ **808/WILD-WAY.** www.hawaiianwaters.com. $30 adults; $20 children under 48 in. tall; under 3 years free. 10:30am–6pm daily. Take H-1 west to the Makakilo/Kapolei exit. Turn left on Makakilo Dr., get into the right lane and take a right at the first traffic light onto Farrington Hwy. (Hwy. 93). Stay in the right lane and drive past the Kapolei Shopping Center, and then turn right at the traffic light just after the Tesoro Gas Express station to Farrington Hwy. Go over the overpass and turn right into the Hawaiian Waters Adventure Park parking lot.

Oahu's newest visitor attraction, the 29-acre water-theme amusement park opened in spring 1999 with some $14 million in attractions, including a football field–sized wave pool for bodysurfing, two 65-foot-high free-fall slides, two water-toboggan bullet slides, inner tube slides, body flume slides, a continuous river for floating inner tubes, and separate pools for adults, teens, and children. In addition, there are restaurants, food carts, Hawaiian cultural demonstrations (hula, chanting, arts and crafts), and shops.

BOATING

A funny thing happens to people when they come to Hawaii: Maybe it's the salt air, the warm tropical nights, or the blue Hawaiian moonlight, but otherwise rational people who have never set foot on a boat in their lives suddenly want to go out to sea. You can go out on a "booze cruise" with a thousand loud, rum-soaked strangers, or you can sail on one of these special yachts, all of which can take you **whale watching** in season (roughly December to April). For fishing charters, see "Sportfishing," below.

Captain Bob's Adventure Cruises. Kaneohe Bay. ☎ **808/942-5077.** No cruises Sun and holidays. $69 adults; $59 children 13–17; $49 children 12 and under. Prices include all-you-can-eat barbecue lunch and transportation from Waikiki hotels. TheBUS: 55 or 56.

See the majestic Windward Coast the way it should be seen—from a boat. Captain Bob will take you on a 4-hour, lazy-day sail of Kaneohe Bay aboard his 42-foot catamaran, which skims across the almost-always calm water above the shallow coral reef, lands at Ahu o Laka, a disappearing sandbar, and takes you past two small islands and to snorkel spots full of tropical fish and, sometimes, turtles. The color of the water alone is worth the price. A shuttle will pick you up at your Waikiki hotel between 9 and 9:30am and return you there at about 4pm, which is a lot quicker than taking TheBUS (no. 55 or 56).

Dream Cruises. Kewalo Basin and Waianae Small Boat Harbor. ☎ **800/400-7300** or 808/592-5200. www.dream-cruises.com. Variety of cruises: dolphin watching, snorkeling, Pearl Harbor coast sightseeing, and dinner/dance cruise. Prices range from $19.95–$45.95 adults; $12.95–$24.95 children 2–11. Rates include hotel pickup and drop-off, plus some meals.

If you aren't lucky enough to be in Hawaii during humpback-whale season (December to March) you can go dolphin-watching instead. Dream Cruises offer year-round cruises to view bottle-nosed and spinner dolphins near Yokohama Bay on the northern end of Oahu. During the whale season, they offer a sighting guarantee—you can sail again for free if you don't see whales. From Kewalo Basin they have a range of cruises, including a snorkel/splash tour where they anchor off Waikiki for snorkeling, swimming, and lunch; a 3-hour Pearl Harbor coastal cruise; and a 2-hour sunset dinner and dancing cruise with views of the Waikiki skyline.

Honolulu Sailing Co. Pier 2, Honolulu Harbor (across from Restaurant Row). ☎ **800/829-0114** or 808/239-3900. Fax 808/239-9718. www.honsail.com. For all-day cruises, park at Restaurant Row, 500 Ala Moana Blvd. (entrance is on Pohukaina St., between South and Punchbowl sts.), for $6 all day; for half-day cruises, park in metered spaces in front of pier 2 (50¢ per hour). TheBUS: 19, 20, or 47.

From a 2-hour sunset sail to a daylong adventure on the waves, Honolulu Sailing Co. offers a variety of sailing activities, including sailing lessons—picture yourself at the helm! They've been in the business for nearly two decades, providing everything from weddings at sea to honeymoon cruises, sail/snorkel trips, private lessons, and exclusive charters. The fleet ranges from 36- to 70-foot yachts; charters start at $50 per person, and lessons start at $125 per person per day.

Hawaii Ocean Thrills. Kewalo Basin (the floating island is located a half-mile offshore between Honolulu International Airport and Sand Island). ☎ **808/539-9400.** Complete package: $89 adults, $49 children 6–14; package without Formula One racing and Jet Skis $69 adults, $49 children 6–14. Boat to floating island departs 9am and returns at 1pm daily. Park on street at the end of Ala Moana Beach Park or in Kewalo Basin. TheBUS: 19 or 20.

If speed is your thing, here's the only place in Hawaii to sit behind the wheel of a Formula One raceboat, a sleek 12-foot-long racing machine that zips up to 30 m.p.h. in a quarter-mile oval track. The speedboats are just part of the 32,000-square-foot water park in the middle of Keehi Lagoon. Package tours include pickup from Waikiki hotels, a cruise on a catamaran out to the island, bumper boat soccer, basketball boat game, fishing, kayaking, paddle boats, swimming, a water slide, barbecue lunch, and, if you pick the deluxe package, Formula One racing boats and Jet Skis.

Navatek I. Aloha Tower Marketplace, Pier 6. c/o Royal Hawaiian Cruises Ltd. ☎ **800/852-4183** or 808/848-6360. Prices vary depending on cruise. Parking $3 with validation. TheBUS: 8, 19, 20, 55, 56, or 57; or the Waikiki Trolley to stop no. 7.

You've never been on a boat, you don't want to be on a boat, you are being dragged aboard a boat to view the sunset you can see perfectly well from your hotel lanai. Why are you boarding this weird-looking boat? It guarantees that you'll be "seasick-free," that's why. The 140-foot-long *Navatek I* isn't even called a boat; it's actually a SWATH (Small Waterplane Area Twin Hull) vessel. That means the ship's superstructure—the part you ride on—rests on twin torpedolike hulls that cut through the water so you don't bob like a cork and spill your mai tai. It's the smoothest ride on Mamala Bay. In fact, *Navatek I* is the only dinner cruise ship to receive U.S. Coast Guard certification to travel beyond Diamond Head.

Sunset dinner cruises leave Pier 6 (across from the Hawaii Maritime Museum) 7 nights a week. If you have your heart set on seeing the city lights at night, your best bet is to take the Skyline dinner cruise, which runs nightly from 8:15 to 10:15pm and costs $75 ($55 for children 2 to 11 years) for a three-course gourmet dinner in a romantic, candlelit setting with a great jazz band. An upscale dinner (four courses for $125, $95 for children 2 to 11 years) is served upstairs. There's an even more expensive dinner cruise from 5 to 7:30pm; it's $120 to $140 for adults, $82 to $115 for kids 2 to 11, and features top local entertainers and gourmet meals designed by award-winning Chef George Mavrothalassitis.

The best deal is the **lunch cruise** (noon to 2pm), with a full buffet lunch, live Hawaiian music, and a great view of Oahu offshore for $45 adults, $26.50 kids ages 2 to 11.

In whale season (roughly January to April), morning **whale-watching cruises** depart at 8:30am and return at 11am. The cost is $49 adults, $28.50 kids 2 to 11, and includes a breakfast buffet, Hawaiian entertainment, and commentary by a naturalist. Or you can choose the whale-watch lunch, noon to 2 pm; $47 adults and $28.50 children 2 to 11 years.

BODYBOARDING (BOOGIE BOARDING) & BODYSURFING

Bodysurfing—riding waves without a board, becoming one with the rolling water—is immensely popular in Hawaii. Some bodysurfers just rely on their outstretched hands (or hands at their sides) to ride the waves. Others use handboards (flat, paddle-like gloves). An excellent beach at which to learn bodysurfing is Kailua. The best beaches for experts are Makapuu and Sandy Beach.

For additional maneuverability, try a **boogie** or **bodyboard** (also known as belly boards or paipo boards). These 3-foot-long vehicles, which support the upper part of the body, are easy to carry and are very maneuverable in the water. The same open-heel fins used in bodysurfing are used in bodyboarding.

The best place to learn boogie boarding is in the calm waters of Waikiki, Kailua Beach, and Bellows Field Beach Park, off Kalanianole Highway (Hi. 72) in Waimanalo, which is open to the public on weekends (from noon on Friday to midnight on Sunday and holidays); to get to Bellows Field, turn toward the ocean on Hughs Road, then right on Tinker Road, which takes you right to the park. The consistently gentle waves and generally placid conditions at these spots allow beginners to practice under ideal conditions. Once you get the feel of boogie boarding and are ready to test your skills against more aggressive waves, check out those at Point Panic (by Kewalo Basin) or Makapuu. When the waves are right, advanced boogie boarders will relish the challenge at Sandy Beach or Banzai Beach.

You can rent boogie boards and fins for as little as $10 to $20 a day in Waikiki from **Aloha Beach Service,** at the Sheraton Moana Surfrider Hotel, 2365 Kalakaua Ave., Waikiki (☎ **808/922-3111,** ext. 2341), and **Blue Sky Rentals,** Inn on the Park, 1920 Ala Moana Blvd., Waikiki (☎ **808/947-0101**). On the way to Hanauma Bay, check out **Local Motion** in the Koko Marina Shopping Center, 7192 Kalanianaole Hwy., Hawaii Kai (☎ **808/396-7873;** TheBUS: 22); and on the windward side, the best boogie boards can be rented from **Kailua Sailboards & Kayaks,** 130 Kailua Rd., a couple of blocks from Kailua Beach Park (☎ **808/262-7341;** TheBUS: 56 or 57). On the North Shore, get equipment from **Surf-N-Sea,** 62–595 Kamehameha Hwy., Haleiwa (☎ **808/ 637-9887;** TheBUS: 52). See also "Shopping A to Z," in chapter 9, "Shopping."

OCEAN KAYAKING

Gliding along the ocean, with only the sound of your paddle dipping into the water to disturb your peace, is what kayaking is all about. A popular sport on Oahu, there are several kayak clubs that have regularly scheduled outings and can provide visitors with useful information. Contact **Hui Waa Kaukahi,** P.O. Box 88143, Honolulu, HI 96744; **Kanaka Ikaika,** P.O. Box 438, Kaneohe, HI 96744; and **Women's Kayak Club of Hawaii,** P.O. Box 438, Kaneohe, HI 96744.

First-timers should go to the North Shore's **Kayak Oahu Adventures,** in Waimea Valley and Adventure Park at 59–864 Kamehameha Hwy. (☎ **808/638-8189;** e-mail: kayak@lava.net), where kayak lessons, including equipment, are $15 per person. The kayaking takes place along the Waimea River; you'll paddle out to the golden sands of Waimea Bay, where you can rest or swim. They also offer a couple of guided tours: down the Waimea River for $35 each and, between June and August, an hour-long guided snorkel trip to Shark's Cove for $25. All equipment and instruction is provided. TheBUS no. 52 will get you there.

For a wonderful adventure, rent a kayak, arrive at Lanikai Beach just as the sun is appearing, and paddle across the emerald water to the pyramid-shaped islands called Mokulua—it's an experience you won't forget. Kayak equipment rental starts at $10 an hour or $37 for a day. In Waikiki, call **Prime Time Sports,** Fort DeRussy Beach, Waikiki (☎ **808/949-8952**); on the windward side, check out **Kailua Sailboards & Kayaks,** 130 Kailua Rd., a couple of blocks from Kailua Beach Park (☎ **808/ 262-7341;** TheBUS: 56 or 57).

SCUBA DIVING

Oahu is a wonderful place to scuba dive, especially for those interested in wreck-diving. One of the more famous wrecks in Hawaii is the ✪ *Mahi,* a 185-foot former mine sweeper easily accessible just south of Waianae. Abundant marine life makes this a great place to shoot photos—schools of lemon butterfly fish and ta'ape are so comfortable with divers and photographers that they practically pose. Eagle rays, green sea turtles, manta rays, and white-tipped sharks occasionally cruise by, and eels peer from the wreck.

For non-wreck diving, one of the best dive spots in the summer is ✪ **Kahuna Canyon.** In Hawaiian, *Kahuna* translates as priest, wise man, or sorcerer. This massive amphitheater, located near Mokuleia, is a perfect example of something a sorcerer might conjure up: Walls rising from the ocean floor create the illusion of an underwater Grand Canyon. Inside the amphitheater, crabs, octopi, and slipper and spiny lobsters abound (be aware that taking them in the summer is illegal), and giant trevally, parrotfish, and unicorn fish congregate. Outside the amphitheater, you're likely to see the occasional shark in the distance.

Since Oahu's best dives are offshore, your best bet is to book a two-tank dive from a dive boat. In Waipahu, try **Ocean Concepts Scuba,** 91–444 Komohana St., Suite C, Kapolei, HI 96707 (☎ **808/808-3483**); they'll take you diving in local lava caves, volcanic ledges, and the *Mahi* wreck. Two-tank dives range from $55 to $285; add another $16 for complete equipment rental. Transportation from Waikiki hotels is available at no extra charge.

Hawaii's oldest and largest dive shop is **Aaron's Dive Shop,** 602 Kailua Rd., Kailua (☎ **808/262-2333;** www.aloha.com/~aarons; TheBUS: 56 or 57). Aaron's offers boat and beach dive excursions off the coast of Oahu. The boat dives start at $80 per person; they include two tanks, all gear, and transportation from the Kailua shop or the Pearl City location. The beach dive off the North Shore in summer and the Waianae Coast in winter is the same price as a boat dive, including all gear and transportation, so Aaron's recommends the boat dive.

On the North Shore, **Surf-N-Sea,** 62–595 Kamehameha Hwy., Haleiwa (☎ **808/ 637-9887;** TheBUS: 52), has dive tours from the shore (starting at $65) or from a boat (starting at $75) and night dives ($80). They also rent scuba diving equipment and can point you to the best dive sites in the area.

SNORKELING

You don't need to take courses to enjoy snorkeling—all you need is a mask, fins, and a snorkel. A word of advice on equipment: Many tour operators provide equipment for free, but if your equipment doesn't fit properly, it's all but worthless. There's nothing worse than having a snorkeling trip ruined by a leaky mask. The mask should stick to your face, without the strap, when you inhale (make sure all hair is away from the mask—men with moustaches often have leakages in that area). You might want to make the investment (about $15 a week) and rent snorkel gear that fits. If you wear eyeglasses, you should be able to rent a suitable prescription mask for an extra charge. Fins should fit comfortably and float (you're snorkeling, not swimming long distances, so monstrous fins are not necessarily better, unless you're a swimmer in training).

Some of Oahu's best snorkeling is at Hanauma Bay. It's crowded and sometimes it seems there are more people than fish, but Hanauma has clear, warm, protected waters and an abundance of friendly reef fish—including Moorish idols, butterfly fish, damsel fish, and wrasses. Hanauma Bay has two reefs, an inner and an outer—the first for novices, the other for experts. The inner reef is calm and shallow (less than 10 ft.); in some places you can just wade in and put your face in the water. Go early; it's packed by 10am, and closed on Tuesdays. It's easy to get to Hanauma Bay; for details, see "Beaches," above.

The braver snorkelers among us may want to head to ✪ **Shark's Cove,** on the North Shore just off Kamehameha Highway, between Haleiwa and Pupukea. Sounds risky, we know, but we've never seen or heard of any sharks in this cove, and in summer this big, lava-edged pool is one of Oahu's best snorkel spots. Waves splash over the natural lava grotto and cascade like waterfalls into the pool full of tropical fish. There are deep-sea caves to explore to the right of the cove. TheBUS no. 52 will get you there.

The uninitiated might feel better after a lesson and a snorkel tour. **Surf-N-Sea,** 62–595 Kamehameha Hwy., Haleiwa (☎ **808/637-9887;** TheBUS: 52), has 2-hour tours, with equipment, starting at $45 for adults and $35 for children under 12. If you like it, they'll rent you snorkel gear.

Snorkel rentals are available at most dive shops and beach activity centers. In Waikiki, call **Blue Sky Rentals,** Inn on the Park, 1920 Ala Moana Blvd. (☎ **808/ 947-0101**); **Aloha Dive Shop,** Koko Marine Shopping Center (☎ **808/395-5922;** TheBUS: 22), the closest dive shop to Hanauma Bay; **Snorkel Bob's,** also on the way to Hanauma Bay at 700 Kapahulu Ave. (at Date Street), Honolulu (☎ **808/ 735-7944;** www.snorkelbob.com); and, on the North Shore, **Haleiwa Surf Center,** 66–167 Haleiwa Rd., Haleiwa (☎ **808/637-5051;** TheBUS: 52), which also teaches snorkeling and offers guided snorkel tours.

SPORTFISHING

The waters surrounding Hawaii are known the world over as one of the best places for big game sportfishing. The largest blue marlin ever captured on rod and reel anywhere on the planet was landed on a charter boat operated by Captain Cornelius Choy off Oahu. The monstrous fish weighed in at 1,805 pounds!

In addition to marlin (which, unlike other places, are caught in all 12 months of the year in Hawaii), you can try for sailfish, swordfish, tuna, rainbow runner, mahi-mahi, wahoo, barracuda, trevally, bonefish, and various snappers, groupers, and other bottom fish. Some 28 current world fishing records were set in Hawaii for marlin, swordfish, tuna, rainbow runner, and trevally. (No saltwater fishing license is required in Hawaii.)

You can contact charter boats through most activity desks or by walking the docks and talking with the captains; the latter method also allows you to make sure they do the type of fishing you're interested in—fishing styles can range from bottom fishing to trolling for big game fish. Charter fishing boats range both in size—from small 24-foot open skiffs to luxurious 50-foot-plus yachts—and in price, from a low of less than $50 per person to "share" a boat with other anglers to more than $800 a day to book an entire luxury sportfishing yacht on an exclusive basis.

Kewalo Basin, between the Honolulu International Airport and Waikiki, is the main location for charter fishing boats on Oahu. Top sportfishing boats from Kewalo Basin include the *Fish Hawk* (☎ 808/596-8338), *Maggie Joe* (☎ 808/591-8888), and *Mary I* **Sportfishing** (☎ 808/596-2998). From Waikiki, take Kalakaua *Ewa* (west) beyond Ala Moana Shopping Center; Kewalo Basin is on the left, across from Ward Centre. Look for charter boats all in a row in their slips; on lucky days, the captains display the catch of the day in the afternoon. You can also take TheBUS no. 19 or 20 (Airport).

SUBMARINE DIVING

Here's your chance to play Jules Verne and experience the underwater world in the comfort of a submarine. It'll take you on a 2-hour ride 60 feet below the surface. The entire trip is narrated, and professional divers feed the tropical fish just outside the sub so you can get a better look at them. Subs leave from Hilton Hawaiian Village Pier. The cost is $89 to $99 for adults, $39 for kids 12 and younger (children must be at least 36 inches tall); call **Atlantis Submarines** (☎ **800/548-6262** or 808/973-9811; www.goatlantis.com) to reserve. To save money, ask about the shorter "Discovery Adventure," which is only $59 for adults (the same $39 for children). *A word of warning:* The ride is safe for everyone, but skip it if you suffer from severe claustrophobia.

Voyager Submarines Hawaii, 1085 Ala Moana Blvd., Honolulu (☎ **808/592-7850**), also offers tours of the deep sea. Passengers board a 90-foot catamaran at Kewalo Basin for a 6-minute ride, with views of Waikiki and Diamond Head, to the submarine moored offshore. As the submarine descends to Kewalo Reef, an ancient lava flow 80 feet beneath the surface, passengers can see the underwater world through 30-inch-wide viewports or via the color video monitors at each seat. For the next 35 minutes, the submarine explores the reef. The first stop is Trumpetfish Cove, a lava outcropping with cauliflower coral and flittering tropical reef fish. Next stop: Urchin Hill, covered with hundreds of red spiny urchins. The sub then begins its trip across the face of the reef, passing volcanic rocks and boulders, clouds of reef fish, colorful corals, and occasionally dolphins. The 73-foot sub weighs 99 tons and is certified by the U.S. Coast Guard to dive to 150 feet. Price (which includes round-trip bus transfers from Waikiki) is $89 for adults and $29 for children 12 and under. Children must be at least 30 inches tall to board the submarine.

SURFING

In the summertime, when the water is warm and there's a soft breeze in the air, the south swell comes up. It's surf season in Waikiki—the best place to learn how to surf on Oahu. At last count, Oahu had more than 100 surf sites, so this is the place to be when the waves are happening. Winter in Hawaii also means monstrous waves on the North Shore. These are not the gentle swells of summer, lapping lazily on the shore. These mountains of water, 20-plus feet tall, explode when they collapse on the beach and the ground rumbles.

Surfing is the sport Hawaii has given to the world. The ancient origins of surfing in Hawaii can be seen in carved petroglyphs and in ancient chants tracing back to the 15th century. The Hawaiians looked upon surfing not only as a sport (a betting sport, at that, with spectators wagering property on their favorite wave rider), but also as a religious experience. The Hawaiian word for surfing, *he'e nalu,* can be translated literally to mean "wave sliding," but a more poetic translation—and one favored by surfers—summons up a metaphor of a newborn baby slipping from a terrifying, roaring, surging saltwater womb.

While you're on Oahu, don't pass up the opportunity to learn to surf—go early to **Aloha Beach Service,** next to the Sheraton Moana Surfrider Hotel, 2365 Kalakaua Ave., in Waikiki (☎ **808/922-3111**). The beach boys offer surfing lessons for $25 an hour; board rentals are $8 for an hour and $12 for 2 hours. Of course, you must know how to swim. **Surf & Sea,** 62–595 Kamehameha Hwy., Haleiwa (☎ **808/637-9887**) offers surfing lessons for $65 for 2 hours or $150 all day, equipment included.

Surfboards are also available for rent (expect to pay about $5 to $10 an hour and $18 to $25 for the day) at **Local Motion,** 1714 Kapiolani Blvd., Honolulu (☎ **808/955-7873**); **Plant Surf,** 412 Nahua, Waikiki (☎ **808/926-2060**); or **Surf & Sea,** 62–595 Kamehameha Hwy., Haleiwa (☎ **808/637-9887**).

More experienced surfers should drop in at any surf shop around Oahu, or call the **Surf News Network Surfline** at ☎ **808/596-SURF** or 808/836-1952 to get the latest surf conditions. A good spot for advanced surfers is The Cliffs, at the base of Diamond Head. The 4- to 6-foot waves churn here, allowing high-performance surfing—and the view of Diamond Head is great.

During the months of November and December, the world championship of surfing, the **Triple Crown,** is held in Hawaii, a three-event series that concludes the yearlong Association of Surfing Professional's World Tour. Even if you've never given surfing much thought, this event is exciting. It's the Super Bowl of surfing; more than 60 surfing competitions held throughout the world lead up to this event. Some $2.5 million in prize money is given away to the men and women, the greatest surfers in the world, who can best the monstrous waves.

If you're in Hawaii in the winter and want to see serious surfers catch really big waves, bring your binoculars and grab a front-row seat on the beach near Kalalua Point. To get there from Waikiki, take the H-1 toward the North Shore, veering off at H-2, which becomes Kamehameha Highway (Hi. 83). Keep going to the funky surf town of Haleiwa and Waimea Bay; the big waves will be on your left, just past Pupukea Beach Park.

SWIMMING

For a quiet, peaceful place to swim, **Malaekahana Bay,** near Kahuku, is one of the best Oahu beaches. This milelong, white-sand, crescent-shaped beach is about a 90-minute drive and a million miles from the crowds at Waikiki. To get there, take Kamehameha Highway past Laie and follow the signs to Malaekahana State Recreational Area. Or take TheBUS no. 52 (Circle Island). Another good swimming beach is **Lanikai;** secluded and calm, this beach is great for families. From Waikiki, take TheBUS no. 56 or 57 (Kailua), and then transfer to the shuttle bus. (See also "Beaches," above.)

WATER-SKIING

Believe it or not, there's water-skiing on Oahu. To learn to water-ski, or to just go out and have a good time, call the oldest water-ski company in Hawaii, **Suyderhoud Water Ski Center,** at Koko Marina Shopping Center (☎ **808/395-3773;** TheBUS: 58). Lessons and boat rental are $49 for a half-hour lesson and $98 for an hour, including the boat and all equipment rental (maximum of five people).

WHALE WATCHING

From December to April, 45-foot humpback whales—Hawaii's most impressive visitors—come to spend the winter. They make the journey from Alaska to calve and mate in Hawaii's calm, warm waters. Once nearly hunted to extinction, humpback whales are now protected by federal law. The mammals may not be approached by any individual or watercraft within 100 yards.

Whales can frequently be seen off the island on calm days. If you spot the familiar spout of water—a sign the mammal is exhaling—there's a good chance you'll see the whale on the surface. If you're in a car, please pull over, as many accidents have occurred when visitors try to spot whales and drive at the same time.

For whale-watching cruises, see "Boating," above.

WINDSURFING

This is another ocean activity that combines two sports: sailing and surfing. Windsurfers stand on a surfboard that has a sail attached to it, thus bringing the wind and the waves together in a ride that enthusiasts claim is a real adrenaline rush. Windward Oahu's Kailua Beach Park is the home of champion and pioneer windsurfer Robbie Naish; it's also the best place to learn to windsurf. The oldest and most established windsurfing business in Hawaii is **Naish Windsurfing Hawaii,** 155-C Hamakua Dr., Kailua (☎ **808/261-3539;** www.naish.com). The company offers everything: sales, rentals, instruction, repair, and free advice on where to go when the wind and waves are happening. Private lessons start at $55 for one, $75 for two; equipment rental is $25 for a half day and $30 for a full day. The **Kailua Sailboard Co.,** 130 Kailua Dr., across the street from Kailua Beach Park (☎ **808/262-2555**), offers 3½-hour small-group lessons for $49 per person; rentals are also available. To get to Kailua Beach Park, take TheBUS no. 56 or 57 and shuttle no. 70.

Windsurfer wanna-bes on the North Shore can contact **North Shore Windsurf School,** 59–452 Makana Rd. (Kamehameha Highway), Haleiwa (☎ **808/638-8198;** TheBUS: 52). Experts give 2½-hour lessons in a protected area on the North Shore for $40. Some people can get up and sail away in one lesson, but it usually takes about three lessons to be sailing over the waves. Another place on the North Shore for lessons ($65 for 2 hours and $150 for the day) and equipment rental is **Surf & Sea,** 62–595 Kamehameha Hwy., Haleiwa (☎ **808/637-9887;** TheBUS: 52).

3 Nature Hikes

Everyone has the notion that Oahu is one big urban island, so you'll be surprised to discover that the great outdoors is less than an hour away from downtown Honolulu. The island's 33 major trails take you across razor-thin ridge backs and deep into valleys with waterfalls.

Check out Stuart Ball's *The Hikers Guide to Oahu* (Honolulu: University of Hawaii Press, 1993) before you hike. For a free **Oahu Recreation Map,** listing all 33 trails, write to the **Department of Land and Natural Resources,** 1151 Punchbowl St., Room 130, Honolulu, HI 96813 (☎ **808/587-0300;** www.hawaii.gov). They'll also send you free topographic trail maps on request and issue camping permits. Another good source of information is the **Hiking/Camping Information Packet** from **Hawaii Geographic Maps and Books,** 49 S. Hotel St., Suite 218, Honolulu, HI 96813 (☎ **808/538-3952**), for a cost of $7 (postage included). Also, be sure to get a copy of *Hiking on Oahu: The Official Guide,* which is a hiking safety guide that includes instructions on hiking preparation, safety procedures, emergency phone numbers, and necessary equipment. The brochure was created in response to the somewhat frequent disappearance of hikers and the deaths of two police officers and a firefighter who were searching for lost hikers. For a copy of the brochure, contact Erin Lau, Trails and Access Manager, **City and County of Honolulu** (☎ **808/ 973-9782**); the **Hawaii Nature Center,** 2131 Makiki Heights Dr. (☎ **808/ 955-0100**); or **The Bike Shop,** 1149 S. King St. (☎ **808/596-0588**). Another good source of hiking information on Oahu is the state's **Na Ala Hele (Trails to Go On) Program;** call ☎ **808/973-9782** or 808/587-0058.

The **Hawaiian Trail and Mountain Club,** P.O. Box 2238, Honolulu, HI 96804, offers regularly scheduled hikes on Oahu. You bring your own lunch and drinking water, and join up with the club at the Iolani Palace. For a schedule of all upcoming hikes and an information packet on hiking and camping in Hawaii, send $1.25, plus a legal-sized, self-addressed, stamped envelope to the address above.

The **Sierra Club,** P.O. Box 2577, Honolulu, HI 96803 (www.hi.sierraclub.org), also offers regularly scheduled hikes on which they welcome visitors. The **Hawaii Nature Center,** 2131 Makiki Heights Dr. (☎ **808/955-0100;** open Monday through Friday, from 8am to 4:30pm) is another organization that offers organized hikes, as well as "Sunday Adventures" for children.

HONOLULU AREA
✪ DIAMOND HEAD CRATER

This is a moderate, but steep, walk to the summit of Hawaii's most famous landmark. Kids love the top of the 761-foot volcanic cone, where they have 360-degree views of Oahu, from the leeward coast to Waikiki. The 1.4-mile round-trip takes about an hour.

Diamond Head was created by a volcanic explosion about a half-million years ago. The Hawaiians called the crater *Leahi* (meaning "the brow of the ahi," or tuna, referring to the shape of the crater). Diamond Head was considered a sacred spot; King Kamehameha offered human sacrifices at a *heiau* (temple) on the western slope. It wasn't until the 19th century that Mount Leahi got its current name. A group of sailors found what they thought were diamonds in the crater; it turned out they really found worthless calcite crystals, but the Diamond Head moniker stuck.

Before you begin your adventure hiking to the top of the crater, put on some decent shoes (rubber-soled tennies are fine) and gather a flashlight (you walk through several dark tunnels), binoculars (for better viewing at the top), drinking water (very important), a hat to protect you from the sun, and your camera. You might want to put all your gear in a pack to leave your hands free for the climb. If you don't have a flashlight or your hotel can't lend you one, you can buy a small one for a few dollars as part of a Diamond Head climbers "kit" at the gift shop at the New Otani Kaimana Beach Hotel, on the Diamond Head end of Kalakaua Avenue, just past the Waikiki Aquarium and across from Kapiolani Park.

Start your hike to the summit of Diamond Head at Monsarrat and 18th avenues on the crater's inland (or mauka) side. To get here, take TheBUS no. 58 from the Ala Moana Shopping Center; get off at Diamond Head Road/18th Avenue (ask the bus driver and he will tell you when to get off). If you're driving, head to the intersection of Diamond Head Road and 18th Avenue. Follow the road through the tunnel (which is closed from 6pm to 6am) and park in the lot. The trailhead starts in the parking lot and proceeds along a paved walkway (with handrails) as it climbs up the slope. You'll pass old World War I and II pillboxes, gun emplacements, and tunnels built as part of the Pacific defense network. Several steps take you up to the top observation post on Point Leahi. The views are indescribable.

Go early: We recommend arriving just after the 6:30am opening, before the noonday sun starts beating down. Honolulu Fire Deputy Chief John Clark said that of the estimated 2,000 people who hike the trail daily, most are ill prepared: "It's not just a walk in the park—it's a moderately strenuous hike that takes you 761 feet above sea level."

If you want to go with a guide, the **Clean Air Team** leads a free guided hike to the top of Diamond Head every Saturday. They gather at 9am, near the front entrance to the Honolulu Zoo (look for the rainbow windsock). Hikers should bring a flashlight. Each hiker will be given a litter bag and asked to help keep the trail clean by picking up litter. For more information, call ☎ **808/948-3299.**

Factoid

Amelia Earhart was the first woman to fly solo from Hawaii to the U.S. mainland in 1935. A plaque on Diamond Head Road memorializes her 12-hour, 50-minute flight from Honolulu to Oakland, California.

KANEALOLE TRAIL

This is the starting place for some of Oahu's best hiking trails; miles of trails converge through the Makiki Valley–Tantalus–Round Top–Nuuanu Valley area. To get a general feel for the hikes in the region, take this 1½-mile round-trip moderate hike, which climbs some 500 feet and takes less than an hour. If you're interested, stop at the **Hawaii Nature Center,** located by the trailhead at 2131 Makiki Heights Dr. (☎ **808/ 955-0100;** open Monday to Friday, from 8am to 4:30pm), where you can find information on the environmental and conservation needs of Hawaii, displays of plants and animals, hands-on exhibits, and numerous maps and pamphlets about this hiking area. They also sponsor organized hikes on weekends.

To get here, take McCully Avenue north out of Waikiki; cross over the H-1 freeway and turn left on Wilder Avenue. Make a right turn on Makiki Street and continue until the road forks at the park. Take the left fork past the Makiki Pumping Station; the road is now called Makiki Heights Drive. Follow it up to the hairpin turn and make a right onto the small spur road that goes into Makiki Valley; park just beyond the green trailers that house the Hawaii Nature Center. If you are taking the bus, it's a little trickier: From Waikiki, take TheBUS no. 8, 19, 20, or 58 to the Ala Moana Shopping Center and transfer to TheBUS no. 17. Tell your driver where you're going, and he'll let you off near the spur road just off Makiki Heights Drive; you'll have to walk the rest of the way.

After stopping at the Hawaii Nature Center, continue up the path, which wanders under the protection of kukui trees and lush vines. The road gets smaller and smaller until it's just a footpath. Along this narrow path, look for the tall, bushy grasslike plant called Job's tears. It's considered a weed in Hawaii, but this is no ordinary grass; it can grow up to 5 feet high and produces a gray, tear-shaped seed. The trail continues through an abandoned valley where there once was a thriving Hawaiian community. Occasionally you'll spot the remains of stone walls and even a few coffee plants; Makiki Valley supported a coffee plantation in the previous century. When you meet the Makiki Valley Trail, you can retrace your steps or choose from the dozens of trails in the area.

✪ MAKIKI–MANOA CLIFFS

From rainforests to ridgetop views, this somewhat strenuous loop trail is one you'll never forget. The hike is just over 6 miles, gains 1,260 feet in elevation, and takes about 3 hours. This trail is part of the labyrinth of trails found in this area (see "Kanealole Trail," above). To get to these trails, follow the directions for the Kanealole Trail (see above).

The trail starts by the rest rooms of the Hawaii Nature Center. Look for the paved path that crosses Kanealole Stream via a footbridge (Maunalaha Trail). Stay on the trail, following it up the hill into the forest, where you'll pass bananas, Norfolk and Cook Island pines, ti plants, and even a few taro patches. Cross over Moleka Stream and look for the four-way junction with the Makiki Valley and Ualakaa trails; turn right on the **Makiki Valley Trail.** This takes you through a dense forest, past a giant banyan tree, and then joins with the Moleka Trail. Turn left on the **Moleka Trail**— now you're in the rainforest: Ancient guava trees reach overhead, maidenhair ferns cling to rocks, and tiny white-flowered begonias crop up.

Further on, the kukui and koa give way to a bamboo-filled forest, which opens up to a parking lot on Round Top Drive at the end of the Moleka Trail. Cross Round Top Drive to the **Manoa Cliffs Trail,** which emerges on Tantalus Drive. Turn right on Tantalus and walk about 100 yards down the street to the **Nahuina Trail** on the left side of Tantalus. As you walk downhill, you'll have breathtaking views of downtown

Outdoor Etiquette

Act locally, think globally, and carry out what you carry in. Find a rubbish container for all your litter (including cigarette butts—it's very bad form to throw them out your car window). Observe kapu and no trespassing signs. Don't climb on ancient Hawaiian heiau walls and temples or carry home rocks, all of which belong to the Hawaiian volcano goddess Pele. Some say it's just a silly superstition or coincidence, but each year the U.S. Park Service gets boxes of lava rocks sent back to Hawaii by visitors who've experienced unusually bad luck.

Honolulu. At the junction of Kanealole Trail, turn right and continue back to where you started.

✪ MANOA FALLS TRAIL

This easy, .8-mile (one-way) hike is terrific for families; it takes less than an hour to reach idyllic Manoa Falls. The trailhead, marked by a footbridge, is at the end of Manoa Road, past Lyon Arboretum. The arboretum prefers that hikers do not use their lot, so the best place to park is in the residential area below the former Paradise Park; you can also get to the arboretum via TheBUS no. 5. The often-muddy trail follows Waihi Stream and meanders through the forest reserve past guava, mountain apple, and wild ginger. The forest is moist and humid and inhabited by giant bloodthirsty mosquitoes, so bring repellent.

PUU OHIA TRAIL TO NUUANU VALLEY VIEW

This moderate hike takes you through a rainforest, up to the top of Tantalus (Puu Ohia) cinder cone, and down through Pauoa Flats to view Nuuanu Valley. Plan about 2 hours for this 3½-mile round-trip hike, which gains about 1,200 feet in altitude.

To get here, follow the directions for the Kanealole Trail, above, but turn to the right at the park fork in Makiki Street. The fork to the right is Round Top Drive. Drive to the top and park in the turnout on the ocean side of the street. Unfortunately, bus service is not available.

The Puu Ohia trailhead is across the street from where you parked. As you head up (a series of switchbacks and, at the steepest part, hand-cut stairs in the dirt), you pass night-blooming jasmine, ginger, Christmas berry, and avocado trees. After dense guava trees and bamboo, the vegetation parts for a magnificent view of Honolulu and Diamond Head. Just as quickly, as you continue along the trail, the bamboo once again obstructs the view. At the next junction, stay on the main trail by bearing to the left; you'll pass through ginger, koa, and bamboo. At the next junction, bear left again, and climb up the steps around the trunk of an old koa tree. At the top is a paved road; turn right and walk downhill. The road leads to an old telephone relay station, and then turns into a footpath. Passing through bamboo, koa, ti, and strawberry guava, turn left onto the Manoa Cliffs Trail. At the next junction, turn right on the Puu Ohia Trail, which leads to the Pauoa Flats and to the view of the Nuuanu Valley. Retrace your steps for your return.

UALAKAA LOOP

The same series of volcanic eruptions that produced Diamond Head and Koko Crater also produced the cinder cones of Round Top (Puu Ualakaa), Sugarloaf (Puu Kakea), and Tantalus (Puu Ohia). *Puu,* as you may have already guessed, means "hill"; these three hills overlook Honolulu and offer spectacular views. The easy Ualakaa Loop Trail is a half-hour hike of about a mile that traverses through woods, offering occasional panoramic views of Honolulu.

There's no bus service to this trailhead. Follow the directions for the Puu Ohia hike, above, but instead of driving to the top of Round Top Drive, turn off on the fourth major hairpin turn (look for it after a long stretch of panoramic straightaway). The turn will go through the gate of the **Puu Ualakaa State Wayside Park.** Continue a little more than 4 miles inside the park; look for a stand of Norfolk pine trees and park there. The trailhead is on the right side of the Norfolk pines. The park is open 7am to 7:45pm from April 1 to Labor Day; after Labor Day, the park closes at 6:45pm.

The loop trail, lined with impatiens, passes through Norfolk pines, palm trees, iron-woods, and Christmas berry trees. The once-native forest now has many foreign intrusions—including all of the foregoing—as well as ti, banana, banyan, guava, and mountain apple. At two points along the trail, you emerge on Round Top Drive; just walk about 100 feet to continue on the trail on the opposite side of the road. The loop will bring you back to where you started.

PEARL CITY
UPPER WAIMANO TRAIL

This is a strenuous, 14-mile round-trip with an altitude gain of nearly 2,000 feet. The rewards are worth the effort: magnificent views from the top of windward Oahu's Koolau Mountains, and a chance to see rare native Hawaiian plants. Plan a full day for this 8-hour hike.

To get here from Waikiki, take the H-1 to the Pearl City exit (Exit 10) on Moanalua Road; head north and turn right on Waimano Home Road; follow it to the end, just over 22 miles. Park on the road. Or take TheBUS no. 8, 19, 20, or 58 from Waikiki to the Ala Moana Shopping Center and transfer to TheBUS no. 53. Tell your driver where you are going and he will take you as far as he can on Waimano Home Road; you'll have to walk the rest of the way to the trailhead (about 1½ miles).

You'll pick up the trailhead at the dirt path to the left of the gate, outside the fence surrounding the Waimano Home. Follow the trail through swamp mahogany trees to the first junction; turn right at the junction to stay on the upper Waimano Trail. At the second junction, turn right again to stay on the upper trail. The Christmas berry becomes denser, but as you move up the mountain, koa, kukui, hau, mango, guava, mountain apple, and ginger start to appear. You'll know you are getting closer to the stream bed when the mosquitoes begin buzzing. Cross the stream bed and climb the switchbacks on the eucalyptus-covered ridge. More native plants will appear: ohia, uluhe, and koa. Just before you reach the crest of the next ridge, look for rarely seen plants like yellow-flowered *ohia lehua, kanawao* (a relative of the hydrangea), and mountain *naupaka.* The trail ends on the sometimes rainy—and nearly always windy—peak of the Koolaus, where you'll have views of Waihee Valley and the entire windward side from Kahaluu to Kaneohe Bay. It's very clear that this is the end of the trail; retrace your steps to the trailhead.

EAST OAHU
MAKAPUU LIGHTHOUSE TRAIL

You've seen this famous old lighthouse on episodes of "Magnum P.I." and "Hawaii Five-O." No longer manned by the Coast Guard (it's fully automated now), the light-house is the goal of hikers who challenge a precipitous cliff trail to gain an airy perch over the Windward Coast, Manana (Rabbit) Island, and the shimmering Pacific. It's about a 45-minute, mile-long hike from Kalanianaole Highway (Hi. 72), along a paved road that begins across from Hawaii Kai Executive Golf Course and winds around the 646-foot-high sea bluff to the lighthouse lookout.

To get to the trailhead from Waikiki, take Kalanianaole Highway (Hi. 72) past Hanauma Bay and Sandy Beach to Makapuu Head, the southeastern tip of the island. Look for a sign that says NO VEHICLES ALLOWED on a gate to the right, a few hundred yards past the entrance to the golf course. The trail isn't marked, but it's fairly obvious: Just follow the abandoned road that leads gradually uphill to a trail that wraps around Makapuu Point. It's a little precarious, but anyone in reasonably good shape can handle it. You can also take TheBUS no. 57–58; get off the bus just past Sandy Beach (ask the bus driver to let you know when you pass the entrance to Hawaii Kai Golf Course).

Blow hole alert: When the south swell is running, usually in summer, there are a couple of blow holes on the south side of Makapuu Head that put the famous Halona Blow Hole to shame.

WINDWARD OAHU
HAUULA LOOP

For one of the best views of the coast and the ocean, follow the Hauula Loop Trail on the windward side of the island. It's an easy, 2½-mile loop on a well-maintained path that passes through a whispering ironwood forest and a grove of tall Norfolk pines. The trip takes about 3 hours and gains some 600 feet in elevation.

To get to the trail, take TheBUS no. 55 or follow Hi. 83 to Hauula Beach Park. Turn toward the mountains on Hauula Homestead Road; when the road forks to the left at Maakua Road, park on the side of the road. Walk along Maakua Road to the wide, grassy trail that begins the hike into the mountains. The climb is fairly steep for about 300 yards, but continues on to easier-on-the-calves switchbacks as you go up the ridge. Look down as you climb: You'll spot wildflowers and mushrooms among the matted needles. The trail continues up, crossing Waipilopilo Gulch, where you'll see several forms of native plant life. Eventually you reach the top of the ridge, where the views are spectacular.

Although the Division of Forestry permits camping along the trail, it's difficult to find a place to pitch a tent on the steep slopes and in the dense forest growth. There are a few places along the ridge, however, that are wide enough for a tent. Contact the **Division of Forestry and Wildlife,** 1151 Punchbowl St., Honolulu, HI 96813 (☎ **808/587-0166;** www.hawaii.gov), for information on camping permits.

PALI (MAUNAWILI) TRAIL

For a million-dollar view of the Windward Coast, take this easy 11-mile (one-way) foothill trail. The trailhead is about 6 miles from downtown Honolulu, on the windward side of the Nuuanu Pali Tunnels, at the scenic lookout just beyond the hairpin turn of the Pali Highway (Hi. 61). Just as you begin the turn, look for the SCENIC

Sacred Falls: News Bulletin

In May 1999, a landslide above Sacred Falls sent tons of jagged boulders, some the size of a compact car, hurling down into Sacred Falls pool, killing 6 people and injuring 36 others. When this book went to press, the State Department of Land and Natural Resources had closed the park indefinitely until geologists could assess the threat of future landslides. But even if the park reopens, the slide appears to have altered the appearance of the pool area and it may not be exactly as we describe it here. For information on the status of the Sacred Falls trail and pool, call the Department of Land and Natural Resources, Parks Division Information, at ☎ **808/587-0300.**

OVERLOOK sign, slow down, and pull off the highway into the parking lot (sorry, no bus service available).

The mostly flat, well-marked, easy-to-moderate trail goes through the forest on the lower slopes of the 3,000-foot Koolau Mountain Range and ends up in the backyard of the coastal Hawaiian village of Waimanalo. Go halfway to get the view and return to your car, or have someone meet you in 'Nalo.

✪ SACRED FALLS

It's easy to see why this place was given the name "Sacred": Clear, cold water, originating from the top of the Koolau Mountains, descends down the Kaluanui Stream and cascades over Sacred Falls into a deep, boulder-strewn pool. The hike to this awe-inspiring waterfall passes under guava and mountain apple trees and through a fern-filled narrow canyon that parallels the streambed.

A few words of warning before you grab your hiking boots: First, do not attempt this hike in wet weather. In fact, the State Parks Division closes the falls if there's a danger of flash floods. This is no idle warning—in 1987, five hikers attempting to reach the falls died in three separate incidents when the normally babbling stream was flooded; in October 1993, a Boy Scout troop had to be rescued by helicopter during a flash flood. Second, go in a group—there have been a few muggings along the 2.2-mile trail in recent years.

The best time to take this hike is in the morning, when the light is good. Be prepared with rain gear and insect repellent. The easy 4.4-mile round-trip takes about 2 to 3 hours. To get to the trail, drive north on the Kamehameha Highway (Hi. 83) to the turnoff for Sacred Falls State Park, or take TheBUS no. 55. The trail begins at the parking lot and heads for the mountains, paralleling the Kaluanui Stream. About a mile into the trail is a grassy area with emergency warning equipment inside a cyclone fence; the trailhead is to the left of the fence. The beginning is a bit rough—the trail is muddy and passes under tangled branches and through a tunnel of Christmas berry. About a half-mile beyond the trailhead, you'll cross the Kaluanui Stream; if the water is high or muddy, don't cross—you could become trapped in the canyon during a flash flood. As you continue up the trail, the canyon becomes increasingly narrow, with steep walls on either side. Be on the lookout for falling rocks. At the end of the trail are the majestic falls and an extremely cold pool, home to spidery Malaysian prawns.

LEEWARD OAHU
KAENA POINT

At the remote western tip of Oahu lie the dry, barren lands of Kaena Point State Park: 853 acres of wild wind- and surf-battered coastline with jagged sea cliffs, deep gulches, sand dunes, and endangered plant life. *Kaena* means "red-hot" or "glowing" in Hawaiian; the name refers to the brilliant sunsets visible from the point.

Kaena is steeped in legends. A popular one involves the demigod Maui, who had a famous hook he used to raise islands from the sea. He decided that he wanted to bring the islands of Oahu and Kauai closer together, so one day he threw his hook across the Kauai Channel and snagged the island of Kauai (which actually is visible from Kaena Point on clear days). Using all his might, Maui was only able to pull loose a huge boulder, which fell into the waters very close to the present lighthouse at Kaena. The rock is still called Pohaku o Kauai (the rock from Kauai). Like Black Rock in Kaanapali on Maui, Kaena is thought of as the point on Oahu from which souls depart.

To get to the trailhead from Honolulu or Waikiki, take the H-1 freeway west to its end; continue on Hi. 93 past Makaha and follow Hi. 930 to the end of the road. There's no bus service.

To start the hike, take the clearly marked trail from the parking lot of the Makua–Kaena Point State Park. The moderate, 5-mile round-trip hike to the point will take a couple of hours. The trail along the cliff passes tide pools, which is abundant in marine life, and rugged protrusions of lava reaching out to the turbulent sea; seabirds circle overhead. There are no sandy beaches and the water is almost always turbulent. During the winter months, when a big north swell is running, the waves at Kaena are the biggest in the state, averaging heights of 30 to 40 feet. Even when the water appears calm, offshore currents are powerful, so don't plan to swim. Go early in the morning to see the school of porpoises that frequent the area just offshore.

4 Great Golf

Oahu has nearly three dozen golf courses, ranging from bare-bones municipal courses to exclusive country club courses with annual membership fees in the six figures. It is possible to play some top-notch golf in Hawaii without having to take out a second mortgage on your home. Golfers unfamiliar with Hawaii's courses will be dazzled by some of the spectacular views—the shimmering ocean and majestic mountains, to name a few.

Golfers will also come to know that the windward golf courses play much differently than the leeward courses. On the windward side, the prevailing winds blow from the ocean to shore and the grain direction of the greens tends to run the same way—from the ocean to the mountains. Leeward golf courses have the opposite tendency; the winds usually blow from the mountains to the ocean, and the grain direction on the greens matches. Below are a variety of courses, with greens fees (cart costs included) and notes on scenic views, challenges, and a taste of what golfing in paradise is like.

For last-minute and discount tee times, call **Stand-by Golf** (from Hawaii, call ☎ **888/645-BOOK;** from the mainland, call 808/874-0600), which offers discounted and guaranteed tee times for same-day or next-day golfing. You can call between 7am and 9pm Hawaii Standard Time, to book one of the seven semiprivate and resort courses they handle and get a guaranteed tee time for the next day at a 10% to 40% discount.

EAST OAHU

Hawaii Kai Golf Course. 8902 Kalanianaole Hwy., Honolulu, HI 96825. ☎ **808/ 395-2358.** Championship course fees: $100 weekdays; $120 weekends; $60 twilight rate weekdays 1–2:30pm. Executive course fees: $37 weekdays; $42 weekends; $12 twilight rate after 4pm. From Waikiki, go east on H-1, past Hawaii Kai; the course is immediately past Sandy Beach on the left. TheBUS: 58.

How to Avoid the Crowds & Save Money

Oahu's golf courses tend to be crowded, so we suggest that you go during midweek. Also, most island courses have twilight rates with substantial discounts if you're willing to tee off in the afternoon, usually between 1 and 3pm. Look for this feature in the golf listings.

No Bags on TheBUS

TheBUS does not allow golf bags onboard. If you don't have another means of transportation, you're going to have to rent clubs at the course.

Actually, there are two golf courses in one here: the par-72, 6,222-yard **Hawaii Kai Championship Golf Course** and the par-3 **Hawaii Kai Executive Golf Course.** Both are between Sandy Beach and Makapuu Point on the island's eastern tip. The Championship course is moderately challenging, with scenic vistas. It's forgiving to high-handicap golfers, although it does have a few surprises. The par-3 Executive golf course is fun for beginners and those just getting back in the game. It has lots of hills and valleys, but no water hazards and only a few sand traps. Lockers are available.

THE NORTH SHORE

✪ **Kahuku Golf Course.** P. O. Box 417, Kahuku, HI 96731. ☎ **808/293-5842.** Fees: $20. From Waikiki, take the H-1 west to H-2; follow H-2 through Wahiawa and Schofield Barracks to Kamehameha Hwy. (Hi. 99, then Hi. 83); follow it to Kahuku. TheBUS: 55.

We admit that this nine-hole budget golf course is a bit funky. Except for a few pull carts that disappear with the first handful of golfers, there are no facilities: no club rentals, no clubhouse. But playing here, among the scenic beauty of this oceanside course and the tranquility of the North Shore, is quite an experience, nonetheless. Duffers will love the ease of this recreational course, and weight watchers will be happy to walk the gently sloping greens. Don't forget to bring your camera for the views (especially at holes 3, 4, 7, and 8, which are right on the ocean). No reservations are taken; tee times are doled out on a first-come, first-served basis—with plenty of retirees happy to sit and wait. The competition is fierce for early tee times. Bring your own clubs and call ahead to check the weather. *Note:* During the summer, this is a sizzling hot course—there are very few shade trees and the sun constantly beats down on you.

✪ **Hilton Turtle Bay Resort.** P.O. Box 187, Kahuku, HI 96731. ☎ **808/293-8574.** George Fazio course fees: $50 for 18 holes. Links course fees: $125. Take H-1 west past Pearl City; when the freeway splits, take H-1 and follow the signs to Haleiwa; at Haleiwa, take Hi. 83 to Turtle Bay Resort. TheBUS: 52 or 55.

Here's a chance to play one of Hawaii's top golf courses, about an hour's drive from Waikiki, for just $50 for 18 holes. The budget course is the **George Fazio–designed 9-hole course**—the only one Fazio designed in Hawaii—which can be played twice for a regulation par-71, 6,200-yard course. The course has two sets of tees, one designed for men and one for women, so you can get a slightly different play if you decide to tackle 18 holes. Larry Keil, pro at Turtle Bay, says that people like the Fazio course because it's a forgiving resort course, without the water hazards and bunkers of the more challenging and expensive Links course, below. "A lot of visitors like the option to just play nine holes," he added. The sixth hole has two greens so you can play the hole as a par 3 or a par 4. The toughest hole has to be the par-3, 176-yard second hole, where you tee off across a lake with the normal trade winds creating a mean cross wind; you have to clear the lake and land on the green and two-putt to make par. The most scenic hole is the seventh, where the ocean is on your left; if you're lucky, you'll see whales cavorting in the winter months.

If you want to splurge, you can play the 18-hole **Links at Kuilima,** designed by Arnold Palmer and Ed Seay—*Golf Digest* rated it the fourth best new resort course in 1994. Turtle Bay used to be labeled a "wind tunnel"; it still is one, but the casuarina (ironwood) trees have matured and they dampen the wind somewhat. Palmer and Seay never meant for golfers to get off too easy; this is a challenging course. The front nine holes, with rolling terrain, only a few trees, and lots of wind, play like a British Isles course. The back nine holes have narrower, tree-lined fairways and water. The course circles Punahoolapa Marsh, a protected wetland for endangered Hawaiian waterfowl.

Facilities include a pro shop, driving range, putting and chipping green, and snack bar. Weekdays are best for tee times. Unfortunately, no twilight rates are available.

CENTRAL OAHU

Hawaii Country Club. 98–1211 Kunia Rd., Wahiawa, HI 96786. ☎ **808/621-5654.** Fees: $30 weekdays, $40 weekends (cart included); $17 twilight rate weekdays after 4pm, $21 weekends. From Waikiki, take the H-1 freeway west for about 20 min. Turn off at the Kunia exit (Exit 5B) and follow it to the course. No bus service.

This public course, located in central Oahu in Wahiawa, is a modest course where golfers usually have no trouble getting a tee time. The 5,861-yard, par-71 course is not manicured like the resort courses, but it does offer fair play, with relatively inexpensive greens fees. Located in the middle of former sugarcane and pineapple fields, the greens and fairways tend to be a bit bumpy and there are a number of tall monkeypod and pine trees to shoot around, but the views of Pearl Harbor and Waikiki in the distance are spectacular. There are a few challenging holes, like the seventh (a 252-yard, par-4), which has a lake in the middle of the fairway and slim pickings on either side. With the wind usually blowing in your face, most golfers choose an iron to lay up short of the water and then pitch it over for par. Facilities include a driving range, practice greens, club rental pro shop, and restaurant.

Mililani Golf Club. 95–176 Kuahelani Ave., Mililani, HI 96789. ☎ **808/623-2222.** Fees: $89 weekdays ($65 after 11am); $95 weekends and holidays; $42 twilight rate weekdays after 1pm. From Waikiki, take the H-1 west (toward Ewa), past Aloha Stadium; at the split in the freeway, turn off onto H-2. Exit at Mililani (Exit 5-B) onto Meheula Pkwy.; go to the third stoplight (about 2 miles from the exit) and make a right turn onto Kuahelani Ave. TheBUS: 52.

This par-72, 6,455-yard public course, which opened in 1966, is the home of the Sports Shinko Rainbow Open, where Hawaii's top professionals compete. Located between the Koolau and Waianae mountain ranges on the Leilehua Plateau, this is one of Oahu's scenic courses, with views of mountains from every hole. Unfortunately, there are also lots of views of trees, especially eucalyptus, Norfolk pines, and coconut palms; it's a lesson in patience to stay on the fairways and away from the trees. The two signature holes, the par-4 no. 4 (a classic middle hole with water, flowers, and bunkers) and the par-3 no. 12 (a comfortable tee-shot over a ravine filled with tropical flowers, that jumps to the undulating green with bunkers on each side) are so scenic, you'll forgive the challenges they pose. Try to catch the $42 twilight (after 1pm) bargain on weekdays.

LEEWARD OAHU
JUST BEYOND PEARL HARBOR: AIEA

Pearl Country Club. 98–535 Kaonohi St., Aiea, HI 96701. ☎ **808/487-3802.** Fees (including cart): $75 weekdays; $80 weekends; $25 twilight rate for 9 holes after 4pm; $35 for 18 holes on Wed after 3pm. From Waikiki, take H-1 freeway past Pearl Harbor to the Hi. 78 (Moanalua Freeway) exit (from the left lane, Hi. 78 becomes Hi. 99 [Kamehameha Hwy.]). Turn right on Kaonohi St. and drive up the hill to the course. TheBUS: 32 (stops at the Pearlridge Shopping Center, Kaonohi and Moanalua sts.; you will have to walk about a half mile uphill from here).

Looking for a challenge? This popular public course, just above Pearl City in Aiea, has all the challenges you can imagine. Sure, the 6,230-yard, par-72 looks harmless enough, and the views of Pearl Harbor and the USS *Arizona* Memorial are gorgeous, but around the fifth hole, you'll start to see what you're in for. That par-5, blind 472-yard hole, doglegs quite seriously to the left (with a small margin of error between the tee and the steep out-of-bounds hillside on the entire left side of the fairway). A water hazard and a forest await your next two shots. Suddenly, this nice public course becomes not so nice. Oahu residents can't get enough of this course, so don't even try to get a tee time on weekends; stick to weekdays—Mondays are usually the best bet. *Tip:* Call at least a week in advance for a tee time. Facilities include a driving range, practice greens, club rental, pro shop, and restaurant.

EWA BEACH

West Loch Municipal Golf Course. 91–1126 Olepekeupe Loop, Ewa Beach, HI 96706. ☎ 808/296-2000. Fees (including carts): $47; $23.50 twilight rate between 1 and 3:30pm. From Waikiki, take H-1 west to the Hi. 76 exit; stay in the left lane and turn left at West Loch Estates, just opposite St. Francis Medical Center. To park, take 2 immediate right turns. TheBUS: 50.

This par-72, 6,615-yard course just 30 minutes from Waikiki, in Ewa Beach, offers golfers a challenge at bargain rates. The challenges on this municipal course are water (lots of hazards), wind (constant trades), and narrow fairways. To help you out, the course features a "water" driving range (with a lake). After a few practice rounds on the driving range, you'll be ready to take on this unusual course, designed by Robin Nelson and Rodney Wright. The first hole starts in front of the clubhouse; the course crosses a freeway for the next 10 holes and then goes back across the freeway for holes 12 to 18. In addition to the driving range, West Loch has practice greens, a pro shop, and a restaurant. We suggest booking a week in advance to get the tee time you want.

KO OLINA

✪ **Ko Olina Golf Club.** 3733 Alii Dr., West Beach, HI 96707. ☎ 808/676-5300. Fees (including carts): $145; $65 twilight rates after 2:30pm. From Waikiki, take H-1 freeway until it ends and becomes Hi. 93 (Farrington Hwy.); turn off at Ko Olina exit. Take exit road (Alinui Dr.) into Ko Olina Resort, and turn left on Alii Dr. to Clubhouse. No bus service.

Golf Digest named this 6,867-yard, par-72 course one of "America's Top 75 Resort Courses" in 1992. The Ted Robinson–designed course has rolling fairways and elevated tee and water features. The signature hole—the 12th, a par-3—has an elevated tee that sits on a rock garden, with a cascading waterfall. Wait until you get to the 18th hole; you'll see and hear water all around you. Seven pools begin on the right side of the fairway and slope down to a lake. A waterfall is on your left off the elevated green. You'll have no choice but to play the left and approach the green over the water.

There is a dress code for the course: Men are asked to wear shirts with a collar. Facilities include a driving range, locker rooms, Jacuzzi/steam rooms, and a restaurant/bar. Lessons and twilight rates are available. This course is crowded all the time. Book in advance.

ON THE WAIANAE COAST

Makaha Valley Country Club. 84–627 Makaha Valley Rd., Waianae, HI 96792. ☎ 808/695-9578. Fees (with cart): $55 weekdays; $65 on weekend. From Waikiki, take H-1 west until it turns into Hi. 93, which winds through the coastal towns of Nanakuli, Waianae, and Makaha. Turn right on Makaha Valley Rd. and follow it to the fork; turn right. TheBUS: 51 and Shuttle: 75.

This beautiful public course offers three tees to choose from. You can probably play your handicap from the middle tee, so for a challenge, you might want to go for the back tee, still a sporting par-69 for the 6,369 yards. The course presents a few challenges along the way: numerous trees and an abundance of water (especially on the third hole, which has a couple of small lakes right at a 90-degree dogleg, followed by a stand of trees). You might want to get an early tee time, as the afternoons in Makaha valley can get windy. The last hole is a doozie, a 494-yard, par-5 with two 90-degree turns to get up to the green. Facilities include driving range, practice greens, club rental, and clubhouse with restaurant.

○ **Sheraton Makaha Golf Club.** 84–626 Makaha Valley Rd., Waianae, HI 96792. ☎ **800/757-8060** or 808/695-9544. Fees: $90 all day for guests of the Sheraton resorts (Moana Surfrider, Royal Hawaiian, Sheraton Waikiki, and Princess Kaiulani); $160 for nonguests; $90 after noon. From Waikiki, take H-1 west until it turns into Hi. 93, which goes through Nanakuli, Waianae, and Makaha. Turn right on Makaha Valley Rd., and follow it to the fork; the course is on the left fork. TheBUS: 51 and Shuttle: 75.

The secret to playing this challenging course—recently named "The Best Golf Course on Oahu" by *Honolulu* magazine and ranked as one of Hawaii's top 10 by the readers of *Golfweek*—without going into debt is to book a tee time after noon on weekdays, when greens fees drop to $90 for 18 holes. This golf course sits some 45 miles (or an hour's drive) west of Honolulu, in Makaha Valley. Designed by William Bell, the par-72, 7,091-yard course meanders toward the ocean before turning and heading into the valley. Sheer volcanic walls tower 1,500 feet above the course, and swaying palm trees and neon-bright bougainvillea surround it; an occasional peacock even struts across the fairways. The beauty of the course would make it difficult to keep your mind on the game if it weren't for the 8 water hazards, 107 bunkers, and frequent and brisk winds. Facilities include a pro shop, bag storage, and a snack shop. This course is packed on weekends, so it's best to try weekdays.

WINDWARD OAHU

○ **Olomana Golf Links.** 41–1801 Kalanianaole Hwy., Waimanalo, HI 96795. ☎ **808/259-7926.** Fees (with cart): $60; $23 twilight fee Mon to Fri after 2:30pm, $13 (without cart). From Waikiki, take H-1 freeway to the Pali Hwy. (Hi. 61). Turn right on Kalanianaole Hwy.; about 5 miles farther, Olomana is on the left. TheBUS: 57.

This is a gorgeous course in Waimanalo, on the other side of the island from Waikiki. The low-handicap golfer might not find this course difficult, but the striking views of the craggy Koolau Mountain Range are worth the trip and the greens fees. The par-72, 6,326-yard course is popular with local residents and visitors alike, so reservations are a must. The course starts off a bit hilly on the front nine, but flattens out by the back nine. The back nine have their own special surprises, including tricky water hazards. The first hole, a 384-yard, par-4 that tees downhill and approaches uphill, is definitely a warm-up. The next hole is a 160-yard, par-3 that starts from an elevated tee to an elevated green over a severely banked, V-shaped gully. Shoot long here—it's longer than you think—as short shots tend to roll all the way back down the fairway to the base of the gully. This course is very, very green; the rain gods bless it regularly with brief passing showers. You can tell the regular players here—they all carry umbrellas and wait patiently for the squalls to pass, then resume play. Facilities include a driving range, practice greens, club rental, pro shop, and restaurant.

Pali Golf Course. 45–050 Kamehameha Hwy., Kaneohe, HI 96744. ☎ **808/296-2000.** Fees: $40 ($14 extra for an optional cart, which carries 2 golfers); $20 twilight rate after 2pm (walking only, no carts). From Waikiki, take the H-1 freeway to the Pali Hwy. (Hi. 61). Turn left at Kamehameha Hwy. at the first traffic light after you are through the Pali Tunnels. The course is immediately on your left after you turn on Kamehameha Hwy. TheBUS: 55.

This beautiful municipal course sits on the windward side of the island near Kaneohe, just below the historic spot where King Kamehameha the Great won the battle that united the islands of Hawaii. The par-72, 6,494-yard course, designed by

Willard G. Wilkinson and built in 1953, makes use of the natural terrain (hills and valleys make up the majority of the 250 acres). The course does not have man-made traps, but a small stream meanders through it. If you're off line on the ninth, you'll get to know the stream quite well. The challenge here is the weather—whipping winds and frequent rain squalls. Because of the potential for rain, you might want to pay for nine holes, and then assess the weather before signing up for the next nine. The views include Kaneohe Bay, the towns of Kailua and Kaneohe, and the verdant cliffs of the Koolau Mountains. Facilities include practice greens, club rental, locker rooms, and a restaurant.

5 Other Outdoor Activities

Oahu is a great place to fulfill all your outdoor needs, and even a dream or two: You can gallop on horseback over a white-sand beach at sunset or parachute out of an airplane. You can play a game of tennis at dawn or watch international racing yachts cross the finish line at Diamond Head. Oahu even has an ice-skating rink. The top professional football players can be seen at the annual Pro Bowl game in Honolulu, and top cowboys from across the country compete in a rodeo that draws people from all over the globe.

BICYCLING

Oahu is great for venturing out on a bicycle; most streets have bike lanes and cycling is a great way to see the island. For information on biking trails, races and tours, check out **www.bikehawaii.com**.

If you're in Waikiki, you can rent a bike for as little as $15 for a half day and $20 for 24 hours at **Blue Sky Rentals,** Inn on the Park, 1920 Ala Moana Blvd., Waikiki (☎ **808/947-0101**). On the North Shore, contact **Waimea Valley Adventure Park,** 59–864 Kamehameha Hwy., Haleiwa (☎ **888/973-9200** or 808/973-9825), which rents mountain bikes starting at $35 for an hour and 45 minutes.

For information on bikeways and maps, contact the **Honolulu City and County Bike Coordinator** (☎ **808/527-5044**). If you'd like to join a club ride, contact the **Hawaii Bicycle League,** P.O. Box 4403, Honolulu, HI 96812 (☎ **808/735-5756**), which offers rides every weekend, as well as several annual events. The league can also give you a schedule of upcoming rides, races, and outings.

GLIDING

Imagine soaring through silence on gossamerlike wings, a panoramic view of Oahu below you. A glider ride is an unforgettable experience, and it's available at Dillingham Air Field, in Mokuleia, on Oahu's North Shore. The glider is towed behind a plane; at the proper altitude, the tow is dropped and you (and the glider pilot) are left to soar in the thermals. You can get the best deal if you go with another person—the price drops to $60 each for a 20-minute ride. We recommend Mr. Bill at **Glider Rides** (☎ **808/677-3404**); he's been offering piloted glider rides since 1970. If Mr. Bill is booked, try **Soar Hawaii** (☎ **808/637-3147**), which offers rides at the same price.

HANG GLIDING

See things from a bird's-eye view (literally) as you and your instructor float high above Oahu on a tandem hang glider. **North Shore Hang/Para Gliding,** at the Dillingham Air Field (☎ **808/637-3178**), offers you an opportunity to try out this daredevil sport. A 20- to 30-minute tandem ride costs $150. If you enjoy it, lessons are available.

HORSEBACK RIDING

You can gallop on the beach at the **Turtle Bay Hilton Golf and Tennis Resort,** 57–091 Kamehameha Hwy., Kahuku, HI 96731 (☎ **808/293-8811;** TheBUS: 52 or 55). The 45-minute rides along sandy beaches with spectacular ocean views and through a forest of ironwood trees cost $35 for adults and $22 for children 9 to 12 (they must be at least 4 ft., 6 in.). Romantic evening rides take place on Friday, Saturday, and Sunday from 5 to 6:30pm, and cost $65 per person. Advanced riders can sign up for a 40-minute trot and canter ride along Kawela Bay for $50.

For guided horseback tours of lush Waimea Valley on the North Shore, contact **Waimea Valley Adventure Park,** 59–864 Kamehameha Hwy., Haleiwa (☎ **888/ 973-9200** or 808/973-9825). They offer a range of tours starting at $35 for a 1-hour tour.

If you've dreamed of learning how to ride, the **Hilltop Equestrian Center,** 41–430 Waikupanaha St., Waimanalo, HI 96895 (☎ **808/259-8463;** TheBUS: 57 or 58), will be happy to teach you. They offer lessons in either British or Western style from British Horse Society–accredited instructors for $40 per lesson (minimum of three lessons).

SKYDIVING

Everything you need to leap from a plane and float to earth can be obtained from **Blue Sky Rentals and Sports Center,** 1920 Ala Moana Blvd. (on the ground floor of Inn on the Park, in Waikiki, on the corner of Ala Moana Boulevard and Ena Road), Honolulu, HI 96815 (☎ **808/947-0101**). The cost is $225 per jump (including suit, parachute, goggles, plane rental, lesson, etc.). For instructions, call **SkyDive Hawaii,** 68–760 Farrington Hwy., Waiawa, HI 96791 (☎ **808/637-9700**). They offer a tandem jump (where you're strapped to an expert who wears a chute big enough for the both of you) for $275. There's no doubt about it—this is the thrill of a lifetime.

TENNIS

Oahu has 181 free public tennis courts. To get a complete list of all facilities or information on upcoming tournaments, send a self-addressed, stamped envelope to **Department of Parks and Recreation,** Tennis Unit, 650 S. King St., Honolulu, HI 96813 (☎ **808/971-7150;** www.co.honolulu.hi.us). The courts are available on a first-come, first-served basis; playing time is limited to 45 minutes.

If you're staying in Waikiki, the **Ilikai Sports Center** at the Ilikai Hotel, 1777 Ala Moana Blvd. (at Hobron Lane) (☎ **808/949-3811;** TheBUS: 19 or 20), has 6 courts, equipment rental, lessons, and repair service. Courts are $9 per person per hour; lessons are $44 per hour. If you're on the other side of the island, the **Hilton Turtle Bay Resort,** 57–091 Kamehameha Hwy., Kahuku, HI 96731 (☎ **808/ 293-8811,** ext. 24; TheBUS: 52 or 55), has 10 courts, 4 of which are lit for night play. You must make advance reservations for the night courts, as they're very popular. Court rates are $12 per person for singles and $10 per person for doubles. *Budget tip:* Book a court between noon and 4pm for half off. Equipment rental and lessons are available.

6 From the Sidelines: Spectator Sports

Don't expect the Chicago Bulls, the San Francisco 49ers, or the New York Yankees. Local people love these sports, and fill the public parks on weeknights and weekends to play them themselves. Although there aren't any major-league sports teams, there are some minor-league teams and a handful of professional exposition games played in Hawaii. Check the schedule at the 50,000-seat **Aloha Stadium,** located near Pearl Harbor (☎ **808/486-9300**), where high school and University of Hawaii football games are also held. There are usually express buses that take you to the stadium on game nights; they depart from Ala Moana Shopping Center (TheBUS no. 47–50 and 52), or from Monsarrat Avenue near Kapiolani Park (TheBUS no. 20). Call TheBUS at ☎ **808/848-5555** for times and fares.

The **Neal Blaisdell Center,** at Kapiolani Boulevard and Ward Avenue (☎ **808/ 521-2911**), features a variety of sporting events, such as professional boxing and Japanese sumo wrestling. In December, the Annual **Rainbow Classic,** a collegiate basketball invitational tournament, takes place at the Blaisdell. For bus information, call TheBUS at ☎ **808/848-5555.**

With Hawaii's cowboy history, **polo** is a popular sport, played every Sunday from March through August in Mokuleia or Waimanalo. Bring a picnic lunch and enjoy the game. Call ☎ **808/637-7656** for details on times and admission charges.

A sport you might not be familiar with is Hawaiian **outrigger canoe racing,** which is very big locally. Every weekend from Memorial Day to Labor Day, canoe races are held around Oahu. The races are free and draw huge crowds. Check the local papers for information on race schedules.

Motor-racing fans can enjoy their sport at **Hawaii Raceway Park,** 91–201 Malakole, in Campbell Industrial Park, in Ewa Beach next to the Barbers Point Naval Air Station (☎ **808/682-7139**), on Friday and Saturday nights. No bus service.

Some of the other spectator sports scheduled during the year are listed in the following calendar:

Calendar of Events: Sports

January

- **Morey World Bodyboard Championships,** Banzai Pipeline, depending on the surf conditions. First week in January. Call ☎ **808/396-2326.**
- **Sony Open,** Waialae Country Club. A $1.2-million PGA golf event featuring some of the game's top pros. Second week in January. Call ☎ **808/734-2151.**
- ✪ **Ala Wai Challenge,** Ala Wai Park, Waikiki. Based on ancient Hawaiian sports, this all-day event features ancient games like *ulu maika* (bowling a round stone through pegs), *oo ihe* (spear throwing at an upright target), *moa pahee* (wooden torpedo slide through two pegs), *huki kaula* (tug of war), and a quarter-mile outrigger canoe race. Great place to hear Hawaiian music. Usually held on the last weekend in January. Call ☎ **808/923-1802.**
- **NFL Pro Bowl Battle of the Gridiron,** Ihilani Resort & Spa. Kicking off the NFL Pro Bowl, a position and skills-oriented challenge between the best of the best in the National Football League. Usually held in late January or early February. Call ☎ **808/521-4322.**

February

- ✪ **Buffalo's Big Board Surfing Classic,** Makaha. This is a colorful, old-style surfing competition—on long boards. Held during the first two weekends in February. The event is free and open to the public. For information, call ☎ **808/ 951-7877.**
- ✪ **NFL Pro Bowl,** Aloha Stadium. The National Football League's best pro players square off in this annual gridiron all-star game. First Sunday in February. Tickets

go on sale the day after Labor Day and sell out quickly. Call ☎ **808/ 486-9300** for tickets and information.

- **The Great Aloha Run,** Honolulu. Thousands run 8.25 miles from Aloha Tower to Aloha Stadium. Always held on Presidents' Day (third Monday in February). Call ☎ **808/528-7388.**

March

✪ **Hawaii Challenge International Sportkite Championship,** Kapiolani Park. The longest running sportkite competition in the world. This event attracts the world's top kite pilots. First weekend in March.

The **International Kite Festival** is held the next weekend at Sandy Beach. Here more than 130 competitors participate in such events as a kite ballet to Taiko drumming and the world's largest kite flying. Just show up on contest day to sign up for the event. Second weekend in March. Call ☎ **808/735-9059.**

April

- **Hawaiian Highland Gathering,** Kapiolani Park, Waikiki. This gathering of the clans for Scottish games, competitions, food, dancing, and pipe bands is open to everyone. First weekend in April. Call ☎ **808/988-7872.**

✪ **Honolulu International Bed Race Festival,** Honolulu. This popular fund-raising event gives visitors a mini taste of Honolulu with food booths sponsored by local restaurants, live entertainment, and a Keiki Carnival with games and rides. Runners, pushing beds through the streets of Honolulu, race to raise money for local charities. Usually held the third Saturday in April. Sit on the bleachers at Kapiolani Park for the best view. Call ☎ **808/696-6262.**

May

- **Outrigger Canoe Season,** various locations. From May to September, canoe paddlers across the state participate in outrigger canoe races nearly every weekend. Call ☎ **808/261-6615** for the year's schedule of events.
- **Outrigger Hotels Hawaiian Oceanfest,** various locations. This weeklong celebration of ocean sports includes the Hawaiian International Ocean Challenge, which features teams of the world's best professional lifeguards; the Outrigger Waikiki Kings Race, an ocean iron-man race; the Diamond Head Wahine Windsurfing Classic, the only all-woman professional windsurfing competition; and the Diamond Head Biathlon, a run/swim event. Serious competition, a variety of evening events, and more. End of May. Call ☎ **808/521-4322.**

July

- **Walter J. McFarlane Regatta and Surf Race,** Waikiki. An outrigger canoe regatta featuring 30 events. July 4. Call ☎ **808/261-6615** or 808/526-1969.
- **Hawaiian Open Ice Skating Competition.** Top skaters compete for honors in July at the Ice Palace. Date varies. For information, call ☎ **808/487-9921.**

August

- **Duke Kahanamoku Beach Doubles Volleyball Championship,** Waikiki. First held in 1958, this is the oldest-running beach volleyball tournament in the state; currently hosted by the Outrigger Canoe Club. Championship-caliber men can enter. Register at least 1 month in advance; fee is $20 per team. Mid-August. Call ☎ **808/923-1585.**

✪ **Kenwood Cup.** This international yacht race is held during July in even-numbered years only (2000, 2002, etc.). Sailors from the United States, Japan,

Australia, New Zealand, Europe, and Hawaii participate in a series of races around the state. For information, call ☎ **808/946-9061.**

September

○ **Waikiki Rough-Water Swim.** This popular 2.4-mile, open-ocean swim from Sans Souci Beach to Duke Kahanamoku Beach in Waikiki takes place on Labor Day. Early registration is encouraged, but they will take last-minute entries on race day. For information, call ☎ **808/988-7788.**

• **Na Wahine O Ke Kai.** This invitational, 41-mile, open-ocean Hawaii outrigger canoe race from Hale O Lono, Molokai, to Duke Kahanamoku Beach, Waikiki, attracts international teams. Usually held the last weekend in September. For information, call ☎ **808/262-7567.**

October

• **Bankoh Molokai Hoe.** Top outrigger canoe teams from around the world compete in a 41-mile, open-ocean race from Molokai to Waikiki. Sunday before Columbus Day. For information, call ☎ **808/261-6615.**

• **Hawaii International Rugby Tournament,** Kapiolani Park, Waikiki. Teams from around the world gather to compete in this exciting tournament. The event has a division for all players including Masters, Social, Championship, 7-side, 9-side, and touch. Second week in October. Call ☎ **808/926-5641.**

November

○ **Triple Crown of Surfing,** Hawaii's top surfing events. These November to December competitions include the Pipeline Masters, the Hawaiian Pro, and the World Cup of Surfing. The world's best surfers compete for $250,000 in prize money. Generally held from mid-November to mid-to-late December. By invitation only. For information, call ☎ **808/638-7266.**

December

• **Honolulu Marathon.** More than 20,000 runners descend on Honolulu for the 26.2-mile race, which is held on the second Sunday in December. Preregistration is recommended, but participants can sign up on race day. For information, call ☎ **808/734-7200;** www.honolulumarathon.org.

○ **Aloha Bowl,** Aloha Stadium. The winner of the PAC 10 plays the winner of the Big 12 in this nationally televised collegiate football classic. Christmas Day. You can purchase tickets year-round; a few are usually available even on game day. Call ☎ **808/947-4141;** www.alohagames.com.

○ **Rainbow Classic,** University of Hawaii, Manoa Valley. Eight of the best NCAA basketball teams compete at the Special Events Arena. Week after Christmas. Call ☎ **808/956-6501** for tickets (ticket packages for the tournament go on sale December 16; individual game tickets go on sale the day of the event).

Seeing the Sights

by Jeanette Foster

In one day you can see and do more in Honolulu than you can in most places in a week. There's historic Honolulu to explore—from the Queen's Summer Palace to the USS *Arizona* Memorial in Pearl Harbor. You can wander through exotic gardens, come face-to-face with brilliantly colored tropical fish, stand on the deck of a four-masted schooner that sailed 100 years ago, venture into haunted places where ghosts are said to roam, take in the spicy smells and sights of Chinatown, and participate in a host of cultural activities from flower lei making to hula dancing. Plus, there are plenty of activities for the youngsters (and the young at heart) to do!

You don't need a huge budget to experience Honolulu's best activities, and you don't really need a car. TheBUS can get you where you need to go for a $1, or you can hop on a moderately priced tour or trolley. Your only obstacle to enjoying all the activities in Honolulu and Oahu might be fitting everything into your schedule!

1 Orientation & Adventure Tours

GUIDED SIGHTSEEING TOURS

If your time is limited, you might want to consider a guided tour: They're informative, entertaining, and you'll probably be surprised at how much you'll enjoy yourself. **E Noa Tours,** 1141 Waimanu St., Honolulu, HI 96814 (☎ **800/824-8804** or 808/591-2561; fax 808/591-9065; www.enoa.com), offers a range of tours. Their 2-hour narrated tour of Honolulu and Waikiki is conducted from an open-air trolley, and includes 20 stops from Waikiki to the Bishop Museum. It's a great way to get the "lay of the land," with the driver not only pointing out the historic sights, but also Honolulu's attractions, shopping locations, and restaurants. You can get on and off the trolley as needed (trolleys come along every 15 minutes). An all-day pass (from 8am to 4:30pm) costs $18 for adults, $8 for children under 11 years; a 5-day pass is $30 for adults and $10 for children.

Other E Noa tours include a "Circle Island" beach and waterfall tour ($47.50 adults, $37 children 6 to 12 years, and $31.50 children 5 and under), which stops at Diamond Head Crater, the Mormon Temple, Sunset Beach, Waimea Valley (admission is included in cost), Hanauma Bay, and various beach sites along the way. Shopping excursions, nightlife tours, and a Pearl Harbor historic tour are also available.

Polynesian Adventure Tours, 1049 Kikowaena Place, Honolulu, HI 96819 (☎ **808/833-3000;** www.polyad.com), also offers a range of guided tours from circling the island to shopping excursions. The all-day island tours start at $39 for adults, $20 for children 6 to 12 years, $16 for children 5 and under; the half-day *Arizona* Memorial Excursion is $14 for adults and $10 for children 3 to 11 years.

GUIDED ECOTOURS

Local boy Darren Akau was Hawaii's tour guide of the year in 1989. He then set out on his own to show Hawaii to visitors in his own way. Spending a day with Darren affords a rare chance to explore the "real" Hawaii. He takes groups of eight or more on guided, active daylong outings. Examples include a hike to Manoa Falls for a splash in the waterfall pool, a beach picnic, or snorkeling and boogie boarding at the very local Waimanalo Beach. Along the way, Darren discusses island ways and local customs, flora and fauna, history and culture, language and food, and more. The day starts at 7am, and usually ends at about 3:30pm. The cost is $75 for adults and $64 for kids; lunch and hotel pickup and return are included. You should be in fairly good shape, be able to hike at least a half mile in a rainforest, and feel at ease in gentle-to-moderate waves. Reservations are required at least a day in advance; call **Darren Akau's Hideaway Tours,** 41–127 Nalu St., Waimanalo, HI 96795 (☎ **808/259-8230**).

WALKING TOURS

Honolulu TimeWalks (☎ **808/943-0371;** fax 808/951-8878) features Glen Grant and his storytelling guides leading a variety of lively 2- to 3-hour walks through Waikiki, Chinatown, and other areas of Honolulu. Much of what they "show" you doesn't exist anymore, so they need to be clever—and you need to have some imagination—to get the picture. Guides appear in turn-of-the-century togs and tell it like it was through lively anecdotes about King Kalakaua, Prince Kuhio, Robert Louis Stevenson, and Mark Twain.

The **Haunted Honolulu Walk,** which takes place two Wednesdays a month from 6 to 9pm, includes the strange and unexplainable happenings around the capitol district; the cost is $8. History buffs will love the **Historic Honolulu Rediscovered: Heritage Trail Tour** of downtown Honolulu, which is offered Saturday from 9am to noon for $8; it starts down by Honolulu Harbor and ends up by Iolani Palace. Another great historical tour is the **Revolution of 1893,** which relives the days of the overthrow of the Hawaiian monarchy, complete with actors in costume; it's offered one Thursday a month from 6 to 8:30pm; the cost is $8 per person.

Honolulu TimeWalks also offers a variety of storytelling and historical theater programs at the Waikiki Heritage Theatre and the International Market Place, as well as excursions around the island. Call for complete information and scheduling.

DOWNTOWN HONOLULU   The **Mission Houses Museum,** 553 S. King St. (at Kawaiahao Street), Honolulu, HI 96813 (☎ **808/531-0481;** TheBUS: 2), offers a walking tour of historic downtown buildings on Thursday and Friday mornings. A guide takes visitors through the capitol district, making stops at sites such as Iolani Palace, the Kamehameha Statue, the Royal Tomb, and James Kekela's grave. The tour

---

Impressions

Thousands have daily lined the wharves to witness the carpenter, Mr. Dibble, in his novel suit of India-rubber with a glass helmet disappear beneath the surface of the water . . .

—1840 Honolulu newspaper article

Bird's-Eye View

To get a feel for why the kings chose Oahu as their place of residence, you have to see it from the air. To do this, contact **Island Seaplane Service** (☎ 808/836-6273; e-mail: seaplane@lava.net), the only company offering seaplane tours in Hawaii.

Passengers board a six-passenger DeHavilland Beaver or a four-passenger Cessna 206, and depart from a floating dock in the protected waters of Keehi Lagoon (parallel to Honolulu International Airport's runway). There's nothing quite like feeling the slap of the waves as the plane skims across the water, then effortlessly lifts into the air. You can almost imagine yourself on one of the famous flying boats like the Pan Am "China Clipper" during the 1930s.

Once in the air, you cruise by Waikiki Beach, getting a bird's-eye view of Diamond Head Crater, and fly on to Kahala's luxury estates and the sparkling waters of Hanauma and Kaneohe bays. The half-hour tour, which costs $79, turns around at Kaneohe Bay and retraces its path back to the dock. The 1-hour tour ($129) continues on to Chinaman's Hat, flies over the grounds of the Polynesian Cultural Center, and continues on to the rolling surf of the North Shore. The flight returns across the island, flying over the historic wartime sites of Schofield Barracks and the *Arizona* Memorial and *Missouri* Memorial in Pearl Harbor.

Captain Pat Magie, company president and chief pilot, has more than 32,000 flight hours without a mishap (26,000 hours in a seaplane in Alaska, Canada, the Arctic, and the Caribbean). He will break the world record for seaplane hours any day now.

---

starts at 9:30am at the museum and lasts until 12:30pm. The Mission Houses Museum also offers a **Women's History Walking Tour,** which tells the stories of women of the Hawaiian *ali'i* (royalty), one Saturday a month. The fee for walking tours is $8 for adults, $7 for seniors, $5 for college students, and $4 for kids 4 to 18, and includes the regular Mission Houses tour (see "Walking Tour: Historic Honolulu," below). Reserve a day ahead in person or by phone.

Kapiolani Community College has a unique series of walking tours into Hawaii's past, including visits to Honolulu's famous cemeteries, the almost-vanished "Little Tokyo" neighborhood, and many more destinations. Tours, which generally cost about $5, are for groups only, but you may be able to tag along. For information and reservations, call ☎ 808/734-9245.

The Hawaii Geographic Society, % Hawaii Geographic Maps and Books, 49 S. Hotel St. (P.O. Box 1698), Honolulu, HI 96808 (☎ 808/538-3952), offers a number of interesting and unusual tours like "A Temple Tour," including Chinese, Japanese, Christian, and Jewish temples, cathedrals, and other houses of worship; an archaeology tour in and around downtown Honolulu; and others. Each tour is guided by an expert from the Hawaii Geographic Society and must have a minimum of three people. Cost is $10 per person.

The Society's brochure, "Historic Downtown Honolulu Walking Tour," is a fascinating self-guided tour of the 200-year-old city center. It's $3, including postage, from the address above.

CHINATOWN HISTORIC DISTRICT   A 3-hour guided tour of Chinatown is offered Tuesdays at 9:30am by the **Chinese Chamber of Commerce,** 42 N. King St.

(at Smith Street), Honolulu, HI (☎ **808/533-3181;** TheBUS: 2). The cost is $5 per person; call to reserve.

The **Hawaii Heritage Center** (☎ **808/521-2749**) also conducts walking tours that focus on the history and culture of Chinatown. Tours are held every Friday at 9:30am and begin at the Ramsay Gallery, 1128 Smith St. (at North King Street; TheBUS: 2); the cost is $5 per person.

You can also do your own walking tour of Chinatown (see "Walking Tour: Historic Chinatown," below).

BEYOND HONOLULU The **Moanalua Gardens Foundation,** 1352 Pineapple Place, Honolulu, HI 96819 (☎ **808/839-5334**), offers a 4- to 5-hour guided walking tour of Kamananui Valley once a month. Historic and natural features include remains of early-20th-century house sites, petroglyph rocks, geological formations, and the effect humans have had on the environment. The 4-mile walk is done at a leisurely pace. You must register in advance, and a $5 donation is requested.

CULTURAL ACTIVITIES

Although most people travel to Hawaii for the sun and the surf, more and more visitors are interested in Hawaiian culture. The best place to learn about and participate in ancient Hawaiian culture is the Hawaiian Hall of the **Bishop Museum,** 1525 Bernice St., Honolulu, HI 96817 (☎ **808/847-3511;** TheBUS: 2). The museum offers a series of free classes in Hawaiian quilt making (Monday and Friday, 9am to 2pm), stone and bone carving (Tuesday, 9am to 2pm), lauhala weaving (Wednesday, 10am to 3pm), feather lei making (Thursday, 10am to 3pm), flower lei making (Saturday, 9am to 3pm), and coconut frond weaving (Sunday, 9am to 3pm).

Hawaiian quilt making is also taught at **Kwilts 'n Koa,** 1126 12th Ave. (between Harding and Waialae avenues in Kaimuki), Honolulu, HI 96816 (☎ **808/735-2300**). Call for class information and times.

If you have ever wanted to learn the hula, the **Waikiki Community Center,** 310 Paoakalani Ave. (Ewa side of the street between Ala Wai Boulevard and Kuhio Avenue), Honolulu, HI 96815 (☎ **808/923-1802**), offers "drop-in" beginner hula classes every Friday night at 7pm; cost is $3.

2 Historic Honolulu

The Waikiki you see today bears no resemblance to the Waikiki of yesteryear, when vast taro fields extended from the ocean into Manoa Valley, and the area was dotted with numerous fishponds and gardens tended by thousands of people. This vision of old Waikiki can be re-created by walking the new **Waikiki Historic Trail,** a meandering 2-mile route, which will eventually include 20 bronze surfboards (standing 6 feet, 5 inches tall; you can't miss 'em) that mark the way and come complete with a description of the historic site and an archive photo. The markers note everything from Waikiki's ancient fishponds to the history of the Ala Wai Canal. As we went to press, about half of the 20 surfboard markers were up, another five of the historic sites were identifiable (like the Moana Surfrider Hotel, Waikiki's first major hotel), and the rest were scheduled to be in position by the end of 2000.

The ✪ **Kodak Hula Show,** hosted by the Eastman Kodak Company, has been a fixture in Waikiki for just about as long as we can remember; it's held at the Waikiki Band Shell in Kapiolani Park (TheBUS: 4, 8, 19, or 20). The show is really more '50s nostalgia than ancient culture, but it's a good bit of fun any way you slice it. Shows begin at 10am every Tuesday, Wednesday, and Thursday, and last until 11:15am. Admission is free. The area seats 1,500 and you'll have a good view no matter where you sit. However, if you want to be front and center (the best spot for photo ops), Kodak suggests that you arrive around 9:15am. For more information, call ☎ **808/627-3300.** (See also "Walking Tour: Kapiolani Park," below.)

For a more genuine Hawaiian hula experience, catch the hula *halau* that performs weekdays at 1pm at the Bishop Museum (see below).

✪ **Bishop Museum.** 1525 Bernice St., just off Kalihi St. (also known as Likelike Hwy.). ☎ **808/847-3511.** Fax 808/841-8968. www.bishopmuseum.org. Admission $14.95 adults; $11.95 children 4–12 and seniors. Daily 9am–5pm. TheBUS: 2.

This forbidding, four-story Romanesque structure (it looks like something out of a Charles Addams cartoon) houses the world's greatest collection of natural and cultural artifacts from Hawaii and the Pacific. The museum was founded by the Hawaiian princess, Bernice Pauahi, who collected priceless artifacts. In her will she instructed her husband, Charles Reed Bishop, to establish a Hawaiian museum "to enrich and delight" the people of Hawaii. The museum is now world-renowned, and home to Dr. Yosihiko Sinoto, the last in a proud line of adventuring archaeologists who has explored more of the Pacific than Captain Cook and traced Hawaii's history and culture through its fishhooks.

The museum is jam-packed with more than 20 million acquisitions—there are 12 million insect specimens alone—from ceremonial spears to calabashes to old photos of topless hula dancers. A visit here will give you a good basis for understanding Hawaiian life and culture. You'll see the great feathered capes of kings, the last grass shack in Hawaii, pre-industrial Polynesian art, even the skeleton of a 50-foot sperm whale. There are seashells, koa-wood bowls, nose flutes, and Dr. Sinoto's major collection of fishhooks.

A hula *halau* performs weekdays at 1pm, and Hawaiian crafts such as lei making, feather working, and quilting are demonstrated on different days.

✪ **Hawaii Maritime Center.** Pier 7 (near Aloha Tower), Honolulu Harbor. ☎ **808/536-6373.** Admission $7.50 adults; $4.50 children 6–17. Daily 8:30am–5pm. TheBUS: 19, 20, 55, 56, or 57.

From the ancient journey of Polynesian voyagers to the nostalgic days of the *Lurline,* which once brought tourists from San Francisco on 4-day cruises, the story of Hawaii's rich maritime heritage is told through artifacts and exhibits at the Hawaii Maritime Center's Kalakaua Boat House, which is patterned after His Majesty King David Kalakaua's own canoe house.

Outside, the *Hokule'a,* a double-hulled sailing canoe that reenacted the Polynesian voyage of discovery in 1976, is moored next to the *Falls of Clyde,* a four-masted schooner that once ran tea from China to the West Coast. Inside, the more than 30 exhibits include Matson cruise ships, which brought the first tourists to Waikiki; flying boats that delivered the mail; and the skeleton of a Pacific humpback whale that beached itself on Kahoolawe. The museum's open-air harborfront restaurant is a popular downtown lunch spot with its view of passing tugboats, sampans, and cargo and cruise ships. *Tip:* Parking at or near the Aloha Tower is expensive; we suggest you take the bus instead.

✪ **Iolani Palace.** At S. King and Richards sts. ☎ **808/522-0832.** Admission $8 adults; $3 children 5–13. Guided tours conducted Wed–Sat 9am–2:15pm. Call ahead to reserve. You must be booked on a guided tour to enter the palace; children under 5 not permitted. TheBUS: 2.

This royal palace was built by King David Kalakaua, who spared no expense. The 4-year project, completed in 1882, cost $360,000—and nearly bankrupted the Hawaiian kingdom. The four-story Italian Renaissance palace, complete with Corinthian

Honolulu Attractions

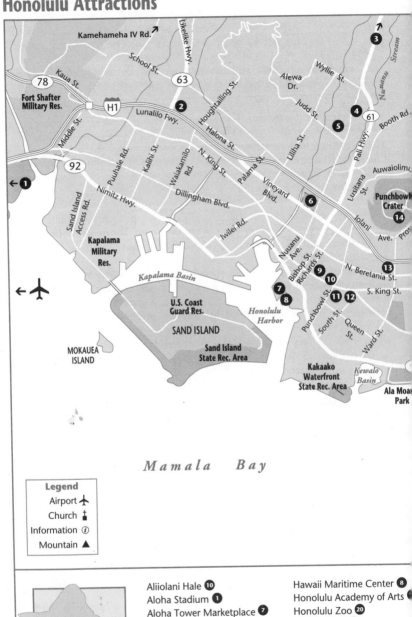

Legend
Airport ✈
Church ⛪
Information ⓘ
Mountain ▲

Mamala Bay

OAHU
Honolulu ★

Aliiolani Hale ⑩
Aloha Stadium ①
Aloha Tower Marketplace ⑦
Bishop Museum ②
The Contemporary Museum ⑮
Diamond Head ㉓
Father Damien Museum ⑲
Foster Garden ⑥

Hawaii Maritime Center ⑧
Honolulu Academy of Arts
Honolulu Zoo ⑳
Iolani Palace ⑨
Kapiolani Park ㉑
Kawaiahao Church ⑪
Kodak Hula Show ㉑
Lyon Arboretum ⑰

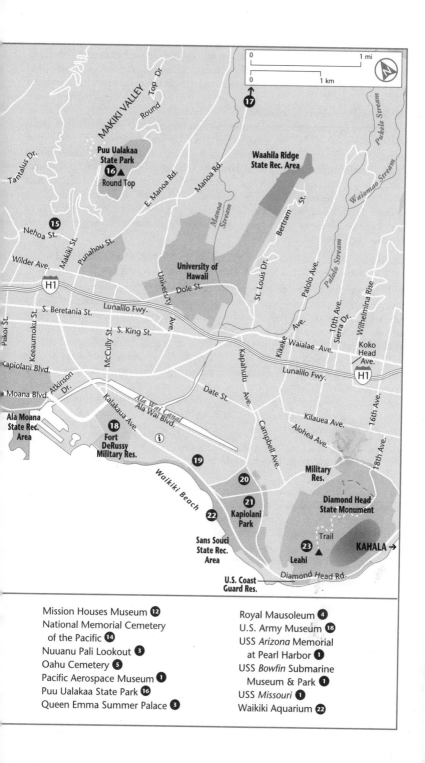

MAKIKI VALLEY

Top Dr.

Round

Tantalus Dr.

Puu Ualakaa
State Park
16 ▲
Round Top

E. Manoa Rd.

Manoa Rd.

Waahila Ridge
State Rec. Area

Pukele Stream

Waiomao Stream

17

0 _____ 1 mi
0 _____ 1 km

N

15

Nehoa St.

Makiki St.

Punahou St.

University of
Hawaii

Manoa Stream

Bertram St.

Palolo Stream

Wilder Ave.

H1

University Ave.

Dole St.

St. Louis Dr.

Patolo Ave.

10th Ave.

Sierra Dr.

Wilhelmina Rise

Piikoi St.

Keeaumoku St.

S. Beretania St.

S. King St.

McCully St.

Lunalilo Fwy.

Kikeke

Waialae Ave.

Koko
Head
Ave.

Kapiolani Blvd.

Atkinson Dr.

Kapahulu Ave.

Lunalilo Fwy.

H1

Moana Blvd.

Ala Wai Canal
Ala Wai Blvd.

Date St.

Campbell Ave.

Kilauea Ave.

Alohea Ave.

16th Ave.

Ala Moana
State Rec.
Area

Kalakaua Ave.

18
Fort
DeRussy
Military Res.

ⓘ

19

Waikiki Beach

20

21
Kapiolani
Park

22

Sans Souci
State Rec.
Area

U.S. Coast
Guard Res.

Military
Res.

Diamond Head
State Monument

Trail

23
Leahi ▲

Diamond Head Rd.

KAHALA →

18th Ave.

Mission Houses Museum **12**
National Memorial Cemetery
 of the Pacific **14**
Nuuanu Pali Lookout **3**
Oahu Cemetery **5**
Pacific Aerospace Museum **1**
Puu Ualakaa State Park **16**
Queen Emma Summer Palace **3**

Royal Mausoleum **4**
U.S. Army Museum **18**
USS *Arizona* Memorial
 at Pearl Harbor **1**
USS *Bowfin* Submarine
 Museum & Park **1**
USS *Missouri* **1**
Waikiki Aquarium **22**

175

columns imported from San Francisco, was the first building in Honolulu to have electricity (it had electricity before the White House and Buckingham Palace). Royals lived here for 11 years, until Queen Liliuokalani was deposed, and the Hawaiian monarchy fell in a January 17, 1893, palace coup led by U.S. Marines at the demand of sugar planters and missionary descendants.

Cherished by latter-day royalists, the 10-room palace stands as a flamboyant architectural statement of the monarchy period. (Iolani, often identified as the only royal palace on American soil, actually shares that distinction with the Big Island's Hulihee Palace, which also served as a royal house.) Open to the public since 1970, Iolani Palace attracts 100,000 visitors a year in groups of 20, who must don denim booties to scoot across the royal floors. The 45-minute tour is well worth your time. Some areas are unfurnished, but the State Dining Room, Throne Room, King's Library, and Privy Council Chamber are complete. The two-story staircase is the largest koa-wood staircase in the world.

Kawaiahao Church. 957 Punchbowl St. (at King St.). ☎ **808/522-1333.** Free admission (small donations appreciated). Mon–Sat 8am–4pm; Sun services 10:30am. TheBUS: 2.

In 1842, Kawaiahao Church stood at last, the crowning achievement of missionaries and Hawaiians working together for the first time on a common project. Designed by Rev. Hiram Bingham and supervised by Kamehameha III, who ordered his people to help build it, the project took 5 years. Workers quarried 14,000 thousand-pound coral blocks from the offshore reefs and cut timber in the forests for the beams.

The proud stone church, complete with bell tower and colonial colonnade, was the first permanent Western house of worship in the islands. It became the church of the Hawaiian royalty and remains in use today by Hawaiians who conduct services in the Hawaiian language (which probably sets old Rev. Bingham spinning in his grave). Some fine portraits of Hawaiian royalty hang inside. Hawaiian-language services are conducted on Sundays at 10:30am.

Mission Houses Museum. 553 S. King St. (at Kawaiahao St.). ☎ **808/531-0481.** Fax 808/545-2280. www.lava.net/~mhm/main.htm. Admission $6 adults; $5 seniors; $3 college students; $2 children. Tues–Sat 9am–4pm. TheBUS: 2.

The Mission Houses Museum tells the dramatic story of cultural change in 19th-century Hawaii. It was here that American Protestant missionaries established their headquarters in 1820. Included in the complex are a visitors center and three historic mission buildings restored and refurnished to reflect the daily life and work of the missionaries. Walking tours of historic downtown buildings are sponsored by the museum on Thursday and Friday mornings. For details, see "Walking Tours," above.

Oahu Cemetery. 2162 Nuuanu Ave. (north of Judd St.). ☎ **808/538-1538.** Free admission. Daily 7am–6pm. TheBUS: 4.

Not Hawaii's oldest, or even its biggest, this 150-year-old, 35-acre cemetery is a burying place in America's rural, monumental tradition—more a garden than a Golgotha. It holds the earthly remains of Honolulu's "Who's Who"—advisors to kings, sugar barons and sea captains, musicians and missionaries, were all buried in a reclaimed taro patch on the outskirts of the mud-and-grass-thatch village that they helped transform into the city of Honolulu. Under shade trees beside old carriage trails are Damons, Judds, and Thurstons, the missionaries who stayed on in the islands; and patriarchs of Hawaii's first foreign families, whose names now appear on buildings and street signs: Blaisdell, Dudoit, Farrington, Magoon, Stangewald, Wilder. Here, too, lies Alexander Joy Cartwright Jr., who some consider to be the real father of baseball; he chaired the committee that adopted the rules of play in 1845 and set base paths at 90 feet. He also umpired in the first official game in 1846. A few grave markers give sketchy details of death: A British sea captain spilled from his horse; a 9-year-old girl drowned off Kauai; a Boston missionary, the victim of consumption; an Army private killed while looking for a leper in Kalalau. It's all there, carved in stone, obituaries and grim reminders of mortality.

Queen Emma Summer Palace. 2913 Pali Hwy. (at Old Pali Rd.). ☎ **808/595-3167.** Admission $5 adults; $4 seniors; $1 children ages 16 and under. Daily 9am–4pm. TheBUS: 4.

"Hanaiakamalama," the country estate of Queen Emma and Kamehameha IV, was once in the secluded uplands of Nuuanu Valley. The Valley is no longer secluded, and a busy six-lane highway now runs adjacent to the palace. The cars going 60 miles per hour sound remarkably—and oddly—like the surf as they zip by. This simple, six-room New England–style house, built in 1847 and restored by the Daughters of Hawaii, holds an interesting mixture of Victorian furniture and hallmarks of Hawaiian royalty, including feather cloaks and *kahili*, the bushy totems that mark the presence of *alii* (royalty). Other royal treasures include a canoe-shaped cradle for Queen Emma's baby, Prince Albert, who died at the age of 4. (Kauai's ultra-ritzy Princeville Resort is named for the little prince.)

Royal Mausoleum. 2261 Nuuanu Ave. (between Wyllie and Judd sts.). ☎ **808/536-7602.** Free admission. Mon–Fri 8am–4:30pm. TheBUS: 4.

In the cool uplands of Nuuanu, on a 3.7-acre patch of sacred land dedicated in 1865—and never surrendered to the United States—stands the Royal Mausoleum, the final resting place of King Kalakaua, Queen Kapiolani, and 16 other Hawaiian royals. Only the Hawaiian flag flies over this grave, a remnant of the kingdom.

JUST BEYOND PEARL HARBOR

Hawaiian Railway. Ewa Station, Ewa. ☎ 808/681-5461. Fax 808/681-4860. http://members.aol.com/hawaiianrr/index.html. Admission $8 adults; $5 seniors and children 2–12. Sun 12:30 and 2:30pm. Take H-1 west to Exit 5a; take Hwy. 76 south for 2.5 miles to Gas Express; turn right on Renton Rd. and drive 1.5 miles to end of paved section. The station is on the left. Bus: 49, 50, 51, 52, 53, or 55 to the State Capitol, then transfer to bus no. 48 (Ewa Mill).

All aboard! This is a genuine train ride back into history. Between 1890 and 1947, the chief means of transportation for Oahu's sugar mills was the Oahu Railway and Land Company's narrow-gauge trains. Not only did the line carry equipment, raw sugar, and supplies, it also transported passengers from one side of the island to the other. You can recapture this experience every Sunday with a 1½-hour narrated ride through Ko Olina Resort and out to Makaha. As an added attraction, on the second Sunday of the month, they hook up the custom-built parlor-observation car belonging to Benjamin F. Dillingham, founder of the Oahu Railway and Land Co.; it costs $15 to ride in this nearly 100-year-old car (no kids under 13).

Hawaii's Plantation Village. Waipahu Cultural Garden Park, 94–695 Waipahu St. (at Waipahu Depot Rd.), Waipahu. ☎ 808/677-0110. Fax 808/677-0110. Escorted Tours available. Mon–Fri 9am–4pm; Sat 10am–4pm. Take H-1 west to Waikele-Waipahu exit (Exit 7); get in the left lane on the exit and turn left on Paiwa St.; at the 5th stoplight, turn right on Waipahu St.; after the 2nd light, turn left. Bus: 47.

This symbolic cornerstone of Hawaii's multi-ethnic society offers a glimpse back in time to when sugar planters from America shaped the land, economy, and culture of territorial Hawaii. From 1852, when the first contract laborers arrived here from China, until 1947, when the plantation era ended, more than 400,000 men, women, and children from China, Japan, Portugal, Puerto Rico, Korea, and the Philippines came to work the sugarcane fields. The village stands as a collective monument to the brave immigrants, who brought their food, culture, language, art, and architecture to

Hawaii, transforming it into the cosmopolitan place it is today. The $2.7 million, 50-acre village was developed from old blueprints, photos, and oral histories; it includes 30 faithfully restored Filipino camp houses, Chinese and Japanese temples, the Plantation Store, and even a sumo-wrestling ring.

WARTIME HONOLULU

✪ **USS *Arizona* Memorial at Pearl Harbor.** Pearl Harbor. ☎ **808/422-0561** (pre-recorded info) or 808/422-2771. www.nps.gov/usar. Daily 7:30am–5pm (boat shuttles run 8am–3pm). Closed Thanksgiving, Christmas, and New Year's Day. Free admission. Children under 12 must be accompanied by an adult. You must wear shoes; no slippers allowed. Drive west on H-1 past the airport; take the USS *Arizona* Memorial exit, and follow the green-and-white signs; there's ample free parking. TheBUS: 20, or Arizona Memorial Shuttle Bus, which picks up at Waikiki hotels 6:50am–1pm ($6 round-trip); ☎ 808/839-0911.

On December 7, 1941, while moored in Pearl Harbor, the USS *Arizona* was bombed in a Japanese air raid. The 608-foot battleship sank in 9 minutes without firing a shot, taking 1,177 sailors and Marines to a fiery death—and plunging the United States into World War II.

No one who visits the memorial will ever forget it. The deck of the ship lies 6 feet below the surface of the sea. Oil still oozes slowly up from the *Arizona*'s engine room to stain the harbor's calm blue water; some say the ship still weeps for its lost crew. The memorial is a stark white 184-foot rectangle that spans the sunken hull of the ship; it was designed by the late Alfred Pries, a German architect interned on Sand Island during the war. It contains the ship's bell, recovered from the wreckage, and a shrine room with the names of the dead carved in stone.

Today, free U.S. Navy launches take visitors to the *Arizona*. To avoid the huge crowds, try to arrive early at the Visitor Center, which is operated jointly by the National Park Service and the U.S. Navy. You'll be issued a number and a departure time, which you must pick up yourself. Waits of 1 to 3 hours are common; no reservations are taken. While you're waiting for the launch to take you out to the ship, you can explore the museum, with personal mementos, photographs, and historical documents. A 20-minute film precedes your trip to the ship. Allow at least 4 hours to visit the memorial. Shirts and shoes are required; no swimsuits or flip-flops are allowed (shorts are okay). Wheelchairs are gladly accommodated.

✪ **USS *Bowfin* Submarine Museum & Park.** 11 Arizona Memorial Dr. (next to the USS *Arizona* Memorial at Pearl Harbor). ☎ **808/423-1342.** Fax 808/422-5201. E-mail: bowfin@aloha.net. Admission $8 adults; $6 active-duty military; $3 children 4–12. Daily 8am–5pm. Closed Thanksgiving, Christmas, and New Year's Day. Drive west on H-1 past the airport; take the USS *Arizona* Memorial exit, and follow the green-and-white signs; there's ample free parking. TheBUS: 20, or Arizona Memorial Shuttle Bus, which stops at Waikiki hotels 6:50am–1pm ($6 round-trip); ☎ 808/839-0911.

Next to the *Arizona* Memorial Visitor Center is the USS *Bowfin*, one of only 15 World War II submarines still in existence today. You can go below deck on this famous submarine—nicknamed the "Pearl Harbor Avenger" for its successful retaliatory attacks on the Japanese—and see how the 80-man crew lived during wartime. The *Bowfin* Museum has an impressive collection of submarine-related artifacts. The Waterfront Memorial honors submariners lost during World War II.

USS *Missouri* Memorial. Battleship Row, Pearl Harbor. ☎ **888/877-6477** or 808/545-2263. Fax 808/545-2265. www.ussmissouri.com. Daily 9am–5pm (hour-long tours 9:30am–4:30pm). $12 adults; $6 children 4–12. Check in at the *Missouri* Visitor Reception Center, between the USS *Bowfin* Memorial and the USS *Arizona* Memorial. Drive west on H-1 past the airport; take the USS *Arizona* Memorial exit, and follow the green-and-white signs; there's ample free parking. TheBUS: 20 and 47.

On the deck of this 58,000-ton battleship (the last one the Navy built), World War II came to an end with the signing of the Japanese surrender on September 2, 1945. The *Missouri* was also part of the force that carried out bombing raids over Tokyo and provided firepower in the battles of Iwo Jima and Okinawa. The Navy decommissioned the ship in 1955 and mothballed it at the Puget Sound Naval Shipyard in Washington state. It was called back into action in 1986 after being modernized, deployed in the Persian Gulf War, and retired to Puget Sound once again in 1992. Here she sat until another battle ensued, this time over who would get the right to be caretaker of this living legend. Hawaii won that battle and brought the ship to Pearl Harbor in 1998. The next year, the 887-foot ship opened to visitors as a living museum and a memorial to the past.

The tours begin at the visitors center where guests are then shuttled to Ford Island on military-style buses. A radio program, complete with news clips, wartime commercials, and music from the 1940s, is broadcasted during the bus ride. Once on the ship, visitors watch a film that explains the ship's history and the exhibits aboard the ship. Guests are then free to explore on their own or take a guided tour. Highlights of this massive (more than 200 feet tall) battleship include the forecastle (or *foc's'le* in Navy talk), where the 30,000-pound anchors are "dropped" on 1,080 feet of anchor chain; the 16-inch guns, each 65 feet long and weighing 116-tons, can accurately fire a 2,700-pound shell some 23 miles in 50 seconds; and the spot where the Instrument of Surrender was signed as Douglas MacArthur, Chester Nimitz, and "Bull" Halsey looked on.

National Cemetery of the Pacific. Punchbowl Crater, 2177 Puowaina Dr. (at the end of the road). ☎ 808/541-1434. Free admission. Daily 8am–5:30pm; Mar–Sept to 6:30pm. TheBUS: 15.

Go in the morning when the air is still and listen—Punchbowl is as silent as a tomb.

The National Cemetery of the Pacific, as it's officially known, is an ash-and-lava tuff cone that exploded about 150,000 years ago—it's like Diamond Head, only smaller. Early Hawaiians called it Puowaina, or "hill of sacrifice." The old crater is a burial ground for 35,000 victims of three American wars in Asia and the Pacific: World War II and the Korean and Vietnam wars. Among the graves you'll find many unmarked ones—only December 7, 1941 is carved in stone. Others are famous, like that of war correspondent Ernie Pyle, who was killed by a Japanese sniper on Okinawa in April 1945. The others buried here are remembered only by family and surviving military buddies, who are now in their mid-70s. The Courts of the Missing, white stone tablets, bear the names of 28,788 Americans missing in action from World War II.

Veterans come here often to reflect on the meaning of war and remember those, like themselves, who stood in harm's way to win peace a half century ago.

3 Fish, Flora & Fauna

✪ **Foster Garden.** 50 N. Vineyard Blvd. (at Nuuanu Ave.). ☎ 808/522-7065. Fax 808/ 522-7050. Admission $5 adults; $1 children 6–12. Daily 9am–4pm; guided tours Mon–Fri at 1pm. TheBUS: 2, 4, or 13.

A leafy oasis amid the high-rises of downtown Honolulu, this 14-acre garden on the north side of Chinatown was founded in 1853 with the planting of a single tree on royal land by German physician and botanist William Hillenbrand. Today, it showcases 24 native Hawaiian trees, and is home to the last stands of several rare trees, including an East African tree whose white flowers bloom only at night. There are orchids galore, a primitive cycad garden, a palm collection, plus all kinds of spices and herbs.

Honolulu Zoo. 151 Kapahulu Ave. (between Paki and Kalakaua aves.), at the entrance to Kapiolani Park. ☎ **808/971-7171.** Fax 808/971-7173. www.hawaii.rr.com/zoo. Admission $6 adults; $1 children 6–12, when accompanied by an adult ($6 without an adult); children under 6 are not allowed in without an adult). Daily 9am–4:30pm. TheBUS: 2, 8, 19, 20, or 47.

Nobody comes to Hawaii to see an Indian elephant or African lions and zebras. Right? Wrong. This 43-acre municipal zoo in Waikiki attracts droves of visitors, who come to see the new African Savannah, a 10-acre wild preserve/exhibit with more than 40 uncaged African critters roaming around in the open. The zoo, which now offers night walks—when the nocturnal beasties are out—has a rare Hawaiian nene goose, a Hawaiian pig, and Mouflon sheep. (Only the goose, an evolved version of the Canadian honker, is considered to be indigenous; all the other animals are imported from Polynesia, India, and elsewhere.)

For a real treat, take the "Zoo by Moonlight" tour, which offers you a rare behind-the-scenes look into the lives of the zoo's nocturnal creatures. Tours are offered 2 days before, during, and 2 days after the full moon from 7 to 9pm; the cost is $7 for adults and $5 for children.

Kapiolani Park. Bordered by Kalakaua Ave. on the ocean side, Monsarrat Ave. on the Ewa side, and Paki Ave. on the mountain side. TheBUS: 2.

In 1877 King David Kalakaua gave 130 acres of land to the people of Hawaii and named it after his beloved wife, Queen Kapiolani. This truly royal park has something for just about everyone: tennis courts, soccer and rugby fields, archery, picnic areas, wide-open spaces for kite flying and frisbee throwing, and a jogging path with aerobic exercise stations. On Sundays in the summer, the Royal Hawaiian Band plays in the bandstand, just as they did during Kalakaua's reign. The Waikiki Shell, located in the park, is host to a variety of musical events, from old Hawaiian songs to rock and roll.

Lyon Arboretum. 3860 Manoa Rd. (near the top of the road). ☎ **808/988-7378.** Fax 808/988-4231. $1 donation requested. Mon–Sat 9am–3pm. TheBUS: 5.

Six-story-tall breadfruit trees . . . yellow orchids no bigger than a bus token . . . ferns with fuzzy buds as big as a human head: Lyon Arboretum is 125 budding acres of botanical wonders. A whole different world opens up to you along the self-guided 20-minute hike through Lyon Arboretum to Inspiration Point. You'll pass more than 5,000 exotic tropical plants full of birdsong in this cultivated rainforest (a research facility that's part of the University of Hawaii) at the head of Manoa Valley.

Guided tours for serious plant lovers are offered one or two Saturdays a month. Led by a resident botanist, the tour may take up to 3 hours and focus on one species. Call ☎ **808/988-3177** for tour schedules and reservations.

✪ **Waikiki Aquarium.** 2777 Kalakaua Ave. (across from Kapiolani Park). ☎ **808/ 923-9741.** Fax 808/923-1771. www.waquarium.mic.hawaii.edu. Admission $6 adults; $4 seniors and students; $2.50 children 13–17. Daily 9am–5pm. Closed Christmas Day. TheBUS: 19 or 20.

Behold the chambered nautilus, nature's submarine and inspiration for Jules Verne's *20,000 Leagues Under the Sea.* This tropical aquarium, located in Diamond Head of Waikiki, is worth a peek if only to see the only living chambered nautilus born in captivity. Its natural habitat is the deep waters of Micronesia, but Bruce Carlson, director of the aquarium, succeeded not only in trapping the pearly shell in 1,500 feet of water by dangling chunks of raw tuna, but also in managing to breed this ancient relative of the octopus. The aquarium was also the first to successfully display the cuttlefish and Hawaii's own mahi-mahi.

There are plenty of other fish in this small but first-class aquarium, located on a live coral reef. Owned and operated by the University of Hawaii, the aquarium, after a $3 million upgrade, now features a Hawaiian reef habitat with sharks, eels, a touch tank, and habitats for the endangered Hawaiian monk seal and green sea turtle. Recently added: a rotating Biodiversity Special Exhibit, which discusses the diversity of sea life, and interactive exhibits focusing on corals and coral reefs.

IN NEARBY EAST OAHU

✪ **Sea Life Park.** 41–202 Kalanianaole Hwy. (at Makapuu Point), Honolulu. ☎ **808/ 259-7933.** Admission $24 adults; $12 children 4–12; children under 4 free. Daily 9:30am–5pm. Parking $3. TheBUS: 22 or 58.

This 62-acre ocean theme park is one of Oahu's main attractions. It features orca whales from Puget Sound, Atlantic bottle-nosed dolphins, California sea lions, and penguins going through their hoops to the delight of kids of all ages. There's a Hawaiian Reef Tank full of tropical fish, a "touch" pool where you can grab a real sea cucumber (commonly found in tide pools), and a Bird Sanctuary where you can see birds like the red-footed booby and frigate bird that usually fly overhead. There's also a whaling museum that tells how New England whalers harpooned whales and made scrimshaw from their bones. The chief curiosity, though, is the world's only "wolphin"—a cross between a false killer whale and an Atlantic bottle-nosed dolphin. On site, marine biologists from the National Marine Life Fisheries operate a recovery center for endangered marine life; during your visit, you can see the restored Hawaiian monk seals and seabirds.

4 Spectacular Views

✪ **Diamond Head.** Diamond Head Rd. Daily 6am–6pm. To get here from Waikiki, take Kalakaua Ave. toward Kapiolani Park. Turn left onto Monsarrat Ave. at the Park. Monsarrat Ave. becomes Diamond Head Rd. after Campbell Ave. Continue on Diamond Head Rd. to turnoff to crater. Turn right into turnoff, follow to parking lot. TheBUS: 22 or 58.

The 360-degree view from atop Diamond Head Crater is worth the 560-foot ascent and is not to be missed. You can see all the way from the Koko Crater to Barbers Point and the Waianae Mountains. The 760-foot-tall volcano, which has become the symbol for Hawaii, is about 350,000 years old. The trail to the summit was built in 1910 to service the military installation along the crater; it's about a 30-minute hike to the top, but it's quite manageable by anyone of any age.

Diamond Head has always been considered a "sacred sight" by Hawaiians. According to legend, Hi'iaka, the sister to the volcano goddess Pele, named the mountain Leahi (meaning the "brow of the ahi") when she saw the resemblance to the yellowfin tuna (called "ahi" in Hawaiian). Kamehameha the Great built a "luakini heiau" on the top where human sacrifices were made to the god of war, Ku.

The name *Diamond Head* came into use around 1825 when a group of British sailors (some say they were slightly inebriated) found some rocks sparkling in the sun. Absolutely sure they had struck it rich, the sailors brought these "diamonds" back into Honolulu. Alas, the "diamonds" turned out to be calcite crystals. The sailors didn't become fabulously rich, but the name Diamond Head stuck.

✪ **Lanikai Beach.** Mokulua Dr., Kailua. To get here from Honolulu, take Hi. 61 (Pali Hwy.) into Kailua. Follow the street (which becomes Kailua Rd., then becomes Kuulei Rd.) until it ends. Turn right on Kalaheo Ave. (which will become Kawailoa Rd. in a few blocks). Follow the road over the canal. At the stop sign, turn left on Kaneapu Place. At the fork in the road, bear left on the one-way Aalapapa Dr. Turn right at any cross street onto Mokulua Dr. No bus service.

This is one of the best places on Oahu to greet the sunrise. Watch the sky slowly move from pitch black to wisps of gray to burnt orange as the sun begins to rise over the two tiny offshore islands of Mokulua. Use your five senses for this experience: hear the birds sing, feel the gentle breezes on your face, taste the salt in the air, smell the ocean, and see the kaleidoscope of colors as another day dawns.

✪ **Nuuanu Pali Lookout.** Near the summit of Pali Hwy. (Hi. 61). To get here directly from downtown Honolulu, turn left off Nimitz Hwy. (Hi. 92) onto Nuuanu Ave. or Bishop St. Follow it to Pali Hwy., which takes you to the Lookout. No bus service.

Sometimes gale-force winds howl through the mountain pass at this 1,186-foot-high perch guarded by 3,000-foot peaks, so hold on to your hat—and small children. Take the short walk up from the parking lot to the precipice, and you'll be rewarded with a view that'll blow you away—no pun intended. At the railing's edge, the dizzying panorama of Oahu's windward side is breathtaking—pinnacles of the *pali* (cliffs), green with ferns, often disappear into the mist; the vertical slopes of the Koolaus end in lush green valleys that become the town of Kaneohe; and the Pacific, a magnificent blue, dotted with whitecaps, beckons in the distance. Definitely take a jacket with you; it can be quite misty at the lookout. On very windy days, you'll notice that the waterfalls look as though they are flowing up rather than down.

In 1898 John Wilson built the road up to the lookout using 200 laborers. Even before the road existed, the Nuuanu Pali (which translates as "cool heights") was infamous because legend claims it was the location of Kamehameha the Great's last battle. Although some academic scholars scoff at this, the story alleges that in 1795, Kamehameha pursued Oahu's warriors up Nuuanu to these cliffs and waged a battle in his attempt to unite the Hawaiian islands. Supposedly, the Oahu warriors were driven over the cliffs by Kamehameha's men. Some say the battle never happened, some say it happened but there were only a few men fighting, and some say thousands were forced over the cliff, plunging to their deaths. Others say at night you can still hear the cries of these long-dead warriors coming from the valley below.

Puu O Mahuka Heiau. One mile past Waimea Bay; take Pupukea Rd. mauka off Kamehameha Hwy. at Foodland, and drive .7 mile up a switchback road. TheBUS: 52 and walk up Pupukea Rd.

From this 18th-century heiau overlooking Waimea Bay, you can see 25 miles of Oahu's wave-lashed north coast—all the way to Kaena Point, where the Waianae Range ends. Once the largest sacrificial temple on Oahu, today Puu O Mahuka Heiau is a National Historical Landmark. Located on a 300-foot bluff, the grounds encompass some 5 acres. The heiau is a huge rectangle of rocks twice as big as a football field (170 feet by 575 feet) and has an altar often covered by the flower and fruit offerings from native Hawaiians. People still come here to pray, so be respectful and don't disturb the offerings or walk on the stones.

Go to the heiau near sundown to feel the *mana* of this sacred place, the construction of which is attributed to the *menehune* (the legendary small people who accomplished amazing construction feats). Chieftesses were sent here to give birth. But the largest sacrificial temple on Oahu became infamous with the great *kahuna* Kaopulupulu, who sought peace between Oahu and Kauai. The prescient kuhuna predicted that the island would be overrun by strangers from a distant land. In 1794, three of Capt. George Vancouver's men of the *Daedalus* supposedly were sacrificed here. In 1819, the year before New England missionaries landed in Hawaii, King Kamehameha II ordered all idols at the heiau be destroyed.

✪ **Puu Ualakaa State Park.** Round Hill Dr. Take the H-1 freeway going Ewa, and get off on the Punahou St. exit (Exit 23). Turn left on Punahou. Make a left onto Wilder Ave. Turn right on Makaki St. When the road forks, bear left onto Round Top Dr. The park entrance is 2½ miles up Round Top from Makaki. Once in the park, it's a half mile to the lookout. No bus service.

Don't miss the sweeping views from this 1,048-foot hill—the panorama extends from Diamond Head across Waikiki and downtown Honolulu, over to the airport and Pearl City, and all the way to the Waianae Range. There are great photo opportunities during the day, romantic sunset views in the evening, and starry skies at night. *Puu Ualakaa* translates into "rolling sweet potato hill," which was how the early Hawaiians harvested the crop. The park gates open at 7am and close at 6:45pm (7:45pm in the summer).

5 More Museums

Aliiolani Hale. 417 S. King St. (between Bishop and Punchbowl sts.). ☎ **808/539-4999.** Fax 808/539-4996. Free admission. Mon–Fri 10am–3pm; reservations for group tours only. TheBUS: 1, 2, 3, 4, 8, 11, or 12.

Don't be surprised if this place looks familiar; you probably saw it on "Magnum P.I." or "Hawaii Five-O." Hollywood always uses it as the Honolulu Police Station, although the made-for-TV movie *Blood and Orchids* correctly used it as the courthouse where Clarence Darrow defended the perpetrators in the famed Massie case in 1931. This gingerbread Italianate, designed by Australian Thomas Rowe in the Renaissance Revival style, was built in 1874 and originally intended to be a palace. Instead, Aliiolani Hale ("House of Kings" in Hawaiian) became the Supreme Court and Parliament government office building.

Aliiolani Hale operates a **Judiciary History Center,** open Monday through Friday from 10am to 3pm. The Center, located on the ground floor of the building, is free and features a multimedia presentation, a restored historic courtroom, and exhibits tracing Hawaii's transition from Hawaiian law (pre-western contact) to western law.

Damien Museum. 130 Ohua St. (between Kuhio and Kalakaua aves., behind St. Augustine's Catholic Church, on Kalakaua Ave.). ☎ **808/923-2690.** Donations accepted. Mon–Fri 9am–3pm. TheBUS: 8, 19, or 20.

This is a tiny museum about a large subject in Hawaii's history: Father Damien's work with leprosy victims on the island of Molokai. The museum contains prayer books used by Father Damien in his ministry as well as his personal items. Don't miss the award-winning video about Father Damien's story.

Pacific Aerospace Museum. In the Central Waiting Lobby, Honolulu International Airport, 300 Rodgers Blvd., Honolulu, HI 96819. ☎ **808/839-0767.** Fax 808/836-3267. Admission $3 adults; $2.50 children 6–12, military, and students; children 5 and under free. Daily 9am–6pm. TheBUS: 19 or 20.

While you're waiting for your flight to depart, check out the history of flight in the Pacific at this $3.8 million shrine to flying. You can trace elapsed time and distance of all direct flights from Honolulu on a 6-foot globe using fiber optics; watch old film clips of NASA astronauts splashing down in Hawaiian waters after landing on the moon; see models of early planes and flying boats (including a life-size replica of the Flight Deck of the space shuttle *Challenger*), and hear the heroic stories of the aviators who pioneered flying routes to the islands and beyond.

U.S. Army Museum. Fort DeRussy Park. ☎ **808/438-2822.** Free admission. Tues–Sun 10am–4:30pm. TheBUS: 8.

This museum, built in 1909, was used in defense of Honolulu and Pearl Harbor. Military memorabilia ranging from ancient Hawaiian warfare to today's high-tech munitions is on display inside. On the upper deck, the photographs at the Corps of Engineers Pacific Regional Visitors Center show how the corps works with the civilian community in managing water resources in an island environment.

ⓘ Especially for Kids

Shop the Aloha Flea Market *(see p. 216)* Most kids hate to shop, but the Aloha Flea Market, a giant outdoor bazaar at the Aloha Stadium on Wednesday, Saturday, and Sunday, is more than shopping. It's an experience akin to a carnival, full of interesting food, odd goods, and bold barkers. Nobody ever leaves this place empty-handed—or without having had lots of fun.

Explore the Bishop Museum *(see p. 173)* There are some 1,180,000 Polynesian artifacts; 13,500,000 different insect specimens; 6,000,000 marine and land shells; 490,000 plant specimens; 130,000 fish specimens; and 85,000 birds and mammals, all in the Bishop Museum. Kids can explore interactive exhibits, see a 50-foot sperm whale skeleton, and check out a Hawaii grass hut. There's something for everyone here.

Walk Through a Submarine *(see p. 178)* At the USS *Bowfin* Submarine Museum Park, an interactive museum offers kids the chance to experience a real submarine—one that served in some of the fiercest naval battles in World War II. Kids can explore the interior of the tightly packed submarine that housed some 90 to 100 men and see the stacked shelves where they slept, the radar and electronics in the command center, and the storage place of the torpedoes.

Dream at the Hawaii Maritime Center *(see p. 173)* Kids will love the Kalakaua Boathouse, the two-story museum of the Maritime Center. Exhibits include such topics as the development of surfing, the art of tattooing, and artifacts from the whaling industry. Next door you'll find the fully-rigged, four-masted *Falls of Clyde*. Built in 1878, this vessel served as a cargo and passenger liner and a sailing tanker before being declared a National Historic Landmark; it is permanently docked as a museum. If it's not out sailing, you'll find the *Hokule'a* moored next to the *Falls of Clyde*. The *Hokule'a* is a re-creation of a traditional double-hulled sailing canoe, which in 1976 made the 6,000-mile round-trip voyage to Tahiti using only ancient navigation techniques—the stars, the wind, and the sea.

Watch the Fish and Sharks at the Waikiki Aquarium *(see p. 180)* Much more than just a big fish tank, the Waikiki Aquarium will astound and educate your youngsters. They can probably sit for hours staring at the sharks, turtles, eels, rays, and fish swimming in the main tank. For a few laughs, wander out to the monk seal area and watch the antics of these seagoing clowns.

Snorkel in Hanauma Bay *(see p. 148)* Kids will be enthralled with the teeming tropical fish and the underwater world at this marine park. The shallow waters near the beach are perfect for neophyte snorkelers to learn in, and the long (2,000-foot) beach has plenty of frolicking room for kids. Get there early; it can get very crowded.

Hike to the Top of Diamond Head Crater *(see p. 181)* The entire family can make this easy 1.4-mile round-trip walk to the top of the 750-foot volcanic cone with its rewarding view of Oahu. Bring a flashlight for the entry tunnel and a camera for the view.

Explore the Depths in a Submarine Dive *(see p. 149)* Better than a movie, more exciting than a video game, the *Atlantis* or *Voyager* submarines journey down 100 feet below the water's surface to explore the Neptunian world of tropical reef fish and even an occasional shark or two.

Walking Tour: Historic Chinatown

Chinese laborers from the Guangdong Province first came to work on Hawaii's sugar and pineapple plantations in the 1850s. Once their plantation contracts were finished, a few of the ambitious ones started up small shops and restaurants in the area around River Street. At the time, the community that became known as Chinatown wasn't much— mainly a handful of dirt streets—but it was in a good location, close to the docks and the newly developing businesses around Iolani Palace in downtown Honolulu.

Chinatown was twice devastated by fire, once in 1886 and again in 1900. It's the 1900 fire that still intrigues historians: In December 1899, bubonic plague broke out in the area, and the Board of Health immediately quarantined its 7,000 Chinese and Japanese residents, but the plague continued to spread. On January 20, 1900, the Board decided to burn down plague-infected homes, starting at the corner of Beretania Street and Nuuanu Avenue. But the fire department wasn't quite ready; a sudden wind quickly spread the flames from one wooden building to the next in the densely built area, and soon Chinatown's entire 40 acres were leveled, all the way to the waterfront. Many historians believe that the "out-of-control" fire may have been purposely set to drive the Chinese merchants—who were becoming economically powerful and controlled prime real estate—out of Honolulu. If this was indeed the case, it didn't work: To everyone's surprise, the determined merchants built a new Chinatown out of the ashes.

Chinatown reached its peak in the 1930s. In the days before air travel, visitors arrived by cruise ship, and they often headed straight for the exotic shops and restaurants of Chinatown. In the 1940s, military personnel on leave flocked to Chinatown looking for excitement in the form of pool halls, beer parlors, tattoo joints, and houses of ill-repute. Over the years Chinatown deteriorated into a tawdry red-light district with seedy bars, drug dealing, and homeless people, but it has recently undergone extensive urban renewal. There's still just enough sleaze on the fringes (a few peep shows and topless bars) to keep it from being a novelty tourist attraction.

Today Chinatown is a jumble of streets that's teeming with busy residents and meandering visitors from all over the world. You'll hear the high-pitched bleating of vendors in the open market, and you'll see retired men talking story over games of mahjong. Brilliant colors and pungent aromas will also challenge your senses. This isn't quite Hawaii, but it's not really a microcosm of China, either—rather, what you'll find is a mixture of Asian cultures.

Getting There: From Waikiki, take TheBUS no. 2 or 20 toward downtown; get off on North Hotel Street (after Maunakea Street). If you're driving, take Ala Moana Boulevard and turn right on Smith Street; make a left on Beretania Street and a left again at Maunakea Street. The City Parking Garage (50¢ per hour) is located on the Ewa (west) side of Maunakea Street, between North Hotel and North King streets.
Start: North Hotel and Maunakea streets.
Finish: Same intersection.
Time: Approximately 1 to 2 hours, depending on how much time you spend browsing.
Best Times: Daylight hours.

Start your walk on the Ewa (west) side of Maunakea Street at:

1. **Hotel Street.** During World War II, Hotel Street was synonymous with "good times." Pool halls and beer joints lined the blocks, and prostitutes were plentiful. Today the nefarious establishments have been replaced with small shops, from art galleries to specialty boutiques. Urban professionals and recent immigrants now walk where the sailors once roamed, looking for bargains.

After you're done wandering through the shops, head back to the intersection with Maunakea Street. On the Diamond Head side of Smith, you'll notice stones in the sidewalk; they are taken from the sandalwood ships, which came to Hawaii empty of cargo, except for these stones that were used as ballast on the trip over. The stones were removed and the ships' hulls were filled with sandalwood and returned to the mainland.

Continue down Hotel Street and turn right on Maunakea; proceed to the corner of King Street and the:

2. Bank of Hawaii. At King and Maunakea streets sits this very unusual-looking bank; not the conservative edifice you'd expect, but one guarded by two fire-breathing dragon statues.

Continue down King Street. As you go, you'll pass the shops of various Chinese herbalists, such as the:

3. Viet Hoa Chinese Herb Shop, 162 N. King St. Chinese herbalists act as both doctors and dispensers of herbs. Patients tell the herbalist what ails them; the herbalist then decides which of the myriad herbs he'll mix together. Usually there's a wall of tiny drawers labeled with Chinese characters; the herbalist selects from the drawers ground, powdered, and dried items, such as flowers, roots, and antelope antler. The patient then takes the mixture home and brews it into a strong tea.

Another interesting shop on North King Street is the:

4. Yat Tung Chow Noodle Factory, 150 N. King St. The delicious, delicate noodles that star in numerous Asian dishes are made here, ranging from threadlike noodles (literally no thicker than embroidery thread) to fat udon noodles. There aren't any tours of the factory, but you can look through the window, past the white cloud of flour that hangs in the air, and watch as dough is fed into rollers at one end of the noodle machines. Perfectly cut noodles emerge at the other end.

On the Ewa side of Kekaulike Street, on King Street, lies the most visited part of Chinatown, the open-air market known as:

5. Oahu Market Place. If you're interested in Asian cooking, you'll find everything you could possibly want here, including pig's heads, poultry (some still squawking), fresh octopus, salted jellyfish, pungent fish sauce, fresh herbs, and thousand-year-old eggs. The friendly vendors are happy to explain their wares and give instructions on how to prepare these exotic treats. The market is divided into meats, poultry, fish, vegetables, and fruits. Past the open market are several grocery stores with fresh produce on display on the sidewalk. You're bound to spot some varieties here that you're not used to seeing at your local supermarket.

Follow King down to River Street and turn right toward the mountains and the:

6. River Street Pedestrian Mall. Before you reach the pedestrian mall, you'll pass a range of inexpensive restaurants that line River Street from King Street to Beretania Street. You can get the best Vietnamese and Filipino food in town in these blocks, but go early—lines for lunch start at 11:15am.

When you get to Beretania Street, River Street ends and the pedestrian mall begins with the **statue of Chinese revolutionary leader Sun Yat-Sen.** The wide mall, which borders the Nuuanu Stream, is lined with shade trees, park benches, and tables where senior citizens gather to play mahjong and checkers. Lots of take-out restaurants are nearby if you'd like to eat outdoors.

Along the River Street Mall, extending nearly a block over to Maunakea Street, is the:

7. Chinatown Cultural Plaza. This modern complex is filled with shops featuring everything from tailors to calligraphers (most somewhat more expensive than

Walking Tour: Historic Chinatown

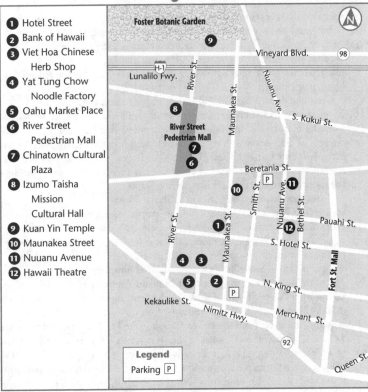

1. Hotel Street
2. Bank of Hawaii
3. Viet Hoa Chinese Herb Shop
4. Yat Tung Chow Noodle Factory
5. Oahu Market Place
6. River Street Pedestrian Mall
7. Chinatown Cultural Plaza
8. Izumo Taisha Mission Cultural Hall
9. Kuan Yin Temple
10. Maunakea Street
11. Nuuanu Avenue
12. Hawaii Theatre

Foster Botanic Garden

Vineyard Blvd. 98

Lunalilo Fwy. H-1

River St.

Maunakea St.

Nuuanu Ave.

S. Kukui St.

River Street Pedestrian Mall

Beretania St.

Smith St.

Nuuanu Ave.

Bethel St.

Pauahi St.

S. Hotel St.

Fort St. Mall

N. King St.

Kekaulike St.

Nimitz Hwy.

Merchant St.

92

Queen St.

Legend
Parking P

their street-side counterparts), as well as numerous restaurants. Although the plaza is a nice idea, most people prefer to wander and explore the streets than be in a complex. If you're looking for Asian magazines, you'll find a couple of shops specializing in them here. Or if you want to mail postcards home with the "Chinatown" postmark, there's a small post office tucked away in a corner of the plaza. The plaza does have one excellent feature: In the center of the plaza sits the **Moongate Stage,** the site of many cultural presentations, especially around Chinese New Year.

Continue up the River Street Mall and cross the Nuuanu Stream via the bridge at Kukui Street, which will bring you to:

8. **Izumo Taisha Mission Cultural Hall.** This small wooden Shinto shrine, built in 1923, houses a male deity (look for the X-shaped crosses on the top). Members of the faith ring the bell out front as an act of purification when they come to pray. Inside the temple is a 100-pound sack of rice, symbolizing good health. During World War II, the shrine was confiscated by the city of Honolulu and wasn't returned to the congregation until 1962.

If temples are of interest to you, walk 1 block toward the mountains to Vineyard Boulevard; cross back over Nuuanu Stream, past the entrance of Foster Botanical Gardens, to:

9. **Kuan Yin Temple.** This Buddhist temple, painted a brilliant red with a green ceramic-tiled roof, is dedicated to Kuan Yin Bodhisattva, the goddess of mercy, whose statue towers in the prayer hall. The piquant aroma of burning incense is

your clue that the temple is still a house of worship, not an exhibit, so enter with respect and leave your shoes outside. You might see people burning paper "money," which is for prosperity and good luck, or leaving flowers and fruits at the altar (also gifts to the goddess). A frequent offering is the *pomelo,* a grapefruit-like fruit that's a fertility symbol as well as a gift indicating a request for the blessing of children.

Continue down Vineyard and then turn left toward the ocean on:

10. Maunakea Street. Between Beretania and King streets, numerous **lei shops** (with lei makers working right on the premises) line both sides of Maunakea Street. The air is heavy with the aroma of flowers being woven into beautiful treasures. Not only is this the best place in all of Hawaii to get a deal on leis, but the size, color, and design of the leis made here are exceptional. Wander through all the shops before you decide which lei you want.

If you have a sweet tooth, stop in at **Shung Chong Yuein,** 1027 Maunakea St. (near Hotel Street), for delicious Asian pastries like moon cakes and almond cookies, all at very reasonable prices. They also have a wide selection of dried and sugared candies (like ginger, pineapple, lotus root) that you can eat as you stroll, or give as an exotic gift to friends back home.

Turn up Hotel Street in the Diamond Head direction, and walk to:

11. Nuuanu Avenue. On the corner of Nuuanu Avenue and Hotel Street is the **Chinatown Police Station,** located in the Perry Block building. Built in 1888, it looks like something straight out of a film noir.

Across the street from the Police Station is the **Lai Fong Department Store,** a classic Chinatown store owned by the same family for more than three-quarters of a century. Walking into Lai Fong is like stepping back in time. The old store sells everything from precious antiques to god-awful knickknacks to rare turn-of-the-century Hawaiian postcards—but it has built its reputation on the fabulous selection of Chinese silks and brocades and custom dresses it carries.

Between Hotel and Pauahi streets is the **Pegge Hooper Gallery,** 1164 Nuuanu Ave., where you can admire Pegge's well-known paintings of beautiful Hawaiian women.

At Pauahi Street, turn toward Diamond Head and walk up to Bethel Street and the:

12. Hawaii Theatre. This restored 1920 art deco theater is a work of art in itself. It hosts a variety of programs, from the Hawaii International Film Festival to beauty pageants (see "The Classics," in chapter 10, "Oahu After Dark," for details on how to find out what's on while you're in town).

Walk toward the ocean on Bethel Street and turn right on Hotel Street, which will lead you back to where you started.

Walking Tour: Honolulu Waterfront

For a walk into Honolulu's past when Polynesians first came to Hawaii, take this leisurely stroll along the waterfront and the surrounding environs.

Until about 1800, the area around Honolulu Harbor (from Nuuanu Avenue to Alakea Street and from Hotel Street to the ocean) was known as *Koa.* Some scholars say it was named after a dedicated officer to Chief Kakuhihewa of Oahu; others say it comes from the koa tree, which flourishes in this area. In 1793, Captain William Brown, on the British frigate *Butterworth,* sailed the first foreign ship into Honolulu harbor. Like most British explorers, he didn't bother to ask about the name of the

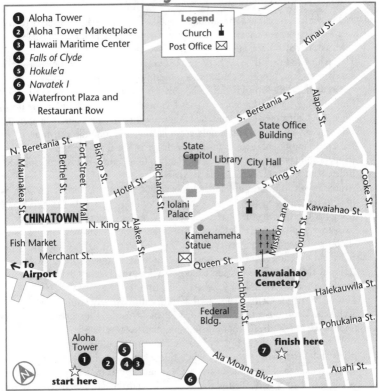

Walking Tour: Honolulu Waterfront

Legend
1. Aloha Tower
2. Aloha Tower Marketplace
3. Hawaii Maritime Center
4. *Falls of Clyde*
5. *Hokule'a*
6. *Navatek I*
7. Waterfront Plaza and Restaurant Row

Church †
Post Office ⊠

Kinau St.

S. Beretania St.

State Office Building

Alapai St.

N. Beretania St.

Fort Street

Bishop St.

Hotel St.

Richards St.

State Capitol

Library

City Hall

S. King St.

Cooke St.

Bethel St.

Maunakea St.

Mall

N. King St.

Alakea St.

Iolani Palace

Kamehameha Statue

Mission Lane

Kawaiahao St.

South St.

CHINATOWN

Fish Market

Merchant St.

⊠ Queen St.

Kawaiahao Cemetery

← **To Airport**

Punchbowl St.

Federal Bldg.

Halekauwila St.

Pohukaina St.

Aloha Tower

finish here ☆

7

5

1 2 4 3

Ala Moana Blvd.

Auahi St.

6

start here ☆

N

---

harbor; instead, he just called it Fair Haven. Other ships that followed started to call the harbor "Brown's Harbor." Luckily, the name the Hawaiians gave the harbor, Honolulu, which translates into "sheltered bay," became the popular name.

The waterfront area played a vital role in the history of Honolulu. King Kamehameha I moved his royal court here in 1809 to keep an eye on the burgeoning trade from the numerous ships that were coming here. The royal residence was at the makai end of Bethel Street, just 1 block from the start of our tour at the Aloha Tower.

Getting There: From Waikiki, take Ala Moana Boulevard in the Ewa direction. When Ala Moana ends, turn left on Nimitz Highway. There is parking on the ocean side of Nimitz at Bishop Street. TheBUS: 19 or 20.

Start: Aloha Tower, ocean end of Fort Street Mall at Pier 9.

Finish: Waterfront Plaza and Restaurant Row, Punchbowl Street/Ala Moana Boulevard.

Time: About 1 to 2 hours, depending on how long you linger in museums and shops.

Best Time: Daylight, when the Hawaii Maritime Museum is open (8:30am to 5pm daily).

Park in the parking lot on Bishop Street and Nimitz Highway and walk over to Pier 9 to:

1. **Aloha Tower.** One of the reasons that the word *aloha* is synonymous with Hawaii is because of the Aloha Tower. Built in 1926 (for the then-outrageous sum of $160,000), this 184-foot, 10-story tower (until 1959 the tallest structure in Hawaii) has clocks on all four of its sides with the word *aloha* under each clock.

Aloha, which has come to mean both "hello" and "farewell," was the first thing steamship passengers saw when they entered Honolulu Harbor. In the days when tourists arrived by steamer, "boat days" were a very big occasion. The Royal Hawaiian band would be on hand to play, crowds would gather, flower leis were freely given, and Honolulu came to a standstill to greet the visitors.

Go up the elevator inside the Aloha Tower to the **10th floor observation deck** for a bird's-eye view that encompasses Diamond Head and Waikiki, the downtown and Chinatown areas, and the harbor coastline to the airport. On the ocean side you can see the harbor mouth, Sand Island, the Honolulu reef runway, and the Pearl Harbor entrance channel. No charge to see the view; the Aloha Tower is open Sunday through Wednesday, 9am to 6pm, and Thursday through Saturday, 9am to 10pm. Next to the Tower is the:

2. Aloha Tower Marketplace. In the early 1990s, city officials came up with the idea to renovate and restore the waterfront with shops, restaurants, and bars to bring back the feeling of "boat days." The shops, restaurants, and bars inside the two-story Aloha Tower Marketplace offer an array of cuisines, one-of-a-kind shops, and even a microbrewery. Most shops open at 9am daily and the restaurants and bars don't shut down until the wee hours of the morning.

From the Aloha Tower Marketplace, walk in the Diamond Head direction along the waterfront to Pier 7, where you'll find the:

3. Hawaii Maritime Center, composed of three entities: the museum, which is in the **Kalakaua Boathouse;** the *Falls of Clyde,* the four-masted ship moored next door; and the *Hokule'a,* the 60-foot Polynesian sailing canoe, also moored at Pier 7.

When you enter the two-story Boathouse, stop to look at the glass case of trophies and artifacts from the days when the boathouse really did belong to King David Kalakaua. The museum has great exhibits on Hawaii's maritime history, whaling, the history of surfing in the islands, and the cultural art of tattooing. There's also an auditorium with videos of Hawaii's seagoing culture, and a reproduction of a Matson Liner stateroom. Moored next door is the:

4. Falls of Clyde. The world's only remaining fully rigged, four-masted ship is on display as a National Historic Landmark. Still afloat, the 266-foot, iron-hulled ship was built in 1878 in Glasgow, Scotland. Matson Navigation bought the ship in 1899 to carry sugar and passengers between Hilo and San Francisco. When that became economically unfeasible, in 1906 the boat was converted into a sail-driven oil tanker. After 1920, it was dismantled and became a floating oil depot for fishing boats in Alaska.

She was headed for the scrap pile when a group of Hawaii residents raised the money to bring her back to Hawaii in 1963. Since then she has been totally restored, and now visitors can wander across her decks and through the cargo area below. After viewing the *Falls of Clyde,* wander over to the:

5. Hokule'a. If you're lucky, the 60-foot Polynesian canoe will be docked, but it's often out on jaunts. In 1976, this reproduction of the traditional double-hulled sailing canoe proved to the world that the Polynesians could have made the 6,000-mile round-trip from Tahiti to Hawaii, navigating only by the stars and the wave patterns. Living on an open deck (9 feet wide by 40 feet long), the crew of a dozen, along with a traditional navigator from an island in the Northern Pacific, made the successful voyage. Since then there has been a renaissance in the Pacific among native islanders to relearn this art of navigation.

Next door, at Pier 6, you'll find:

6. Navatek I. From ancient Polynesian sailing canoes to today's high-tech, *Navatek I* is the latest specimen in naval engineering. The 140-foot-long vessel isn't even called a boat; it's actually a SWATH (Small Waterplane Area Twin Hull) vessel. That means the ship's superstructure—the part you ride on—rests on twin torpedolike hulls that cut through the water so you don't bob like a cork. It's the smoothest ride in town and guarantees you will not get seasick or spill your mai tai.

From Pier 6, walk down Ala Moana Boulevard and turn mauka at Punchbowl, where you'll come to:

7. **Waterfront Plaza and Restaurant Row.** Eateries serving an array of cuisines from gourmet Hawaii regional to burgers, shops, and theaters fill this block-long complex. This is a great place to stop for lunch or dinner, or for a cool drink at the end of your walk.

Walking Tour: Historic Honolulu

The 1800s were a turbulent time in Hawaii. By the end of the 1790s, Kamehameha the Great had united all the islands. Foreigners then began arriving by ship—first explorers, then merchants, and in 1820, missionaries. The rulers of Hawaii were hard-pressed to keep up. By 1840 it was clear that the capital had shifted from Lahaina, where the Kingdom of Hawaii was actually centered, to Honolulu where the majority of commerce and trade was taking place. In 1848 the Great Mahele (division) enabled commoners and eventually foreigners to own crown land, and in two generations, more than 80% of all private lands had shifted to foreign ownership. With the introduction of sugar as a crop, the foreigners prospered, and in time they put more and more pressures on the government.

By 1872, the monarchy had run through the Kamehameha line and in 1873 David Kalakaua was elected to the throne. Known as the "Merrie Monarch," Kalakaua redefined the monarchy by going on a world tour, building Iolani Palace, having a European-style coronation, and throwing extravagant parties. By the end of the 1800s, however, the foreign sugar growers and merchants had become extremely powerful in Hawaii. With the assistance of the U.S. Marines, they orchestrated the overthrow of Queen Liliuokalani, Hawaii's last reigning monarch, in 1893. The United States declared Hawaii a territory in 1898.

You can witness the remnants of these turbulent years in just a few short blocks.

Getting There: From Waikiki, take Ala Moana Boulevard in the Ewa direction. Ala Moana Boulevard ends at Nimitz Highway. Turn right on the next street on your right (Alakea Street). Park in the parking garage across from St. Andrews Church after you cross Beretania Street. TheBUS: 1, 2, 3, 4, 11, 12, or 50.

Start: St. Andrew's Church, Beretania and Alakea streets.

Finish: Same place.

Time: 2 to 3 hours, depending on how long you linger in museums.

Best Times: Wednesday through Saturday, daytime, when the Iolani Palace has tours.

Cross the street from the church parking lot and venture back to 1858 when you enter:

1. **St. Andrew's Church.** The Hawaiian monarchs were greatly influenced by the royals in Europe. When King Kamehameha IV saw the grandeur of the Church of England, he decided to build his own cathedral. He and Queen Emma founded the Anglican Church of Hawaii in 1858. The king, however, didn't live to see the church completed; he died on St. Andrew's Day, 4 years before King Kamehameha V oversaw the laying of the cornerstone in 1867. The church was named St. Andrew's in honor of King Kamehameha IV's death. This French-Gothic structure was shipped in pieces from England and reassembled here. Even

if you aren't fond of visiting churches, you have to see the floor-to-eaves handblown stained-glass window that faces the setting sun. In the glass is a mural of Reverend Thomas Staley, the first bishop in Hawaii; King Kamehameha IV; and Queen Emma. There's also an excellent thrift shop on the grounds with some real bargains, open Monday, Wednesday, and Friday 9:30am to 4pm and Saturday 9am to 1pm.

Next, walk down Beretania Street in the Diamond Head direction to the gates of:

2. **Washington Place.** Today this is the residence of the Governor of Hawaii (sorry, no tours; just peek through the iron fence), but it occupies a distinguished place in Hawaii's history. Originally the colonial-style home was built by a U.S. sea captain named John Dominis. The sea captain's son, also named John, married a beautiful Hawaiian princess, Lydia Kapaakea, who later became Hawaii's last queen, Lili-uokalani. When the queen was overthrown by U.S. businessmen in 1893, she moved out of Iolani Palace and into her husband's inherited home, Washington Place, where she lived until her death in 1917. On the left side of the building, near the sidewalk, is a plaque inscribed with the words to one of the most popular songs written by Queen Liliuokalani, "Aloha Oe" ("Farewell to Thee").

Cross the street and walk to the front of the Hawaii State Capitol, where you'll find the:

3. **Father Damien Statue.** The people of Hawaii have never forgotten the sacrifice this Belgian priest made to help the sufferers of leprosy when he volunteered to work with them in exile on the Kalaupapa Peninsula on the island of Molokai. After 16 years of service, Father Damien died of leprosy, at the age of 49. The statue is frequently draped in leis in recognition of Father Damien's humanitarian work.

Behind Father Damien's statue is the:

4. **Hawaii State Capitol.** Here's where Hawaii's state legislators work from mid-January to the end of April every year. This is not your typical white dome structure, but a building symbolic of Hawaii. Unfortunately, it symbolizes more of Hawaii than the architect and the state legislature probably bargained for. The building's unusual design has palm tree–shaped pillars, two cone-shaped chambers (representing volcanoes) for the legislative bodies, and in the inner courtyard, a 600,000-tile mosaic of the sea (Aquarius) created by a local artist. A reflecting pool (representing the sea) surrounds the entire structure. Like a lot of things in Hawaii, it was a great idea, but no one considered the logistics. The reflecting pond also draws brackish water, which rusts the hardware; when it rains, water pours into the rotunda, dampening government business; and the Aquarius floor mosaic became so damaged by the elements that it became a hazard. The entire building was closed for a couple of years (forcing the legislature to set up temporary quarters in several buildings) while the entire building (built in 1969) was renovated in the early 1990s. It's open again, and you are welcome to go into the rotunda and see the woven hangings and murals at the entrance, or take the elevator up to the fifth floor for a spectacular view of the city's historical center.

Walk down Richards Street toward the ocean and stop at the:.

5. **Iolani Palace.** Hawaii is the only state in the U.S. to have not one, but two royal palaces; one in Kona where the royals went during the summer, and Iolani Palace (*Iolani* means "royal hawk"). Don't miss the opportunity to see this grande dame of historic buildings. Tours are limited (Wednesday through Saturday, 9am to 2pm; admission $8 adults, $3 children 5 to 13) and very popular. You must reserve in advance; call ☎ **808/522-0832.**

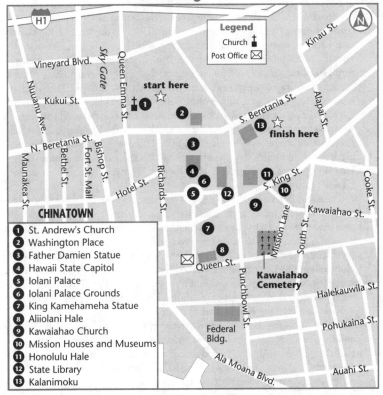

Legend
† Church
⊠ Post Office

H1

Vineyard Blvd.

Sky Gate

Queen Emma St.

Kukui St.

Nuuanu Ave.

N. Beretania St.

Bethel St.

Maunakea St.

Fort St. Mall

Bishop St.

Hotel St.

Richards St.

CHINATOWN

start here

S. Beretania St.

Kinau St.

Alapai St.

finish here

S. King St.

Cooke St.

Kawaiahao St.

Mission Lane

South St.

Punchbowl St.

Queen St.

⊠

Kawaiahao Cemetery

Halekauwila St.

Pohukaina St.

Federal Bldg.

Ala Moana Blvd.

Auahi St.

1 St. Andrew's Church
2 Washington Place
3 Father Damien Statue
4 Hawaii State Capitol
5 Iolani Palace
6 Iolani Palace Grounds
7 King Kamehameha Statue
8 Aliiolani Hale
9 Kawaiahao Church
10 Mission Houses and Museums
11 Honolulu Hale
12 State Library
13 Kalanimoku

In ancient times a heiau stood in this area. When it became clear to King Kamehameha III that the capital should be transferred from Lahaina to Honolulu, he moved to a modest building here in 1845. The construction of the palace was undertaken by King David Kalakaua and was begun in 1879; it was finished 3 years later at a cost of $350,000. The king spared no expense: You can still see the glass and iron work imported from San Francisco. The palace had all the modern conveniences for its time: Electric lights were installed 4 years before the White House had them; every bedroom had its own full bath with hot and cold running water and copper-lined tubs, a flush toilet, and a bidet. The king had a telephone line from the palace to his boathouse on the water a year after Alexander Graham Bell introduced it to the world.

It was also in this palace that Queen Liliuokalani was overthrown and placed under house arrest for 9 months. Later, the territorial and then the state government used the palace until it outgrew it. When the legislature left in 1968, the palace was in shambles and has since undergone a $7 million overhaul to restore it to its former glory.

After you visit the palace, spend some time on the:

6. **Iolani Palace Grounds.** You can wander around the grounds at no charge. The ticket window to the palace and the gift shop are in the former barracks of the Royal Household Guards. The domed pavilion on the grounds was originally built as a Coronation Stand by King Kalakaua (9 years after he took the throne,

he decided to have a formal European-style coronation ceremony where he crowned himself and his queen, Kapiolani). Later he used it as a **Royal Bandstand** for concerts (King Kalakaua, along with Herni Berger, the first Royal Hawaiian Bandmaster, wrote "Hawaii Pono'i," the state anthem). Today the Royal Bandstand is still used for concerts by the Royal Hawaiian Band. The more modern building on the grounds is the **State Archives,** built in 1953, which hold records, documents, and photos of Hawaii's people and its history.

From the palace grounds, walk makai to King Street, and cross the street to the:

7. **King Kamehameha Statue.** At the juncture of King, Merchant, and Mililani streets stands a replica of the man who united the Hawaiian Islands. The striking black and gold bronze statue is magnificent. The best day to see the statue is on June 11 (King Kamehameha Day), when it is covered with leis in honor of Hawaii's favorite son.

The statue of Kamehameha I was cast by Thomas Gould in 1880 in Paris. However, it was lost at sea somewhere near the Falkland Islands. Subsequently, the insurance money was used to pay for a second statue, but in the meantime, the original statue was recovered. The original was eventually sent to the town of Kapaau on the Big Island, the birthplace of Kamehameha, and the second statue was placed in Honolulu in 1883, as part of King David Kalakaua's coronation ceremony. A third statue (all three are very different, but they were supposedly all cast from the same mold) was sent to Washington, D.C., when Hawaii became a state in 1959.

Right behind King Kamehameha's statue is:

8. **Aliiolani Hale,** which translates to "House of Heavenly Kings." This distinctive building, with a clock tower, now houses the State Judiciary Building. King Kamehameha V originally wanted to build a palace here and commissioned the Australian architect Thomas Rowe in 1872. However, it ended up as the first major government building for the Hawaiian monarchy. Kamehameha V didn't live to see it completed, and King David Kalakaua dedicated the building in 1874. Ironically, less than 20 years later, on January 17, 1893, Stanford Dole, backed by other prominent sugar planters, stood on the steps to this building and proclaimed the overthrow of the Hawaiian monarchy and the establishment of a provisional government. Tours are conducted on Tuesday through Thursday, 10am to 3pm, no charge.

Walk toward Diamond Head on King Street; at the corner of King and Punchbowl, stop in at:

9. **Kawaiahao Church.** When the missionaries came to Hawaii, the first thing they did was build churches. Four thatched grass churches (one measured 54 feet by 22 feet and could seat 300 people on lauhala mats; the last thatched church held 4,500 people) had been built on this site through 1837 before Rev. Hiram Bingham began building what he considered a "real" church—a New England–style congregational structure with Gothic influences. Between 1837 and 1842, the building of the church required some 14,000 giant coral slabs (some weighing more than 1,000 pounds). Hawaiian divers literally raped the reefs, digging out huge chunks of coral and causing irreparable environmental damage.

Kawaiahao is Hawaii's oldest church, and it has been the site of numerous historical events, such as a speech made by King Kamehameha III in 1843, an excerpt from which became Hawaii's state motto ("Ua mau ke ea o ka aina i ka pono," which translates as "The life of the land is preserved in righteousness"). The clock tower in the church, which was donated by King Kamehameha III and installed in 1850, continues to tick today. The church is open Monday through

Saturday, from 8am to 4pm; you'll find it to be very cool in temperature. Don't sit in the pews in the back, marked with kahili feathers and velvet cushions; they are still reserved for the descendants of royalty. Sunday service (in Hawaiian) at 10:30am.

Cross the street, and you'll see the:

10. Mission Houses and Museums. On the corner of King and Kawaiahao streets stand the original buildings of the Sandwich Islands Mission Headquarters: the **Frame House** (built in 1821), the **Chamberlain House** (1831), and the **Printing Office** (1841). The complex is open Tuesday through Saturday from 9am to 4pm; admission is $6 adults, $5 seniors, $3 college students, and $2 children. The tours are often led by descendants of the original missionaries to Hawaii.

Believe it or not, the missionaries brought their own prefab house along with them when they came around Cape Horn from Boston in 1819. The Frame House was designed for New England winters and had small windows (it must have been stifling hot inside). Finished in 1921 (the interior frame was left behind and didn't arrive until Christmas 1920), it is Hawaii's oldest wooden structure. The Chamberlain House, built in 1931, was used by the missionaries as a storehouse.

The missionaries believed that the best way to spread the Lord's message to the Hawaiians was to learn their language, and then to print literature for them to read. So it was the missionaries who gave the Hawaiians a written language. The Printing House on the grounds was where the lead-type Ramage press (brought from New England, of course) printed the Hawaiian Bible.

Cross King Street and walk in the Ewa direction to the corner of Punchbowl and King to:

11. Honolulu Hale. The **Honolulu City Hall,** built in 1927, was designed by Honolulu's most famous architect, C. W. Dickey. His Spanish mission–style building has an open-air courtyard, which is used for art exhibits and concerts. Open weekdays.

Cross Punchbowl Street and walk mauka to the:

12. State Library. Anything you want to know about Hawaii and the Pacific can be found here, the main branch of the state's library system. Located in a restored historic building, there is an open garden courtyard in the middle of the building, great for stopping for a rest on your walk.

Head mauka up Punchbowl to the corner of Punchbowl and Beretania streets to:

13. Kalanimoku. This beautiful name, Ship of Heaven, has been given to this dour state office building. Here you can get information on hiking and camping (from the Department of Land and Natural Resources) in state parks.

Retrace your steps in the Ewa direction down Beretania to Alakea back to the parking garage.

Walking Tour: Kapiolani Park

On June 11, 1877, King Kamehameha Day, then-King David Kalakaua donated some 140 acres of land to the people of Hawaii for Hawaii's first park. He asked that the park be named after his beloved wife, Queen Kapiolani, and he celebrated the opening of this vast grassy area with a free concert and "high stakes" horse races (the king loved gambling) on the new horse-racing oval he had built below Diamond Head.

The horse races, and the gambling that accompanied it, were eventually outlawed, but the park—and the free concerts—live on. Just a coconut's throw from the high-rise concrete jungle of Waikiki lies this 133-acre grassy park (the Paki playground and a fire station make up the remaining acreage) dotted with spreading banyans, huge monkeypod trees, blooming royal poincianas, and swaying ironwoods. Throughout the open spaces are jogging paths, tennis courts, soccer and cricket fields, and even an archery range. People come to the park to listen to music, watch ethnic dancing, exercise, enjoy team sports, take long meditative walks, picnic, buy art, smell the roses, and just relax. The park is the site of international kite-flying contests, the finishing line for the Honolulu marathon, and the home of yearly Scottish highland games, Hawaiian cultural festivals, and about a zillion barbecues and picnics every year.

Getting There: From Waikiki, walk toward Diamond Head on Kalakaua Avenue. If you are coming by car, the cheapest parking is metered street parking on Kalakaua Avenue adjacent to the park. TheBUS: 19 or 20.

Start: Waikiki Beach Center, Kalakaua Avenue, Diamond Head side of the Sheraton Moana Hotel, across the street from the Hyatt Regency and Uluniu Avenue.

Finish: Kapiolani Beach Park.

Time: 4 to 5 hours. Allow at least an hour each for walking around the park, wandering around the zoo, exploring the aquarium, and snapping photos at the Kodak Hula Show, plus all the time you want for the beach.

Best Time: Tuesday to Thursday mornings if you want to catch the Kodak Hula Show.

Start at the:

1. **Waikiki Beach Center.** On the ocean side of Kalakaua Avenue, next to the Sheraton Moana Hotel, is a complex of rest rooms, showers, surfboard lockers, rental concessions, and the Waikiki police substation.

On the Diamond Head side of the police substation are the:

2. **Wizard Stones or Healing Stones.** These four basalt boulders, which weigh several tons apiece and sit on a lava rock platform, are held sacred by the Hawaiian people.

The story goes that sometime before the 15th century, four powerful healers from Moaulanuiakea, in the Society Islands, named Kapaemahu, Kahaloa, Kapuni, and Kihohi, lived in the Ulukoa area of Waikiki. After years of healing the people and the alii of Oahu, they wished to return home. They asked the people to erect four monuments made of bell stone, a basalt rock that was found in a Kaimuki quarry and that produced a bell-like ringing when struck. The healers spent a ceremonious month transferring their spiritual healing power, or *mana*, to the stones. The great mystery is how the boulders were transported from Kaimuki to the marshland near Kuhio Beach in Waikiki! Over time a bowling alley was built on the spot, and the stones got buried beneath the structure. After the bowling alley was torn down in the 1960s, tourists used the stones to eat lunch on or to drape their wet towels over. In 1997 the stones were once again given a place of prominence with the construction of a $75,000 shrine that includes the platform and a wrought-iron fence. Since then the stones have become something of a mecca for students and patients of traditional healing.

Just west of the stones you'll find the:

3. **Duke Kahanamoku Statue.** Here, cast in bronze, is Hawaii's most famous athlete, also known as the father of modern surfing. Duke (1890–1968) won Olympic swimming medals in 1912, 1920, 1924, and 1928. He was enshrined in both the Swimming Hall of Fame and the Surfing Hall of Fame. He also traveled around the world promoting surfing. Interestingly, when the city of Honolulu first erected the statue of this lifelong ocean athlete, they placed it with his

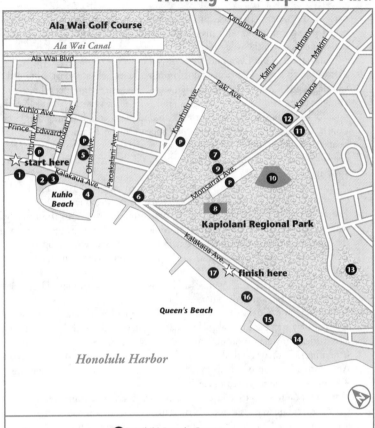

Ala Wai Golf Course

Ala Wai Canal

Ala Wai Blvd.

Kanaina Ave.

Hinano

Makini

Kaina

Kalua

Paki Ave.

Kapahulu Ave.

Kaunaoa

Kuhio Ave.

Prince Edward

Uluniu Ave.

Lihokane Ave.

Ohua Ave.

Paoakalani Ave.

Kalakaua Ave.

Monsarrat Ave.

Kuhio Beach

Kapiolani Regional Park

★ start here

Kalakaua Ave.

★ finish here

Queen's Beach

Honolulu Harbor

1. Waikiki Beach Center
2. Wizard Stones or Healing Stones
3. Duke Kahanamoku Statue
4. Kuhio Beach Park
5. Father Damien Museum
6. Kapiolani Park Kiosk
7. Honolulu Zoo
8. Kapiolani Park Bandstand
9. Art Mart
10. Waikiki Shell
11. Queen Kapiolani Garden
12. People's Open Market
13. Diamond Head Tennis Courts
14. San Souci Beach
15. Natatorium
16. Waikiki Aquarium
17. Kapiolani Beach Park

back to the water. There was public outcry, because no one familiar with the ocean would ever stand with his back to it. To quell the outcry, the city moved the statue closer to the sidewalk.

Continuing in the Diamond Head direction, you'll come to:

4. **Kuhio Beach Park.** The two small swimming holes here are great, but heed the warning sign: WATCH OUT FOR HOLES. There actually are deep holes in the sandy bottom, and you may suddenly find yourself in very deep water. The best pool for swimming is the one on the Diamond Head end, but the water circulation is questionable—there sometimes appears to be a layer of suntan lotion floating on the surface. If the waves are up, watch the boogie boarders surf by the seawall. They ride toward the wall and at the last minute veer away with a swoosh.

After watching the surfers, cross Kalakaua Avenue and walk mauka down Ohua Avenue; behind St. Augustine's Church you'll find the:

5. **Father Damien Museum.** This small museum is a tribute to the priest who worked with the sufferers of leprosy on Molokai. A video of Father Damien and the leprosy colony is available for viewing here. The museum is open Monday through Friday from 9am to 3pm, and Saturday from 9am to noon; admission is free.

Go back to Kalakaua Avenue and walk towards Diamond Head to the entrance of Kapiolani Park, where you'll see the:

6. **Kapiolani Park Kiosk.** On the corner of Kalakaua and Kapahulu avenues, this small display stand contains brochures and actual photos of the park's history. It also carries information on upcoming events at the various sites within the park (Aquarium, Zoo, Waikiki Shell, Kodak Hula Show, and Kapiolani Bandstand). An informative map will help to orient you to the park grounds. Continue up Kapahulu Avenue to the entrance of the:

7. **Honolulu Zoo.** The city's 42-acre zoo is open every day from 9am to 4:30pm, but the best time to go is as soon as the gates open—the animals seem to be more active and it is a lot cooler than walking around at midday in the hot sun.

You can walk or ride the tram to view the animals from around the world, stopping at the new African Savannah exhibit, a 10-acre wild preserve with more than 40 African critters (including lions, cheetahs, white rhinos, giraffes, zebras, hippos, and monkeys) roaming around in the open. There's also a petting zoo of farm animals, an aviary for Hawaii's rapidly disappearing native birds, and an interesting collection of Hawaii's native plants. Admission is $6 adults, $1 children 6 to 12 when accompanied by an adult (if a child isn't with an adult, he or she pays the adult fee; children under 6 are not allowed in without an adult).

For a real treat, take the **"Zoo by Moonlight"** tour, which allows you a rare behind-the-scenes look into the lives of the zoo's nocturnal creatures. Tours are offered 2 days before, during, and 2 days after the full moon from 7 to 9pm; the cost is $7 for adults and $5 for children.

Trace your steps back to Kapahulu and Kalakaua avenues and head mauka down Monsarrat Avenue to the:

8. **Kapiolani Park Bandstand,** where, on the mauka side of the bandstand, the **Kodak Hula Show** has been presenting the hula to visitors since 1937 (and a few of the senior ladies in the show have been dancing since the show started). Some 3,000 people fit into the bleachers around a grassy stage area (with the sun to your back for perfect picture taking). If you forget your camera or run out of film, Kodak has cameras for rent and plenty of film for sale. For a good seat, get there by 8am; to get into the show, be there no later than 9am. Once

the show starts, they admit people only between acts. The show is nonstop entertainment with hula dancers, bedecked in ti-leaf skirts and flower leis, swaying to an assortment of rhythms. Be sure to save some film to photograph the grand finale, which consists of all the dancers lining up on the stage and spelling out A-L-O-H-A and H-A-W-A-I-I with placards. The performances are Tuesday through Thursday, 10 to 11:15am, and are free.

Back on Monsarrat Avenue, on the fence facing the zoo, you'll find the:

9. Art Mart, or Artists of Oahu Exhibit, which is the new official name of this display. Here, local artisans hang their artwork on a fence for the public to view and buy. Not only do you get to meet the artists, but you have an opportunity to purchase their work at a considerable discount from the prices you'll see in galleries. Exhibits are Saturday, Sunday, and Wednesday, 10am to 4pm.

Cross Monsarrat Avenue, and you'll see the:

10. Waikiki Shell. Just mauka of the Kodak Hula Show is the open-air amphitheater that hosts numerous musical shows, from the Honolulu Symphony to traditional Hawaiian music.

Continue walking down to the end of the block to the corner of Monsarrat and Paki avenues to the:

11. Queen Kapiolani Garden. You'll see a range of hibiscus plants and dozens of varieties of roses, including the somewhat rare Hawaiian rose. The tranquil gardens are always open and are a great place to wander and relax.

Across the street on a Wednesday morning, you'll find the:

12. People's Open Market. Open from 10 to 11am, the farmer's market with its open stalls is an excellent spot to buy fresh produce and flowers. After you make your purchases, continue in the Diamond Head direction down Paki Avenue to the:

13. Diamond Head Tennis Courts. Located on the mauka side of Paki Avenue, the free City and County tennis courts are open for play during daylight hours 7 days a week. Tennis etiquette suggests that if someone is waiting for a court, limit your play to 45 minutes.

After watching or playing, turn onto Kalakaua Avenue, and begin walking back toward Waikiki to:

14. San Souci Beach. Located next to the New Otani Kaimana Beach Hotel, this is one of the best swimming beaches in Waikiki. The shallow reef, which is close to shore, keeps the waters calm. Farther out there is good snorkeling in the coral reef by the Kapua Channel. Facilities include outdoor showers and a lifeguard. After a brief swim, keep walking toward Waikiki until you come to the:

15. Natatorium. This huge concrete structure next to the beach is both a memorial to the soldiers of World War I and a 100-meter saltwater swimming pool. Opened in 1927, when Honolulu had hopes of hosting the Olympics, the ornate swimming pool fell into disuse and disrepair after World War II, and was finally closed in 1979. For two decades the state and the City and County of Honolulu have argued about what to do with the Natatorium. Currently, the Mayor of Honolulu wants to reopen the pool, but the project is still bogged down in the political quagmire.

After a brief stop here, continue on to the:

16. Waikiki Aquarium, at 2777 Kalakaua Ave. Try not to miss this stop—the tropical aquarium is worth a peek if only to see the only living **chambered nautilus** born in captivity. Its natural habitat is the deep waters of Micronesia, but Bruce Carlson, director of the aquarium, succeeded not only in trapping the pearly shell in 1,500 feet of water by dangling chunks of raw tuna, but also managed to breed this ancient relative of the octopus. The aquarium was also the first to successfully display the cuttlefish and Hawaii's favorite eating fish, the mahi-mahi. There are plenty of other fish in this small but first-class aquarium, located at the edge of a live coral reef. Owned and operated by the University of Hawaii, the aquarium, after a $3 million upgrade, now features a Hawaiian reef habitat with sharks, eels, a touch tank, and habitats for the endangered Hawaiian monk seal and green sea turtles. Recently added: a rotating Biodiversity Special Exhibit, which features a look at the diversity of sea life and interactive exhibits focusing on corals and coral reefs. Admission $6 adults, $4 seniors and students, $2.50 children 13 to 17. Open daily 9am to 5pm; closed Christmas Day.

Your final stop is:

17. **Kapiolani Beach Park.** Relax on the stretch of grassy lawn alongside the sandy beach, one of the best-kept secrets of Waikiki. This beach park is much less crowded than the beaches of Waikiki, plus it has adjacent grassy lawns, barbecue areas, picnic tables, rest rooms, and showers. The swimming is good here year-round, a surfing spot known as "Public's," is offshore, and there's always a game going at the volleyball courts. The middle section of the beach park, in front of the pavilion, is known as Queen's Beach or Queen's Surf, and is popular with the gay community.

6 Beyond Honolulu: Exploring the Island

The moment always arrives—usually after 2 or 3 days at the beach, or while enjoying sundown mai tais at the Halekulani—when a certain curiosity kicks in about the rest of Oahu (which is largely unexplored by most visitors). It's time to pick up the rental car and set out around the island. If you don't want to hassle with a car, you can explore the island via TheBUS. There are two buses that "circle the island": no. 52, which goes around the island clockwise (west to east), and no. 55, which goes around the island counterclockwise (east to west). Both run about every 30 minutes. However, be aware that at Turtle Bay Hilton, just outside of Kahuku, the no. 52 becomes the no. 55 and returns to Honolulu via the coast, and the no. 55 becomes the no. 52 and returns to Honolulu on the inland route. *Translation:* You have to get off and switch buses to complete your island tour, which takes about 4 hours, not including stops. If you're interested in one specific area, there are express buses to certain destinations (no. 54 to Pearl City; no. 46 to Kailua-Kaneohe; and nos. 57 and 58 to Sea Life Park); call **TheBUS** for more information at ☎ **808/848-5555.**

For great places to stop for a bite to eat while you're exploring, see chapter 6, "Dining." You also might want to check out chapter 9, "Shopping."

OAHU'S SOUTHEAST COAST

From the high-rises of Waikiki, head down Kalakaua Avenue past Kapiolani Park toward the arid south shore. The landscape here is more moonscape with prickly cacti onshore and, in the winter, spouting whales cavorting offshore. Some call it the South Shore, others Sandy's after the mile-long beach here, but Hawaiians call it **Ka Iwi,** which means "the bone"—no doubt because of the bone-cracking shore breaks along this popular body-boarding coastline. The beaches here are long, wide, and popular with local daredevils.

This open, scenic coast is the best place on Oahu to watch sea, shore, and even land birds. In season, it's also a good whale-watching spot, and the night sky is ideal for amateur astronomers to look for meteors, comets, and constellations.

Eastern Oahu & The Windward Coast

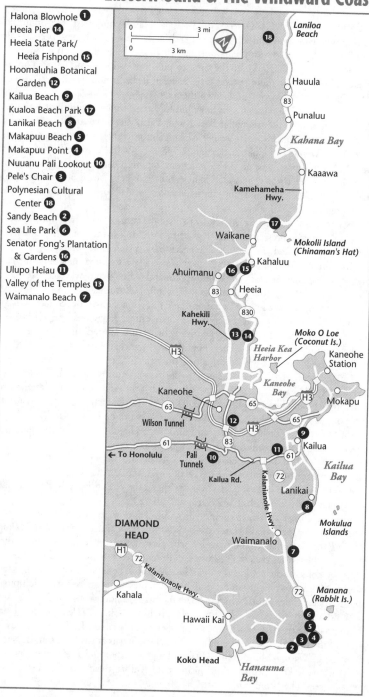

0   3 mi
0   3 km

18 Laniloa
Beach

Hauula

83

Punaluu

Kahana Bay

Kaaawa

**Kamehameha
Hwy.**

17

Waikane
*Mokolii Island
(Chinaman's Hat)*

16 **15** Kahaluu

Ahuimanu
Heeia

830

**Kahekili
Hwy.**

13 **14**
*Moko O Loe
(Coconut Is.)*

*Heeia Kea
Harbor*
Kaneohe
Station

H3

*Kaneohe
Bay*

Kaneohe

63

Wilson Tunnel

65
H3
Mokapu

12

65

← To Honolulu

61

Pali
Tunnels

10

83

9 Kailua

11

61

Kailua Rd.

72

*Kailua
Bay*

Lanikai

8

DIAMOND
HEAD

H1
72

Waimanalo
7

*Mokulua
Islands*

Kahala

Kalanianaole Hwy.

72

*Manana
(Rabbit Is.)*

6

5

Hawaii Kai

1

3 **4**

2

Koko Head
*Hanauma
Bay*

DRIVING INSTRUCTIONS Follow Kalakaua Avenue past the multitiered **Dillingham Fountain** and around the bend in the road, which now becomes Poni Moi Road. Make a right on Diamond Head Road and begin the climb up the side of the old crater. At the top, take the time to pull over at **Diamond Head Lookout,** where the view of the rolling waves is spectacular. If the turnout is jammed with cars, there are two more lookouts just down the road.

Diamond Head Road now rolls downhill into the ritzy community of **Kahala.** At the V in the road at the triangular **Fort Ruger Park,** veer to your right and continue on the palm tree–lined Kahala Avenue. Make a left on Hunakai Street and then a right on Kilauea Avenue and look for the sign H-1 WEST—WAIMANALO. Turn right at the sign. You won't actually be on the H-1 freeway, but on Kalanianaole Highway, a four-lane highway, interrupted by a stop light every few blocks. You'll be passing through one of Honolulu's bedroom communities, marked by malls on the left and beach parks on the right.

About a half hour outside Waikiki, you'll see the turn off to **Hanauma Bay** on the right. This marine preserve is a great place to stop for a swim; you'll find the friendliest fish on the island. *Be warned:* The beach park is closed on Tuesday.

Around the 11-mile marker, through the jagged lava rock that makes up the coastline, waves spout sea foam at **Halona Blowhole.** Look out over the ocean from Halona, over Sandy Beach and across the 26-mile gulf, to neighboring **Molokai** and the faint triangular shadow of **Lanai** on the far horizon. **Sandy Beach** (see "Beaches" in chapter 7, "Fun in the Surf & Sun") is Oahu's most dangerous beach; it's also the only one with an ambulance always standing by to rush injured surfers to the hospital in the event of an emergency. Body boarders love the challenge here.

The coast looks raw and empty along this stretch, but the road weaves past old Hawaiian fishponds and past the famous formation known as **Pele's Chair,** just off Kalanianaole Highway (Hi. 72) above Queen's Beach. From a distance, the lava-rock outcropping looks like a mighty throne; it's believed to be the fire goddess's last resting place on Oahu before she flew off to continue her work on other islands.

Ahead lies 647-foot-high **Makapuu Point,** with a lighthouse that once signaled safe passage for arriving steamship passengers from San Francisco. The automated light now brightens Oahu's south coast for passing tankers, fishing boats, and sailors. You can take a short hike up there for a view of a spectacular vista.

If you're with the kids, you may want to spend the day at **Sea Life Park,** a marine amusement park; see "Fish, Flora & Fauna," above.

Turn the corner at Makapuu and you're on Oahu's windward side, where cooling trade winds propel windsurfers across turquoise bays and the waves at **Makapuu Beach Park** are perfect for bodysurfing. For more details, see "Beaches," in chapter 7.

Ahead, the coastal vista is a profusion of fluted green mountains and strange peaks, edged by golden beaches and the blue, blue Pacific. The 3,000-foot-high sheer green Koolau Mountains plunge almost straight down, presenting an irresistible jumping-off spot for hang-glider pilots, who catch the thermals on hours-long rides.

Winding up the coast, Kalanianaole Highway (Hi. 72) leads through rural **Waimanalo,** a country beach town of nurseries and stables, fresh fruit stands, and some of the island's best conch and triton shell specimens at roadside stands. Nearly 4 miles long, **Waimanalo Beach** is Oahu's longest beach, and the most popular for bodysurfing. Take a swim here or head on to **Kailua Beach,** one of Hawaii's best beaches (see "The Windward Coast," below, and "Beaches," in chapter 7).

If it's still early in the day, you can head up the lush, green Windward Coast by turning right at the Castle Junction, Hi. 72, and Hi. 61 (which is also Kailua Road on the makai side of the junction, Kalanianaole Highway on the mauka side of the junction), and continue down Kailua Road (Hi. 61). After Kailua Road crosses the Kaelepulu Stream, the name of the road changes to Kuulei Road. When Kuulei Road ends, turn left on to Kalaheo Avenue. After Kalaheo Avenue crosses the Kawainui Channel, the name of the road changes to Kaneohe Bay Drive. Follow this scenic drive around the peninsula until it joints the junction of Kaneohe Bay Drive and Kamehameha Highway (Hi. 83). Turn right and continue on Kamehameha Highway for a scenic drive along the ocean.

If you're in a hurry to get back to Waikiki, turn left at Castle Junction and head over the Pali Highway (Hi. 61), which becomes Bishop Street in Honolulu and ends at Ala Moana. Turn left for Waikiki; it's the second beach on the right.

THE WINDWARD COAST

From the **Nuuanu Pali Lookout,** near the summit of Pali Highway (Hi. 61), you get the first hint of the other side of Oahu, a region so green and lovely that it could be an island sibling of Tahiti or Moorea. With many beaches and bays, the scenic 30-mile Windward Coast parallels the corduroy-ridged, nearly perpendicular cliffs of the Koolau Range, which separates the windward side of the island from Honolulu and the rest of Oahu. As you descend on the serpentine Pali Highway beneath often gushing waterfalls, you'll see the nearly 1,000-foot spike of **Olomana,** the bold pinnacle that always reminds us of that mountain in *Close Encounters,* and beyond, the Hawaiian village of **Waimanalo.**

DRIVING INSTRUCTIONS Coming down from Pali Highway, **Kailua** is to the right. It is Hawaii's biggest beach town, with more than 50,000 residents and two special beaches, **Kailua** and **Lanikai,** begging for visitors (for more details, see "Beaches," in chapter 7). Funky little Kailua is lined with $1 million houses next to tar-paper shacks, antiques shops, and bed-and-breakfasts. Although the Pali Highway (Hi. 61) proceeds directly to the coast, it undergoes two name changes, becoming first Kalanianaole Highway—from the intersection of Kamehameha Highway (Hi. 83)—and then Kailua Road as it heads into Kailua town; the road remains Hi. 61 the whole way. Kailua Road ends at the T-intersection at Kalaheo Drive, which follows the coast in a northerly and southerly direction. Turn right on South Kalaheo Drive to get to Kailua Beach Park and Lanikai Beach. No signs point the way, but you can't miss them.

If you spend a day at the beach here, stick around for sunset, when the sun sinks behind the Koolau Range and tints the clouds pink and orange. After a hard day at the beach you work up an appetite, and Kailua has several great, inexpensive restaurants (see "Dining," in chapter 6).

If you want to skip the beaches this time, turn left on North Kalaheo Drive, which becomes Kaneohe Bay Drive as it skirts Kaneohe Bay and leads back to Kamehameha Highway (Hi. 83), which then passes through **Kaneohe.** The suburban maze of Kaneohe is one giant strip mall of retail excess that mars one of the Pacific's most picturesque bays. After clearing this obstacle, the place begins to look like Hawaii again.

Incredibly scenic **Kaneohe Bay** is spiked with islets and lined with gold-sand beach parks like **Kualoa,** a favorite picnic spot (see "Beaches," in chapter 7). The bay has a barrier reef and four tiny islets, one of which is known as **Moku o loe,** or Coconut Island. Don't be surprised if it looks familiar—it appeared in "Gilligan's Island." It's now the United States' only tropical marine research laboratory on a coral reef.

At **Heeia State Park** (☎ 808/247-3156) is **Heeia Fishpond,** which ancient Hawaiians built by enclosing natural bays with rocks to trap fish on the incoming tide. Heeia Fishpond is now being restored. The 88-acre fishpond, made of lava rock, which had four watchtowers to observe fish movement and several sluice gates along the 5,000-foot-long wall, is now in the process of being restored.

Stop by the **Heeia Pier,** which juts onto Kaneohe Bay. You can take a snorkel cruise here, or sail out to a sandbar in the middle of the bay for an incredible view of Oahu that most people, even those who live here, never see. If it's Tuesday through Saturday between 7am and 6pm, stop in and see Ernie Choy at the **Deli on Heeia Kea Pier** (☎ **808/235-2192**). Ernie Choy has served fishermen, sailors, and kayakers the beach town's best omelets, plate lunches, and loco mocos at reasonable prices since 1979.

Everyone calls it Chinaman's Hat, but the tiny island off the eastern shore of Kualoa Regional Park is really **Mokolii.** It's a sacred *puu honua,* or place of refuge, like the restored Puu Honua Honaunau on the Big Island of Hawaii. Excavations have unearthed evidence that this area was the home of ancient *alii* (royalty). Early Hawaiians believed the island of Mokolii (or "fin of the lizard") is all that remains of a *mo'o,* or lizard, slain by Pele's sister, Hiiaka, and hurled into the sea. At low tide, you can swim out to the island, but keep watch on the changing tide, which can sweep you out to sea. The islet has a small sandy beach and is a bird preserve, so don't spook the red-footed boobies.

Little poly-vowelled beach towns like **Kahaluu, Kaaawa, Punaluu,** and **Hauula** pop up along the coast, offering passersby shell shops and art galleries to explore. Famed hula photographer **Kim Taylor Reece** lives on this coast; his gallery at 53–866 Kamehameha Hwy., near Sacred Falls (☎ **808/293-2000**), is open Sunday through Tuesday, from 10am to 6pm. There are also working cattle ranches, fisherman's wharves, and roadside fruit and flower stands selling ice-cold coconuts (to drink) and tree-ripened mangoes, papayas, and apple bananas.

Sugar, once the sole industry of this region, is gone. But **Kahuku,** the former sugar plantation town, has new life as a small aquaculture community with prawn and clam farms that supply island restaurants.

From here, continue along Kamehameha Highway (Hi. 83) to the North Shore.

ATTRACTIONS ALONG THE WINDWARD COAST

Hoomaluhia Botanical Gardens. 45–680 Luluku Rd., Kaneohe. ☎ **808/233-7323.** Free admission. Daily 9am–4pm. From Honolulu, take H-1 to the Pali Hwy. (Hi. 61); turn left on Kamehameha Hwy. (Hi. 83); at the fourth light, turn left onto Luluku Rd. TheBUS: 55 or 56 will stop on Kamehameha Hwy.; you'll have a 1½-mile walk to the Visitors Center.

This 400-acre botanical garden at the foot of the steepled Koolau Mountains is the perfect place for a *mauka* picnic. Its name means "a peaceful refuge." That's exactly what the Army Corps of Engineers created when they installed a flood-control project here, which resulted in a 32-acre freshwater lake and the garden. Just unfold a beach mat, lay back, and watch the clouds race across the rippled cliffs of the majestic Koolau Range. It's one of few public places on Oahu that provides a close-up view of the steepled cliffs. The park has hiking trails, and—best of all—the island's only free inland campground. (See "Oahu's Campgrounds & Wilderness Cabins," in chapter 5, "Accommodations.") Guided nature hikes start at 10am Saturday and 1pm Sunday from the Visitors Center.

Valley of the Temples. 47–200 Kahekili Hwy. (across the street from Temple Valley Shopping Center), Kaneohe. ☎ **808/239-8811.** Admission $2 adults; $1 children under 12 and seniors 65 and older. Daily 8:30am–4:30pm. From Honolulu, take the H-1 to the Likelike Hwy. (Hi. 63); after the Wilson Tunnel, get in the right lane and take the Kahekili Hwy. (Hi. 63); at the sixth traffic light is the entrance to the cemetery (on the left). TheBUS: 65.

The people of Honolulu bury their pets and their grandparents in this graveyard. Awhile back, Ferdinand Marcos, the exiled Filipino dictator, was also here; he occupied a temporary mausoleum until the Philippines relented and let him be buried in his native land. Marcos may be gone now, but dogs and cats and a lot of local folks remain. In a cleft of the pali, the graveyard is stalked by wild peacocks and about 700 curious people a day, who pay to see the 9-foot meditation Buddha, 2 acres of ponds full of more than 10,000 Japanese koi (carp), and a replica of Japan's 900-year-old Byodo-in Temple of Equality. The original, made of wood, stands in Uji, on the outskirts of Kyoto; the Hawaiian version, made of concrete, was erected in 1968 to commemorate the 100th anniversary arrival of the first Japanese immigrants to Hawaii. It's not the same as seeing the original, but it's worth a detour. A 3-ton brass temple bell brings good luck to those who can ring it—although the gongs do jar the Zen-like serenity of this Japan-like setting.

Senator Fong's Plantation & Gardens. 47–285 Pulama Rd., Kaaawa. ☎ **808/239-6775.** www.fonggarden.com. Admission $10 adults; $8 seniors; $6 children 5–12. Daily from 9am–4pm; 45-min. narrated tram tours daily from 10:30am; last tour 3pm. From Honolulu, take the H-1 to the Likelike Hwy. (Hi. 63); turn left at Kahekili Hwy. (Hi. 83); continue on to Kaaawa, and turn left on Pulama Rd. TheBUS: 55; it's a mile walk uphill from the bus stop.

Senator Hiram Fong, the first Chinese-American elected to the U.S. Senate, served 17 years before retiring to tropical gardening years ago. Now you can ride an open-air tram through five gardens named for the American presidents he served. His 725-acre botanical garden includes 75 plants and flowers. It's definitely worth an hour—if you haven't already seen enough botanics to last a lifetime.

Kualoa Ranch & Activity Club. 49–560 Kamehameha Hwy., Kaaawa. ☎ **800/237-7321** or 808/237-7321. Daily 9:30am–3:30pm. Various activity packages $35–$99 adults; $17.50–$65 children 3–11. Reservations required. Take H-1 to the Likelike Hwy. (Hwy. 63); turn left at Kahekili Hwy. (Hwy. 83); continue on to Kaaawa. Bus: 52.

This once-working ranch now has five different adventure packages covering two dozen activities on its 4,000 acres. Depending on the package you buy, you have a selection of activities, including horseback riding, mountain-bike riding, shooting a rifle or a .22-caliber handgun, hiking, dune cycling, jet skiing, canoeing, kayaking, windsurfing, snorkeling, freshwater fishing, and more. We highly recommend the beach activities, where you'll be shuttled to Molii fishpond's outermost bank, which is decked out like a country club: hammocks on the beach, volleyball courts, horseshoe pits, Ping-Pong tables, and beach pavilions. From there, you can take a 45-foot catamaran to Kaneohe Bay for snorkeling.

Ulupoa Heiau. Behind the YMCA on the Kaneohe side of 1200 Kailua Rd. (Hi. 61), at the end of Manuoo Rd. TheBUS: 56 or 57 will get you to the YMCA.

On a street lined with contemporary Christian churches, out of sight behind a YMCA gym and pool, is one of Oahu's most sacred ancient sites, where some believe the world began. Built of stacked rocks, the 30-by-40-foot temple is believed to have been an agricultural temple, since it's next to Kawainui Marsh, the largest body of freshwater in Hawaii. Its name roughly translates to "night inspiration," so go there during a full moon to get the full, eerie effect. Remember, Hawaii's *heiau* are sacred, so don't walk on the rocks or dare to move one.

✪ Polynesian Cultural Center. 55–370 Kamehameha Hwy., Laie. ☎ **800/367-7060,** 808/293-3333, or 808/923-2911. Fax 808/923-2917. www.polynesia.com. Admission only $27 adults; $16 children 5–11. Admission, buffet, and nightly show $47 adults; $30 children. Admission, IMAX, luau, and nightly show $59 adults; $37 children. Ambassador VIP (deluxe) tour $95 adults; $63 children. Mon–Sat 12:30–9:30pm. Take H-1 to Pali Hwy. (Hwy. 61) and turn left on Kamehameha Hwy. (Hwy. 83). Bus: 55. Polynesian Cultural Center coaches $15 round-trip; book at numbers above.

If you, like most people, have reached the end of your geographical leash in Hawaii, then you can satisfy your curiosity about the rest of the far Pacific all in a single day here. The Polynesian Cultural Center makes it easy (and relatively inexpensive, considering the time and distance involved to see the real thing) to experience the authentic songs, dance, costumes, and architecture of seven Pacific islands. The 42-acre lagoon park re-creates villages of Hawaii, Tonga, Fiji, Samoa, the Marquises, New Zealand, and Easter Island.

You "travel" through this kind of living museum of Polynesia by canoe on a man-made freshwater lagoon. Each village is "inhabited" by native students from Polynesia, who attend Hawaii's Bright Young University. Operated by the Mormon Church, the park also features a variety of stage shows, including "Manna! The Spirit of Our People," and "Pageant of the Long Canoes," which celebrate the music, dance, history, and culture of Polynesia. There's also a luau every evening. Since a visit can take up to 8 hours, it's a good idea to arrive before 2pm.

Just beyond the center is a replica of the **Mormon Tabernacle,** built of volcanic rock and concrete in the form of a Greek cross with reflecting pools, formal gardens, and royal palms. It was the first Mormon temple built outside Salt Lake City.

CENTRAL OAHU & THE NORTH SHORE

If you can afford the splurge, rent a bright, shiny convertible—the perfect car for Oahu since you can tan as you go—and head for the North Shore and Hawaii's surf city: **Haleiwa,** a quaint turn-of-the-century sugar plantation town designated as a historic site. A collection of faded clapboard stores with a picturesque harbor, Haleiwa has evolved into a surfer outpost and major roadside attraction with art galleries, restaurants, and shops that sell hand-decorated clothing, jewelry, and sports gear (see chapter 9, "Shopping").

Getting there is half the fun. You have a choice: Cruise up the H-2 through Oahu's broad and fertile central valley, past Pearl Harbor and Schofield Barracks of *From Here to Eternity* fame, and on through the red-earthed heart of the island where pineapple and sugarcane fields once stretched from the Koolau to the Waianae mountains. Or meander north along the lush Windward Coast, through country hamlets with roadside stands selling mangos, bright tropical pareus, fresh corn, and pond-raised prawns (see "The Windward Coast," above).

TAKING THE CENTRAL OAHU ROUTE

If you take the central route, the tough part is getting on and off the H-1 freeway from Waikiki, which is done by maneuvering along convoluted neighborhood streets. Try McCully Street off Ala Wai Boulevard, which is always crowded but usually the most direct route.

Once you're on H-1, stay to the right side; the freeway tends to divide abruptly. Keep following the signs for the H-1 (it separates off to Hi. 78 at the airport, and reunites later on; either way will get you there), then the H-1/H-2. Leave the H-1 where the two "interstates" divide; take the H-2 up the middle of the island, headed north toward the town of Wahiawa. That's what the freeway sign will say—not North Shore or Haleiwa, but Wahiawa.

The H-2 runs out and becomes a two-lane country road about 18 miles out of downtown Honolulu, near Schofield Barracks. The highway becomes Kamehameha Highway (Hi. 99 and later Hi. 83) at Wahiawa. Just past Wahiawa, about half an hour out of Honolulu, the **Dole Pineapple Plantation,** 64–1550 Kamehameha Hwy. (☎ **808/621-8408;** fax 808/621-1926; open daily 9am to 6pm), offers a rest stop with pineapples, pineapple history, pineapple trinkets, and pineapple juice (TheBUS no. 52 can also get you here). "Kam" Highway, as everyone calls it, will be your road for most of the rest of the trip to Haleiwa.

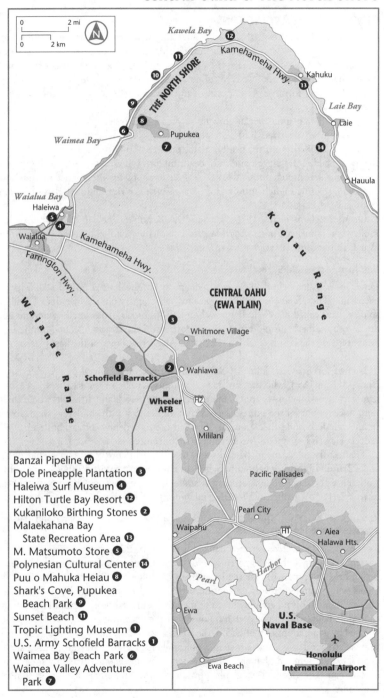

Kawela Bay

Kamehameha Hwy.

THE NORTH SHORE

Waimea Bay

Pupukea

Waialua Bay

Haleiwa

Waialua

Kamehameha Hwy.

Farrington Hwy.

W a i a n a e   R a n g e

K o o l a u   R a n g e

CENTRAL OAHU
(EWA PLAIN)

Whitmore Village

Schofield Barracks

Wahiawa

Wheeler
AFB

H2

Mililani

Kahuku

Laie Bay

Laie

Hauula

Pacific Palisades

Pearl City

Waipahu

Aiea
Halawa Hts.

H1

Pearl

Harbor

Ewa

U.S.
Naval Base

Ewa Beach

Honolulu
International Airport

Banzai Pipeline ⑩
Dole Pineapple Plantation ❸
Haleiwa Surf Museum ❹
Hilton Turtle Bay Resort ⑫
Kukaniloko Birthing Stones ❷
Malaekahana Bay
    State Recreation Area ⑬
M. Matsumoto Store ❺
Polynesian Cultural Center ⑭
Puu o Mahuka Heiau ❽
Shark's Cove, Pupukea
    Beach Park ❾
Sunset Beach ⑪
Tropic Lighting Museum ❶
U.S. Army Schofield Barracks ❶
Waimea Bay Beach Park ❻
Waimea Valley Adventure
    Park ❼

207

Central Oahu Attractions

On the central plains of Oahu, tract homes and malls with factory outlet stores are now spreading across abandoned sugarcane fields. Before the sugarcane, sandalwood grew at the foot of Mount Kaala, the mighty summit of Oahu. Hawaiian chiefs sent commoners into the thick forests to cut down the trees, which were then sold to China traders for small fortunes. The scantily clad natives caught cold in the cool uplands, and many died.

In the 1800s, planters began growing sugarcane and pineapple, and a man named James Campbell discovered artesian wells to irrigate the fields that changed Hawaii forever. In 1908, also on the central plain, the U.S. Army pitched a tent on the site that became Hawaii's biggest and most beautiful fort. On December 7, 1941, Japanese pilots came screaming through Kolekole Pass to shoot up the art deco barracks at Schofield, sending soldiers running for cover in their skivvies, and then flew on to sink ships at Pearl Harbor.

On those plains in the 1950s, an out-of-work pop singer named Sinatra made a Hollywood comeback portraying Maggio, a soldier at Schofield on the eve of World War II in the film classic *From Here to Eternity.*

U.S. Army Schofield Barracks.

James Jones called Schofield Barracks "the most beautiful army post the U.S. has or ever had." The *Honolulu Star Bulletin* called it a country club. More than 1 million soldiers have called Schofield Barracks home. With broad, palm-lined boulevards and art deco buildings, this old army calvary post is still the largest operated by the U.S. Army outside the continental United States. And it's still one of the best places to be a soldier.

Named for Lt. Gen. John M. Schofield, commanding general of the U.S. Army from 1888 to 1895, who first saw Hawaii's strategic value in the Pacific, the 17,597-acre post sprawls across central Oahu on an ancient Hawaiian battlefield where chieftains once fought for the supremacy of Oahu. In the 1930s, the buildings were erected in the art deco style then popular. The red-tile-roofed post office, built in 1939, reflects Hawaii's version of Mediterranean architecture.

The history of Schofield Barracks and the 215th Infantry Division is told in the small **Tropic Lightning Museum,** Schofield Barracks (☎ **808/655-0438;** free admission; open Tuesday through Saturday 10am to 4pm). Artifacts range from relics of the War of 1812 to a replica of Vietnam's infamous Cu Chi tunnels.

Kukaniloko Birthing Stones. Off Kamehameha Hwy. between Wahiawa and Haleiwa, opposite the road to Whitmore Village.

Two rows of 18 lava rocks once flanked a central birthing stone, where women of ancient Hawaii gave birth to potential *alii* (royalty). The rocks, according to Hawaiian belief, held the power to ease the labor pains of childbirth. Birth rituals involved 48 chiefs who pounded drums to announce the arrival of newborns likely to become chiefs. Children born here were taken to the now-destroyed Holonopahu Heiau in the pineapple field, where chiefs ceremoniously cut the umbilical cord.

Used by generations of Oahu's alii, the *pohaku* (or rocks), many in bowl-like shapes, now lie strewn in a coconut grove in a pineapple field at this, the most sacred site in central Oahu. Some think it also may have served as an ancient astronomy site, sort of a Hawaiian Stonehenge. Petroglyphs of human forms and circles appear on some of the stones.

Surf City: Haleiwa

Only 28 miles from Waikiki is Haleiwa, the funky ex–sugar plantation town that's the world capital of big-wave surfing. This beach town really comes alive in winter, when big waves rise up, light rain falls, and temperatures dip into the 70s. Then, it seems, every surfer in the world is here to see and be seen, surfing the big swells.

Officially designated a Historic Cultural and Scenic District, Haleiwa thrives in a time warp recalling the turn of the century, when it was founded by sugar baron Benjamin Dillingham. Dillingham built a 30-mile railroad to link his Honolulu and North Shore plantations, and opened a hotel named Haleiwa, or "house of the Iwa," after the tropical seabird often seen here.

The turn-of-the-century Victorian-style hotel and railroad are gone, but Haleiwa, which was rediscovered in the late 1960s by hippies, resonates with rare rustic charm. Tofu, not taro, is a staple in the local diet. Arts and crafts, boutiques, and burger stands line both sides of the town; there's a busy fishing harbor full of charter boats and captains who hunt the Kauai Channel daily for tuna, mahi-mahi, and marlin. And the bartenders at Jameson's mix the best mai tais (made according to the original recipe by Trader Vic Bergeron) on the North Shore.

Once in Haleiwa, the hot and thirsty traveler reports directly to the nearest shave-ice stand, usually **M. Matsumoto Store,** 66–087 Kamehameha Hwy. For 40 years, this small, humble shop operated by the Matsumoto family has served a popular rendition of the Hawaii-style snow cone flavored with tropical tastes. The cooling treat is also available at neighboring stores, some of which still shave the ice with a hand-crank device.

Just down the road are some of the fabled shrines of surfing—**Waimea Bay, Banzai Pipeline, Sunset Beach**—where the world's largest waves, reaching 20 feet and more, rise up between November and January. They draw professional surfers as well as reckless daredevils and hoards of onlookers, who jump in their cars and head north when word goes out that "surf's up." Don't forget your binoculars. (For more details on North Shore beaches, see "Beaches," in chapter 7.)

North Shore Surf and Cultural Museum. North Shore Marketplace, 66–250 Kamehameha Hwy. (behind Kentucky Fried Chicken), Haleiwa. ☎ **808/637-8888.** Free admission. Tues–Sun noon–5pm. TheBUS: 52.

Even if you've never set foot on a surfboard, you'll want to visit Oahu's only surf museum to trace the history of this Hawaiian sport of kings. The collection of memorabilia includes the evolution of surfboards from an enormous weathered, redwood board made in the 1930s for Turkey Love, one of Waikiki's legendary beach boys to the modern-day equivalent (a light, sleek, racy foam-and-fiberglass board made for big-wave surfer Mark Foo, who drowned while surfing in California in 1994). Other items include classic 1950s surf-meet posters, 1960s surf music album covers, old beach movie posters starring Frankie Avalon and Sandra Dee, the early black-and-white photos by legendary surf photographer LeRoy Grannis, and trophies won by surfing's greatest. Curator Steve Gould is working on a new exhibit of surfing in the ancient Hawaiian culture, complete with Hawaiian artifacts.

More North Shore Attractions

✪ **Waimea Valley & Adventure Park.** 59–864 Kamehameha Hwy. ☎ **808/638-8511.** Fax 808/638-7900. Admission $24 adults; $12 children 4–12; free 3 and under. Various packages available including transportation, camping, kayaking, horseback riding, etc. Daily 10am–5:30pm. Parking $3. Bus: 52. Shuttle service from some Waikiki hotels $5 round-trip.

If you have only a day to spend on Oahu and want to see an ancient hula, sniff tropical flowers, go kayaking along the shore or hiking to archaeological sites and a waterfall, and play the games of ancient Hawaii (spear-throwing, lawn bowling), there's only one place to be: Waimea Falls Park. This is the perfect family place—it takes a whole family to do everything. You can explore remnants of the old Hawaiian settlements in a scenic 1,800-acre river valley that's full of tropical blooms. Or watch authentic demonstrations of the ancient (*kahiko*) hula by the park's own *halau* (school), and see cliff divers swan-dive into a pool fed by a 45-foot waterfall. Everyone is invited to explore the valley. You can ride a mountain bike, paddle a kayak, or run the Elehaha River on an all-terrain vehicle into the jungle.

✪ **Puu O Mahuka Heiau.** One mile past Waimea Bay; take Pupukea Rd. mauka off Kamehameha Hwy. at Foodland, and drive .7 mile up a switchback road. TheBUS: 52; then walk up Pupukea Rd.

Go around sundown to feel the mana of this sacred Hawaiian place, the largest sacrificial temple on Oahu, associated with the great *kahuna* Kaopulupulu, who sought peace between Oahu and Kauai. The prescient kahuna predicted that the island would be overrun by strangers from a distant land. In 1794, three of Captain George Vancouver's men of the *Daedalus* were sacrificed here. In 1819, the year before New England missionaries landed in Hawaii, King Kamehameha II ordered all idols at the heiau to be destroyed.

A National Historical Landmark, this 18th-century heiau, known as the "hill of escape," sits on a 5-acre, 300-foot bluff overlooking Waimea Bay and 25 miles of Oahu's wave-lashed north coast—all the way to Kaena Point, where the Waianae Range ends in a spirit leap to the other world. The heiau is a huge rectangle of rocks twice as big as a football field (170 ft. by 575 ft.), with an altar often covered by the flower and fruit offerings left by native Hawaiians.

Shopping 9

by Jocelyn Fujii

In this land of the alluring outdoors, few people like to admit that shopping is a major temptation. With bodysurfing, hiking on volcanoes, and other invigorating, exotic adventures beckoning, spending time in a shopping mall seems so, well, bourgeois. Truth be known, the proliferation of topnotch made-in-Hawaii products, the vitality of the local crafts scene, and the unquenchable thirst for mementos of the islands lend a new respectability to shopping here. Oahu is also a haven for mall mavens—nearly a thousand stores occupy the 11 major shopping centers on this island. From T-shirts to Versace, posh European to down-home local, avant-garde to unspeakably tacky, Oahu's offerings are wide-ranging indeed.

Shopping on Oahu can be slightly schizophrenic. You must sometimes wade through oceans of schlock to arrive at the mother lode. Nestled amid the Louis Vuitton, Chanel, and Tiffany boutiques on Waikiki's Kalakaua Avenue are plenty of tacky booths hawking airbrushed T-shirts, gold by the inch, and tasteless aloha shirts.

The section that follows is not about finding cheap souvenirs or tony items from designer fashion chains; you can find them on your own. Rather, we offer a guide to finding those special treasures that lie somewhere in between.

1 Shopping A to Z

IN & AROUND HONOLULU & WAIKIKI
ALOHA WEAR

One of Hawaii's lasting afflictions is the penchant tourists have for wearing loud, matching aloha shirts and muumuus. We applaud such visitors' good intentions (to act local), but they are not Hawaiian. No local resident would be caught dead in such a get-up. Muumuus and aloha shirts are wonderful, but the real thing is what island folks wear on Aloha Friday (every Friday), to the Brothers Cazimero Lei Day Concert (every May 1), or to work (where allowed). It's what they wear at home and to special parties when the invitation reads "Aloha Attire."

Aside from the vintage Hawaiian wear (made from the 1930s through 1950s) that one finds only in collectibles shops and swap meets, our favorite contemporary aloha wear designer is **Tommy Bahama.** This is heresy, because the mainland-based Tommy Bahama is not a Hawaiian company, and also because it never calls its shirts "aloha shirts" and claims, instead, a Caribbean influence. Regardless,

Tommy Bahama, available throughout the mainland and Hawaii, stands out because of its high-quality, textured silks and inspired textile prints. They're the priciest, too, from $60 to $90, but no one can dispute their elegance of design and topnotch fabric quality. For the vintage look, **Avanti** has a corner on the market with its stunning line of silk shirts and dresses in authentic 1930s to 1950s fabric patterns. The shirts are the *ne plus ultra* of the genre, with all the qualities of a vintage silkie without the high price or the web-thin fragility of authentic antique shirts. For about $60, you can find a stylish shirt that's wearable long after you leave Hawaii. Women's dresses, tea timers from the 1940s, pant sets, and many other styles are the epitome of comfort and nostalgic good looks. The line is distributed in better boutiques and department stores throughout Hawaii (see below).

Someone has lit a fire under **Tori Richard,** a once stodgy line of aloha shirts that has repositioned and redefined itself as a hip, often-imitated, hardly duplicated manufacturer of aloha shirts. Tori Richard's dragon design on jacquard silk and vintage-inspired motifs have gained them new inroads in an old market. We also love the **Kamehameha Garment Company,** founded in 1936 as one of the two pioneer aloha shirt factories in Hawaii. And it is not just longevity that speaks in Kamehameha's favor; its shirts and fabric patterns are as vibrant and stylish as ever.

Also popular is **Kahala Sportswear,** a well-known local company also established in 1936. Kahala has faithfully reproduced the linoleum-block prints of noted Maui artist Avi Kiriaty and the designs of other contemporary artists, including artist-surfer John Severson. Kahala is sold in department stores (from Liberty House to Nordstrom), surf shops, and stylish boutiques throughout Hawaii and the mainland.

For the most culturally correct aloha wear, check out the aloha shirts, dresses, polo shirts, duffel bags, textiles, and T-shirts of **Sig Zane Designs,** available very spottily on Oahu and most prominently at his Hilo, Hawaii store. Zane, an accomplished hula dancer married to one of Hawaii's most revered hula masters, has an unmistakable visual style and a profound knowledge of Hawaiian culture that bring depth and meaning to his boldly styled renditions: the ti plant, ohia, kukui, koa, kaunaoa, and other prominent Hawaiian flora. Each Sig Zane aloha shirt, in pure cotton, tells a story. No wonder it's the garb of the cultural connoisseurs, who also buy fabrics by the yard for cushions, curtains, and interior accents that bring the rainforest into their homes.

Another name to watch for is **Tutuvi,** whose aloha shirts, T-shirts, dresses, and pareus are distinctive for their brilliant color combinations and witty juxtaposition of design motifs. Tutuvi designs can be found in various shops throughout Hawaii (Native Books & Beautiful Things; ☎ **808/596-8885**), or by appointment at Tutuvi, 2850 S. King St. (☎ **808/947-5950**). Designer Colleen Kimura is a master of surprise, wit, and technical precision whose T-shirts, aloha shirts, pareus, and dresses are immediately recognizable.

Reyn Spooner is another source of attractive aloha shirts and muumuus in traditional and contemporary styles, with stores in Ala Moana Center, Kahala Mall, and the Sheraton Waikiki. The reverse-print aloha shirt—the uniform of downtown boardrooms—was popularized by Reyn's, which has also jumped aboard the vintage-look bandwagon with its old-Hawaii cotton prints, some of them in attractive two-color pareu patterns.

Kamehameha, Diamond Head, Paradise, and Hinahina are other popular aloha shirt lines.

Well-known muumuu labels in Hawaii include **Mamo Howell,** who has a boutique in Ward Warehouse; **Princess Kaiulani** and **Bete** for the dressier muus, sold along with many other lines at Liberty House and other department stores. **Hilo Hattie's** new Ala Moana store (☎ **808/973-3266**) is a gold mine of affordable aloha wear. **Hilo Hattie** (☎ **808/537-2926**) offers free daily shuttle service from Waikiki to its retail outlet on Nimitz Highway and to Aloha Tower Marketplace, Ala Moana Center, and Waikiki. Quality and selection have improved noticeably at Hilo Hattie in recent years. You'll find macadamia nuts, Hawaiian coffees, jewelry, and other Hawaii souvenirs at these Hilo Hattie's stores, as well as live Hawaiian entertainment and free Kona coffee samples.

Our favorite retail stores for aloha shirts include:

✪ **Avanti Fashion.** 2229 Kuhio Ave. (☎ **808/924-1668**); 2250 Kalakaua Ave., Waikiki Shopping Plaza (☎ 808/922-2828); 307 Lewers St. (☎ 808/926-6886); and 2160 Kalakaua Ave. (☎ 808/924-3232).

This is the leading retro aloha shirt label, which turns out stunning silk shirts and dresses in authentic 1930s to 1950s fabric patterns. The shirts, though made of thin silk, are hip and nostalgic, without the web-thin fragility of authentic antique shirts. The line is distributed in better boutiques and department stores throughout Hawaii, but the best selections are at its Waikiki retail stores.

Bailey's Antiques and Aloha Shirts. 517 Kapahulu Ave. ☎ **808/734-7628.**

A large selection (hundreds!) of vintage, secondhand, nearly new, inexpensive, and expensive (rock-star prices) aloha shirts and other collectibles fill this eclectic emporium. It looks like the owners regularly scour Hollywood movie costume departments for old ball gowns, feather boas, fur stoles, leather jackets, 1930s dresses, and scads of other garments from periods past, including one of the largest vintage aloha shirt collections in Honolulu. Prices range from inexpensive to sky-high. Old Levi's jeans, mandarin jackets, vintage vases, household items, shawls, purses, and an eye-popping assortment of bark cloth fabrics (the real thing, not repros) are among the mementos in this monumental collection of high junque to great finds.

Hilo Hattie. 1450 Ala Moana Blvd., Ala Moana Center. ☎ **808/973-3266.** Also at 700 N. Nimitz Hwy., ☎ 808/544-3500.

Hilo Hattie, the largest manufacturer of Hawaiian fashions, attracts more than a million visitors to its ever-expanding empire throughout the state. That number is rising daily since the large new Ala Moana store opened. The new store is a jump up in image, quality and range of merchandise, and overall shopping options. You can find great gifts here, from coconut utensils to food products and aloha shirts in all price ranges and motifs. Hilo Hattie offers complimentary daily shuttle service to most of its stores, including service from Waikiki to its sprawling retail outlet on Nimitz Highway in Iwilei. There are some inexpensive silk aloha shirts as well as brand-name aloha shirts like Tommy Bahamas and the store's own Hilo Hattie label. Also offered here are macadamia nuts, Hawaiian coffees, jewelry, aloha wear, and other Hawaii souvenirs, as well as live Hawaiian entertainment and free Kona coffee samples.

JCPenney. 1450 Ala Moana Blvd., Ala Moana Center. ☎ **808/946-8068.** Other locations throughout Hawaii.

Although not known for its taste, this chain department store has a surprisingly respectable aloha shirt selection that includes all the name brands, and more. Racks and racks of aloha shirts fill the floor with vintage looks, Hawaiian heritage designs, and the usual surf-oriented motifs. Kahala is a big seller here.

Kamehameha Garment Co. In Ward Centre, 1200 Ala Moana Blvd. ☎ **808/597-1503.**

This Ward Centre newcomer carries dresses and aloha shirts by the time-honored Kamehameha label, one of the two original aloha shirt manufacturers established in

Oahu's Vibrant Art Scene

Passionate art lovers find solace and serenity in Hawaii's two top cultural resources: the Contemporary Museum and the Honolulu Academy of Arts. The vastly differing collections are housed in two of Hawaii's most memorable settings, both the legacy of one woman, Mrs. Charles Montague Cooke, who built the Alice Cooke Spalding house in 1925 (which now houses the Contemporary Museum) and, 2 years later, founded the Academy, a beacon in the arts to this day. One shudders to think what Hawaii's art world would have been like without this kamaaina legacy.

The **Honolulu Academy of Arts,** 900 S. Beretania St. (☎ **808/532-8701**), the only general fine arts museum in Hawaii, claims one of the top Asian art collections in the country, including James Michener's collection of Hiroshige's *ukiyoe* prints. Its acclaimed collection also includes American and European masters and prehistoric works of Mayan, Greek, and Hawaiian art. The award-winning architecture is a paragon of graciousness, featuring curved, tiled rooflines, six magnificent courtyards, lily ponds, and wide hallways leading to 30 sensitively organized galleries. Ongoing renovations are expected to continue through 2000. Open Tuesday through Saturday from 10am to 4:30pm, Sunday from 1 to 5pm. Admission is $5 per adult, with discounts for seniors and military personnel; members free.

Located up on the slopes of Tantalus, one of Honolulu's most prestigious residential communities, the **Contemporary Museum,** 2411 Makiki Heights Dr. (☎ **808/526-0232**), is renowned for several features: its 3½ acres of Oriental gardens with reflecting pools, sun-drenched terraces, views of Diamond Head, and stone benches for quiet contemplation; the Cades Pavilion, housing David Hockney's *L'Enfant et les Sortileges,* an environmental installation of his sets and costumes for Ravel's 1925 opera; its excellent cafe and gift shop; and six galleries representing significant work and artists of the past four decades. Equally prominent is the presence of contemporary Hawaii artists in the museum's programs and exhibitions. Open Tuesday through Saturday from 10am to 4pm, Sunday from noon to 4pm. A 1-day membership for adults is $5; seniors and students, $3; members and children free. The third Thursday of each month is free. Ask about the daily docent-led tours.

Galleries   Longevity matters in Hawaii's art world. Like restaurants, galleries come and go in Chinatown, where well-meaning efforts to revitalize the area have moved in fits and spurts, especially in recent years. Two exceptions are the **Ramsay Galleries** in the striking stone Tan Sing Building, 1128 Smith St. (☎ **808/537-2787**), celebrating 200 exhibitions in January 2000; and the **Pegge Hopper Gallery,** 1164 Nuuanu Ave. (☎ **808/524-1160**). Both are housed in historic Chinatown buildings that have been renovated and transformed into stunning showplaces for their and other artists' work.

Nationally known quill-and-ink artist Ramsay, who has drawn everything from the Plaza in New York to most of Honolulu's historic buildings, maintains a vital monthly show schedule featuring her own work. The finest names in contemporary crafts and art appear here, ranging in media from photography to sculpture to glass, clay, painting, prints, and, yes, computer art. When Ramsay's work is exhibited, each drawing is displayed with a magnifying glass to invite intimate viewing of the rich details. A consummate preservationist, Ramsay has added a courtyard garden with exotic varieties of bamboo and an oval pond.

One of Hawaii's most popular artists, Pegge Hopper's widely collected paintings of Hawaiian women with broad, strong features, shown in simple lines and colors in relaxed poses, are displayed in her attractive two-story gallery, which has become quite the gathering place for exhibits ranging from Tibetan sand-painting by saffron-robed monks to the most avant-garde printmaking in the Islands.

Fans (and there are many) of prominent contemporary artist Roy Venters are paying close attention to his downtown gallery and his edgy monthly "Dinners from Hell." (He loves to raise eyebrows.) The **Roy Venters Gallery,** 1160-B Nuuanu Ave. (☎ **808/273-3983**), next door to the Pegge Hopper Gallery, is a showcase and studio for Venters's powerful, unconventional works in two- and three-dimensional art: paintings, sculpture, furniture, interiors, and wearable art. Venters's pieces—avant-garde "shrines," three-dimensional crosses made of sea glass and colored stones, canvases and assemblages taking on taboo subjects—and his execution make him the Andy Warhol of Hawaii.

Next door is Seth Goldstein's **Sisu Gallery,** 1160-A Nuuanu Ave. (☎ **808/ 537-5880**), offering rotating monthly displays of local art, as well as a labyrinthine, two-story space devoted to retro contemporary design. Wander downstairs among the Herman Miller and other designer furniture, the Tamara de Lempicka charcoals, and the restored new '50s furniture and interior accents, and see if you don't agree that Sisu is a repository for works with a designer flair.

Newcomer ✪ **Bibelot** in Kaimuki, upstairs at 1130 Koko Head Avenue, Suite 2 (☎ **808/738-0368**), opened quietly but has a voice that carries. The gallery is wonderful! Small and smart, with an impressive selection of works from new and emerging artists, as well as those who are well established. More than 30 artists, almost all of them from Hawaii, are represented in the gallery, including Charles Higa, Margaret Ezekiel, Doug Britt, Ron Lee, and Kenny Kicklighter.

✪ **Four Calling Birds,** 619 Kapahulu Ave. (☎ **808/735-6133**), a Kapahulu newcomer, gets our vote as the most lovable gallery. Or is it a shop? It doesn't matter; it's wonderful, with great finds made by local artists, at friendly prices. From designer birdhouses to lamps, retro-aloha welcome mats, mochi demonstrations, and objects that are handmade, collectible, antique, or recycled, this unique atelier is a treasure trove of finds. Mailboxes, utensils, leather coats, jewelry, beads are all made or collected by local artists. Open only 2 days a week (Friday 10am to 7pm and Saturday 10am to 5pm), but it is well worth the wait.

At **Art à la Carte** in Ward Centre, 1200 Ala Moana Blvd. (☎ **808/597-8034**), a cooperative gallery of Hawaii artists, all media are represented. What's there: paper, clay, scratchboard, oils, acrylics, watercolors, collages, woodblocks, lithographs, glass, jewelry, and other works.

Hawaii's most unusual gallery is perched on the slopes of Punchbowl. It is the **Tennent Art Foundation Gallery,** 203 Prospect St. (☎ **808/531-1987**), devoted to the *oeuvre* of internationally esteemed artist Madge Tennent, whose work hangs in the National Museum of Women with the work of Georgia O'Keeffe. Tennent's much-imitated style depicts Polynesians through the 1920s to the 1940s. The gallery is open only for limited hours or by appointment, so call before you go. There is no admission charge, and there are Madge Tennent reproductions, prints, notecards, and some original watercolors and drawings for purchase.

—Jocelyn Fujii

1936. Aloha shirts and dresses, many of them with a vintage look, fill the cordial room with a sense of nostalgia. Wide variety, good styling, and striking fabric patterns make this a must for those in search of the perfect aloha shirt.

Liberty House. 1450 Ala Moana Blvd., Ala Moana Center. ☎ **808/941-2345.**

If it's aloha wear, Liberty House has it. The extensive aloha shirt and muumuu departments of Liberty House stores feature every label you can conjure, with a selection that changes with the times, and in all price ranges. The sprawling aloha shirt department in Ala Moana covers a sizable section of the first floor, with rack upon rack of shirts in all price levels.

Reyn's. 1450 Ala Moana Blvd., Ala Moana Center. ☎ **808/949-5929.** Also at 4211 Waialae Ave., Kahala Mall. ☎ 808/737-8313.

The reverse-print aloha shirt, the uniform of downtown boardrooms, was popularized by Reyn's, which has also jumped aboard the vintage-look bandwagon with its old-Hawaii cotton fabric prints, some of them in attractive two-color pareu patterns. Reyn's used to be a prosaic line, but has stepped up its selection of women's and men's aloha wear with contemporary fabric prints and stylings, appealing to a hipper clientele than the Reyn's of yesteryear.

ANTIQUES & COLLECTIBLES

For the best in collectible aloha wear, see "Fashion," under "Shopping the North Shore: Haleiwa," below.

Aloha Antiques and Collectibles. 930 Maunakea St. ☎ **808/536-6187.**

You might find rare Japanese plates or a priceless Lalique among the knickknacks that fill every square inch of this dizzying shop, but you'll have to look hard; there are so many items that they literally spill out onto the sidewalk. The prices are good, and the rewards substantial. Upstairs, downstairs, in adjoining rooms, around corners—the place defies inventory. Jewelry, vintage aloha shirts, vases, silver, ephemera, and countless eclectic items make up this mind-boggling collection of junk, treasures, and nostalgia. The three new shops and more than a dozen new vendors add exponentially to the possibilities here.

Aloha Flea Market. Aloha Stadium. ☎ **808/486-1529.** Admission 50¢. Wed, Sat, and Sun 6am–3pm.

Our advice is to go as early as possible, take a hat, and wear sunscreen. It gets very hot in this neck of the woods, and with more than 1,000 vendors sprawling across the stadium floor, it can be exhausting as well. You'll find the more interesting individuals and estates offering vintage treasures interspersed among produce stands and tacky stalls with cheap sunglasses and T-shirts. You never know when that extra-special 1940s tablecloth, Matson liner menu, vintage silkie aloha shirt, or Roseville vase will appear. These elusive treasures are becoming increasingly rare and are snatched up quickly by flea-market habitués, so serious collectors had best go early.

Anchor House Antiques. 471 Kapahulu Ave. ☎ **808/732-3884.**

This highly eclectic collection of Hawaiian, Oriental, and European pieces sprawls over thousands of square feet. You'll find wooden calabashes, camphor chests, paintings, Hawaiian artifacts, and trinkets, priced from $10 to $2,000.

Antique Alley. 1347 Kapiolani Blvd. ☎ **808/941-8551.**

This narrow shop is chock-a-block with the passionate collections of several vendors under one roof. With its expanded collection of old Hawaiian artifacts and surfing and hula nostalgia, it's a sure winner for eclectic tastes. The showcases include estate jewelry, antique silver, Hawaiian bottles, collectible toys, pottery, Depression glass, linens, plantation photos and ephemera, and a wide selection of nostalgic items from Hawaii and across America. Salt and pepper shakers, Pillsbury dough-boy statuettes, old phones, radios, ivory, china, and cameras spill out across the narrow shop. At the rear is a small, attractive selection of soiree clothing, made by Julie Lauster out of antique kimonos and obis.

Antique House. Royal Hawaiian Hotel, 2259 Kalakaua Ave. ☎ **808/923-5101.**

Small but tasteful, the low-profile Antique House is hidden below the lobby level of the illustrious Royal Hawaiian Hotel. Come here for small items: Oriental antiques, Chinese and Japanese porcelains, and a stunning selection of snuff bottles, bronzes, vases, and china.

✪ **Garakuta-Do.** 1833 Kalakaua Ave, Ste. 100. ☎ **808/955-2099.**

The huge warehouse/store in Iwilei has moved to this new, more convenient location on the Ala Wai Canal, across from the Hawaii Convention Center, with ample free parking and some thoughtful changes: expanded inventory, separate retail and warehouse spaces, and 3,000 square feet on the bottom floor for its sublime collection of Japanese antiques. It's worth finding Garakuta-Do for its late-Edo period (1800s through early 1900s) antiques, collected and sold by cheerful owner Wataru Harada. The selection of gorgeous tansus, Mingei folk art, Japanese screens, scrolls, Imari plates, bronze sculptures, kimonos, obis, modern woodblock prints, and stone objects makes shopping here a treasure hunt.

✪ **Kilohana Square.** 1016 Kapahulu Ave.

If there's any one destination we would recommend for antiques, it's this tiny square in Kapahulu. Kilohana's cluster of antiques shops covers a rich range of Oriental art, Japanese and European antiques, and high-quality collectibles. Many of the shops have loyal clients across the country who know they can find authentic goods, particularly Asian antiques, here. Our favorites include the following three shops.

Carriage House Antiques. Kilohana Square. ☎ **808/737-2622.**

The owner here is an expert in antique silver and European porcelain.

Miko Oriental Art Gallery. Kilohana Square. ☎ **808/735-4503.**

This store has a large repository of Chinese, Japanese, Korean, and Southeast Asian ceramics, bronzes, and furniture, ranging in price from $50 to $22,000.

T. Fujii Japanese Antiques. Kilohana Square. ☎ **808/732-7860.**

A long-standing icon in Hawaii's antiques world and an impeccable source for *ukiyoe* prints, scrolls, obis, Imari porcelain, tansus, tea-ceremony bowls, and screens, as well as contemporary ceramics from Mashiko and Kasama. Prices range from $25 to $18,000.

✪ **Robyn Buntin.** 848 S. Beretania St. ☎ **808/523-5913.**

The gracious and authoritative Robyn Buntin is an expert in netsuke and a highly esteemed resource in Oriental art. Located not far from the Honolulu Academy of Arts, the 2,500-square-foot space, as much a gallery as an antiques store, radiates a tasteful serenity. The offerings include jade; scholar's table items; Buddhist sculpture; Japanese prints; contemporary Chinese, Japanese, and Korean pictorial (graphic) art; and a large and magnificent collection of Hawaiiana. Some pieces are 5,000 years old, and many others are hot off the press from Tokyo, Seoul, and Beijing. The brilliant selection of netsuke and Japanese carvings is augmented by Hawaiian works by Isami Doi, Avi Kiriaty, Guy Buffet, Mark Kadota, and others. Few people know that John

Kelly's legacy includes Oriental works; they're here, along with rare etchings and prints that move swiftly to waiting collectors. Also known for his meticulous craftsmanship and taste in framing, Buntin has a framing operation downtown.

BOOKSTORES

In addition to the local stores below, Honolulu is home to branches of the famous names in bookselling. With more than 150,000 titles, a respectable music department, strong Hawaiiana, fiction, and new-release departments, as well as a popular coffee bar, **Barnes & Noble,** at Kahala Mall, 4211 Waialae Ave. (☎ **808/737-3323**) has become the second home of Honolulu's casual readers and bibliophiles. **Borders Books & Music,** at Ward Centre, 1200 Ala Moana Blvd. (☎ **808/591-8995**), is a beehive of literary activity, with weekly signings, prominent local and mainland musicians at least monthly, and special events almost daily that make it a major Honolulu attraction; there's a second Borders at Waikele Center, 94–821 Lumiaina St. (☎ **808/676-6699**). And **Waldenbooks** still ranks high as a boutique bookseller, with branches at Kahala Mall, 4211 Waialae Ave. (☎ **808/737-9550**); Waikiki Trade Center, 2255 Kuhio Ave. (☎ **808/924-8330**); Waikiki Shopping Plaza, 2270 Kalakaua Ave. (☎ **808/922-4154**); and other Oahu locations.

Book Cellar. 222 Merchant St. ☎ **808/523-3772.**

Located downtown for more than a decade, it's definitely a cellar, spilling over with used and rare books, plus a few new items. This is a good general used-book store, with about 35,000 titles—Hawaiiana, nonfiction, and books of the Pacific are among its stronger categories. Ask for CC (Carl Carroll, the man who knows the inventory).

Pacific Book House. 1249 S. Beretania St. ☎ **808/591-1599.**

Denis Perron, connoisseur of rare books, has moved his venerable Pacific Book House to a new location; kept and expanded the rare and out-of-print book inventory; and expanded into paintings, antiques, and estate jewelry, even offering appraisals of rare books and paintings and handling restorations others are afraid to touch. When you tire of book browsing, look into the expanded selection of antique silver and china. Literati still come here for finds in Hawaiiana, rare prints, collectible books, and other out-of-print treasures.

Rainbow Books and Records. 1010 University Ave. ☎ **808/955-7994.**

A little weird but totally lovable, especially among students and eccentrics (and insatiable readers), Rainbow Books is notable for its selection of popular fiction, records, and Hawaii-themed books, secondhand and reduced. Because it's located in the university area, it's always bulging with textbooks, Hawaiiana, and popular music. It's about the size of a large closet, but you'll be surprised at what you'll find.

CONSIGNMENT SHOPS

comme ci comme ca. 3464 Waialae Ave., Kaimuki. ☎ **808/734-8869.**

Great finds abound here, especially if your timing is good. Brand-new Prada bags, old Hermès jackets and dresses in pristine condition, an occasional Ferragamo purse, Armani suits, and vintage fur-collared sweaters straight out of 1940s Hollywood are some of the pleasures awaiting. Timing is paramount here: Finds—such as a made-in-Italy, brand-new, mostly cashmere Donna Karan for Men jacket—disappear to the early birds.

Consignment Closet. 2970 E. Manoa Rd., Manoa. ☎ **808/988-7442.**

Manoa's neighborhood consignment store is cheaper (much) and funkier than most, with a small yet honorable selection of shoes, dresses, and separates. Don't forget the hidden back room with its racks and racks of secondhand goodies—silk blouses, blazers, separates, sweaters. An entire wall is lined with dresses.

The Ultimate You. 1020 Auahi St., Kakaako. ☎ **808/591-8388.**

As far as prices go, no one can beat the budget-saving Goodwill and Salvation Army stores. But don't compare them with a consignment store like The Ultimate You, a resale boutique where the clothes are current and not always cheap, but always 50% to 90% off retail. When a red star appears on the tag, it means another big chunk off the bill. The joy is in the hunt here, as you peruse the selection of perfectly good clothes of recent vintage (freshly laundered or cleaned). This means designer suits and dresses, often new or barely worn, from such names as Escada, Chanel, Prada, Gianfranco Ferre, Donna Karan, Yves St. Laurent, Armani, Ralph Lauren, and Laura Ashley. You'll also find aisles of separates, cashmere sweaters, dresses, shoes, scarves, and purses. They also carry Ann Taylor, Gap, J. Crew, and Banana Republic clothing, as well as a handsome assortment of handbags and accessories. Shopaholics as far away as the West Coast send their new and barely used clothes here, so the inventory is always intriguing.

EDIBLES

The buzz in the chocolate world is **Sweet Cheeks Chocolate Sushi**—ingenious, and so exquisite you won't want to eat it. Sushi has gone three-dimensional trompe l'oeil, convincing to the last grain of "rice." From the pink curls of ginger to the fleshy red *maguro* (fish), custardy yellow *tamago* (egg), and thin bands of *nori* (seaweed), the "sushi" is handmade of chocolate, marzipan, coconut, and other confections, every bit as delicious as they look. Every orange pearl of *ikura* (salmon roe) is rolled by hand and nestled atop a bed of coconut "rice," enveloped in thin, *nori*-like chocolate, true to color and form. Packed in bento boxes just like the real thing, they won't spoil, and Sweet Cheeks ships everywhere. Sorry, phone orders only: ☎ **888/807-8744.**

In addition to the stores listed below, we also recommend **Executive Chef** in the Ward Warehouse and **Islands' Best** in the Ala Moana Center. Both shops contain wide-ranging selections that include Hawaii's specialty food items.

Asian Grocery. 1319 S. Beretania St. ☎ **808/593-8440.**

Asian Grocery supplies many of Honolulu's Thai, Vietnamese, Chinese, and Filipino eateries with authentic spices, rices, noodles, produce, sauces, herbs, and adventurous ingredients for their native cookery. Browse among the kaffir lime leaves, tamarind and fish pastes, red and green chiles, curry sauces, chutneys, lotus leaves, gingko nuts, jasmine and basmati rices, and shelf upon shelf of medium to hot chili sauces.

Daiei. 801 Kaheka St. ☎ **808/973-4800.**

Stands offering take-out sushi, Korean *kal bi*, pizza, Chinese food, flowers, Mrs. Fields cookies, and other items for self and home ring this huge emporium. Inside, you'll find household products, a pharmacy, and inexpensive clothing, but it's the prepared foods and produce that excel. The fresh-seafood section is one of Honolulu's best bets, not far from where regulars line up for the bento lunches and individually wrapped sushi. When Kau navel oranges, macadamia nuts, Kona coffee, Chinese taro, and other Hawaii products are on sale, savvy locals arrive in droves to take advantage of the high quality and good value.

Fujioka's Wine Merchants. 3184 Waialae Ave. ☎ **808/739-9463.**

It was a long drive for townies to get to Lyle Fujioka's North Shore store (in Haleiwa), where he sells an affordable, wide-ranging selection of wines, particularly California vintages. Now the Dead Liver Society and other wine connoisseurs have only to drive to Fujioka's new Kaimuki location—an honest-to-goodness cellar—to stock up on libations year round. Everyday wines (Cotes du Rhone, $9.95), special-occasion wines (Tignanello, $55), esoteric wines, and a spate of reds and whites from California and Europe are priced more reasonably here than most places, with friendly, knowledgeable service at the ready. New as it is, Fujioka's, with its strong affinity for California wines, is becoming quite the nexus for wine tastings and private parties.

✪ **Honolulu Chocolate Co.** Ward Centre, 1200 Ala Moana Blvd. ☎ **808/591-2997.** Also Restaurant Row, 500 Ala Moana Blvd. ☎ 808/528-4033.

Life's greatest pleasures are dispensed here with abandon: expensive gourmet chocolates made in Honolulu, chocolate-covered macadamia nuts, Italian and Hawaiian biscotti, boulder-size turtles (caramel and pecans covered with chocolate), truffles, chocolate-covered coffee beans, and jumbo apricots in white and dark chocolate. There are tinned biscuits, European candies, and sweets in a million disguises at this Honolulu people-pleaser. *Tip:* You pay dearly for them, but the dark-chocolate-dipped whole macadamia nut clusters are beyond compare.

✪ **It's Chili in Hawaii.** 2080 S. King St., Ste. 105. ☎ **808/945-7070.**

This is *the* oasis for chileheads, a house of heat with endorphins aplenty and good food to accompany the hot sauces from around the world, including a superb selection of made-in-Hawaii products. Scoville units (measurements of heat in food) are the topic of the day in this shop, lined with thousands of bottles of hot sauces, salsas, and other chile-based food products. Although many of the products are made in Hawaii, owners Ken Martinez and Gary Toyama travel regularly throughout the mainland to scout the finest hot sauces and chile products. Not everything is scorching, however; some products, like Dave's Soyabi and the limu-habañero sauce called Makai, are everyday flavor enhancers that can be used on rice, salads, meats, and pasta. (We also love the Tropical Drizzle.) They make great gifts to go. If you're eating in, the fresh frozen tamales, in several varieties including meatless, are now in regular supply. Every Saturday, Martinez and Toyama dish out free samples of green-chile stew as part of their generous hot-sauce tastings.

✪ **Mauna Kea Marketplace Food Court.** 1120 Maunakea St., Chinatown. ☎ **808/ 524-3409.**

Eager patrons line up in front of the no-nonsense food booths proffering everything from pizza to plate lunches and many other types of quick, authentic, inexpensive Vietnamese, Thai, Italian, Chinese, Japanese, and Filipino cuisine. The best seafood fried rice comes from the woks of **Malee Thai/Vietnamese Cuisine** at the mauka end of the marketplace—generous, perfectly flavored, endowed with morsels of fish, squid, and shrimp. Walk the few steps down to the produce stalls (pungent odors, fish heads, and chicken feet on counters—not for the squeamish) and join in the spirit of discovery. Fish counters and produce stalls sell everything from fresh ahi and whole snappers to yams and taro, seaweed, and fresh fruits and vegetables of every shape and size.

✪ **Paradise Produce Co.** 84 N. King St., Chinatown. ☎ **808/533-2125.**

Reasonably priced and very fresh produce, neat rows of mangoes, and top-quality papayas make this a paradise for food lovers. When asparagus is plentiful, it will be inexpensive and fresh. When mangoes are in season, you'll find Yee's Orchard Haydens set apart from the less desirable Mexican mangoes and, if you're lucky, a stash of ambrosial Piries that sell out quickly. Chinese taro, litchis in season, local eggplant, and dozens of fruits and vegetables are offered up fresh, neat, and colorful.

✪ **People's Open Markets.** Various sites around town. ☎ **808/527-5167;** call to find the open market nearest you.

Truck farmers from all over the island bring their produce to Oahu's neighborhoods in regularly scheduled, city-sponsored open markets, held Monday through Saturday at various locations. Among the tables of ong choy, choi sum, Okinawan spinach, opal basil, papayas, mangoes, seaweed, and fresh fish, you'll find homemade banana bread, Chinese *pomelo* (like large grapefruit), fresh fiddleheads (fern shoots) when available, and colorful, bountiful harvests from land and sea. The offerings change by the week and the season, but you'll always find a satisfying sampling of inexpensive, freshly gathered greens.

✪ **R. Field Wine Co.** Foodland Super Market, 1460 S. Beretania St. ☎ **808/596-9463.**

The big news among foodies is that Richard Field, oenophile, gourmet, and cigar aficionado, has moved his shop from Ward Centre to this new location in Foodland, where a special section has been built to accommodate his expanded inventory. A huge hit is the warm, just-baked breads (rosemary-olive oil; olive; whole wheat; potato; and other varieties) baked on the premises with dough flown in from the famous La Brea Bakery in Los Angeles. These breads are fabulous and usually sell out. Field's penchant for finding great wines and gourmet products from around the world continues unbridled. He offers hard-to-find vintages; the classic malts of Scotland; organic, vine-ripened tomatoes; salmon and vegetarian mousses; exotic chutneys and fruit preserves; plum pudding; designer vinegars; Langenstein estate Kona coffee; estate-grown, super-luxe Hawaiian Vintage Chocolate; Petrossian caviar; Waimanalo baby greens; gourmet cheeses; and more.

Shirokiya. Ala Moana Center, 1450 Ala Moana Blvd. ☎ **808/973-9111.**

Shirokiya's upstairs food department is well-known throughout Honolulu as *the* marketplace for Japanese treats and a place to discover the best new made-in-Hawaii products, from Sweet Cheeks chocolate sushi to fern-shoot noodles from the Big Island. Food samples hot off the grill or out of the oven are offered from the counters: Fish, mochi, pickled vegetables, and black beans fill the air with briny, smoky scents. A separate take-out food department sells sushi, udon and noodle soups, and many varieties of boxed bento lunches. Tables are available, or you can order the food to go. In the surrounding retail food department, exotic assortments, from deluxe dried shiitake mushrooms to Japanese teas and rice crackers, call out for your attention.

✪ **Strawberry Connection of Hawaii.** 1931 Kahai St., Kalihi. ☎ **808/842-0278.**

If you love food enough to search for it in the bowels of industrial Honolulu, this place is worth the hunt. And now, with the addition of Lyn Utsugi's new tea salon, **The Way of Tea,** shoppers have another reason to love Strawberry Connection. Epicures swear by this ever-growing showcase of Hawaii's gourmet food products. Chef Nick Sayada, formerly of Nick's Fishmarket, Black Orchid, and Cascada, has transformed the deli into a food-lover's fantasy. Order from the deli for take-out, or dine in the warehouse at minimalist, industrial-chic tables from a menu that includes warm duck salad, truffle potato salad, shrimp curry rice salad, crab cakes with green papaya salad, stuffed chicken breast, and a spate of salads, sandwiches, soups, and entrees. Grab a jacket and venture into the chill boxes for the best portabello or shiitake mushrooms, flawless asparagus spears, plump strawberries, Waimanalo gourmet greens, and stacks of designer produce from throughout the Hawaiian islands. They will also pack and ship produce to the mainland, and at Christmas, custom-made baskets fly out the door.

Taniguchi Store. 2065 S. Beretania St. ☎ **808/949-1489.**

Taniguchi Store's prepared foods—rice balls (*musubi*), salmon/rice bentos, fried saimin, chicken salad, tofu salad, Korean chicken, chicken cutlet, sautéed vegetables, and many other easy treats—are much loved in Honolulu. A small produce section proffers fresh shiso, exotic mushrooms, burdocks, and mountain yams, while the seafood counter is lined with several kinds of ahi and tako poke. A new plate-lunch department, **Stephie's Kitchen,** serves plate lunches at reasonable prices, and the home-baked cookies and sweets, though pricey, are as good as gold.

Bakeries

The **Saint-Germain bakeries** in Shirokiya at Ala Moana Shopping Center (☎ **808/955-1711**), near Times Supermarket (11296 S. Beretania St.; ☎ **808/593-8711**), and at Pearlridge Center (☎ **808/488-4967**) are good sources for French breads, baguettes, country loaves, and oddball delicacies, such as mini mushroom and spinach pizzas in Danish-type shapes and dough. How good are the breads? Many of the fine restaurants in Honolulu serve their French loaves at candlelit tables.

In Ward Warehouse, **Mary Catherine's Bakery** (1050 Ala Moana Blvd.; ☎ **808/591-8525**) is the darling of the gourmet bakeries, and still turns out sinful cakes, fruit tarts, and cookies. Try its new Moiliili location, **Bakery and Café,** too (2820 S. King St.; ☎ **808/946-4333**). In Kaimuki, the rave is **Cafe Laufer** (3565 Waialae Ave.; ☎ **808/735-7717;** see chapter 6, "Dining"), where the baked goods compete with the towering, made-to-order soufflés and inexpensive sandwiches. Nearby, old-timers still line up at **Bea's Pies & Deli** (1117 12th Ave.; ☎ **808/734-4024**), which often runs out of pies (custard-pumpkin is a must) by noon. Across the Pali in Kailua town, **Agnes Portuguese Bake Shop** (46 Hoolai St.; Kailua, ☎ **808/262-5367**) is the favorite of the *malassada* mavens. These sugary Portuguese dumplings, like doughnuts without holes, fly out of the bakery along with a full variety of specialty pastries (see "Kailua" under "Windward Oahu," below).

Fish Markets

Safeway (1121 S. Beretania St.) has a seafood counter with fresh choices and a staff that takes pride in its deftness with prepared foods. (If you're curious, don't be shy about asking for a taste.) The prepared foods (fresh ahi poke, seaweed salad, shrimp cocktail, marinated crab) are popular items among busy working folks heading home, or for potluck gatherings.

Tamashiro Market. 802 N. King St., Kalihi. ☎ **808/841-8047.**

You'll think you're in a Fellini movie amid the tanks of live lobsters and crabs and the dizzying array of counters glistening with fresh slabs of ahi, opakapaka whole and in fillets, onaga, and ehu. Point and ask if you don't know what you're looking at, and one of the fish cutters will explain, and then clean and fillet your selection. Good service and the most extensive selection in Honolulu make Tamashiro the grandfather of fish markets and the ace-in-the-hole for home chefs with bouillabaisse or paella in mind. Also popular is the separate counter of seaweed salads, prepared poke, lau lau, lomi salmon, Filipino and Puerto Rican ti-wrapped steamed rice, Japanese pickles, fresh produce, and dozens of other ethnic food items.

Yama's Fish Market. 2203 Young St., Moiliili. ☎ **808/941-9994.**

Neighbor islanders have been known to drive directly from the airport to Yama's for a plate lunch, one of the best in Honolulu. Robust Hawaiian plates with pork or chicken lau lau (20 combinations!), baked ahi, chili, beef stew, shoyu chicken, and dozens of other varieties stream out to those who line up at the counter and to offices who order by the dozen. But Yama's is also known for its inexpensive fresh fish (fresh mahi-mahi is always less expensive here than in the supermarkets), tasty poke (ahi, aku, Hawaiian-style, Oriental-style, with seaweed), lomi salmon, and many varieties of prepared seafood. Chilled beer, boiled peanuts, and fresh ahi they can slice into sashimi are popular for local-style gatherings, sunset beach parties, and festive *pau hana* (end of work) celebrations.

Health Food

Down to Earth. 2525 S. King St., Moiliili. ☎ **808/947-7678.**

Located in the university district, Down to Earth sells organic vegetables and bulk foods, with a strong selection of supplements, herbs, and cosmetic products. Everything here is vegetarian, down to the last vitamin pill or drop of tincture. Cereals, bulk grains and nuts, breads, many varieties of honey, nonalcoholic beer, teas, snacks, environment-friendly paper and household products, and a vegetarian juice and sandwich bar are among the reasons shoppers of all ages come here.

Hou Ola. 1541 S. Beretania St. ☎ **808/955-6168.**

Tiny but powerful, with a loyal clientele that has stuck by it through management and name changes and a hefty dose of parking problems, Hou Ola has competitive prices and a wide and user-friendly selection of health-food supplements. The supplements are good enough reason to shop here. No produce, but there are frozen vegetarian foods, cosmetics, bulk grains, and healthy snacks.

Huckleberry Farms. 1613 Nuuanu Ave., Nuuanu. ☎ **808/524-7960.**

Located in Nuuanu across town from the university area, Huckleberry Farms has a wide selection of produce, vitamins, cosmetics, and books, with a serviceable selection of prepared vegetarian foods. A few doors down from the Huckleberry Farms grocery store is the new beauty and vitamin retail outlet, a large and dizzyingly stocked room dedicated to beauty creams, cosmetics, nutritional supplements, and nonperishable, nongrocery health products.

Kokua Market. 2643 S. King St., Moiliili. ☎ **808/941-1922.**

Kokua is Honolulu's best source of healthy grinds in all categories but vitamin supplements. They are trying, however: The vitamin selection is expanding noticeably. Voluminous, leafy organic vegetables; an excellent variety of cheeses; pastas and bulk grains; sandwiches, salads, and prepared foods; poi as fresh as can be; and a solid selection of organic wines give Kokua a special place in the hearts of health-minded shoppers. Ample parking is offered behind and makai (toward the beach) of the store.

FLOWERS & LEIS

For a special-occasion, top-of-the-line, designer bouquet or lei, you can't do better than Michael Miyashiro of **Rain Forest Plantes et Fleurs** (phone orders only for now; ☎ 808/942-1550). He is a nature-loving, ecologically aware, and highly gifted lei maker—pricey, but worth it. His nontraditional leis include one-of-a-kind garlands made from ma'o flowers (Hawaiian cotton) entwined with pikake, pakalana with a new twist, a New Guinea blossom brand-new to the islands, or strands of regal native ilima he has specially grown for his creations. He custom-designs the lei for the person and the occasion, and the personalized attention is evident.

The other primary sources for flowers and leis are the shops lining the streets of Moiliili and Chinatown. Moiliili favorites include **Rudy's Flowers** (2722 S. King St.; ☎ 808/944-8844), a local institution with the best prices on roses, Micronesian ginger leis (they can go as low as $8.50 here, while others sell them for $15), and a variety of cut blooms. Across the street, **Flowers for a Friend** (2739 S. King St.; ☎ 808/955-4227) sells leis and cut flowers. In Chinatown, lei vendors line Beretania and Maunakea streets, and the fragrances of their wares mix with the earthy scents of incense and ethnic foods. Our top picks in Chinatown are **Lita's Leis** (59 N. Beretania St.; ☎ **808/521-9065**), which has fresh puakenikeni, gardenias that last, and a supply of fresh and reasonable leis; **Sweetheart's Leis** (69 N. Beretania St.; ☎ **808/537-3011**), with a worthy selection of the classics at fair prices; **Lin's Lei Shop** (1017 A Maunakea St.; ☎ **808/537-4112**), with creatively fashioned, unusual leis (*Kauai mokihana* in season, *Hilo maile,* stefanotis, baby roses); and **Cindy's Lei Shoppe** (1034 Maunakea St.; ☎ **808/536-6538**), a household word with terrific sources for unusual leis such as feather dendrobium, firecracker combinations, and everyday favorites such as ginger, tuberose, orchid, and pikake, which can be purchased in quantity. At this and other lei shops, simple leis sell for $3 and up, deluxe leis, $10 and up. Ask Cindy's about its unique "curb service," available with advance phone orders. Give them your car color and model, and you can pick up your lei at curbside. What a convenience—especially on this street.

HAWAIIANA/GIFT ITEMS

Our top recommendations in this category are the ✪ **Academy Shop** at the Honolulu Academy of Arts (900 S. Beretania St.; ☎ **808/523-8703**) and the ✪ **Contemporary Museum Gift Shop** (2411 Makiki Heights Rd.; ☎ **808/523-3447**), two of the finest shopping stops on Oahu and worth a special trip whether or not you're in a museum mood. As the retail operations of Hawaii's two finest art museums, each is stocked with the best in books, cards, and ethnic and contemporary gift items. The Academy Shop offers art books, jewelry, basketry, beadwork, ikats, saris, and ethnic fabrics from all over the world; posters and books; native crafts; and fiber vessels and accessories. The Contemporary Museum shop focuses on contemporary arts and crafts, such as avant-garde jewelry, cards and stationery, books, home accessories, and gift items made by artists from Hawaii and across the country.

Other good sources for quality gift items are the **Little Hawaiian Craft Shop** (in the Royal Hawaiian Shopping Center) and **Martin and MacArthur** (in the Aloha Tower Marketplace).

✪ **Following Sea.** 4211 Waialae Ave. ☎ **808/734-4425.**

The buyers scour the country for the best representations of fine American craftsmanship in everything from candles and bath products to fine arts and crafts. Incense and candles scent the air to the soothing bubbling of indoor water fountains. Hawaii is well represented in the collection, with handsome hand-turned bowls and accessories made of native and introduced woods, jewelry, ceramics, handmade paper, and hand-bound books. Local artists have crafted a noteworthy selection of koa boxes, and Hawaii-inspired jewelry in gold and silver. For candle lovers, the Terrain candles, scented with ginger and tea, are intoxicating.

Hula Supply Center. 2346 S. King St., Moiliili. ☎ **808/941-5379.**

Hawaiiana meets kitsch in this shop's marvelous selection of Day-Glo cellophane skirts, bamboo nose flutes, T-shirts, hula drums, shell leis, feathered rattle gourds, lauhala accessories, fiber mats, and a wide assortment of pareu fabrics. Although hula dancers shop here for their dance accoutrements, it's not all serious shopping. This is fertile ground for souvenirs and memorabilia of Hawaii, rooted somewhere between irreverent humor and cultural integrity.

✪ **Island Provision Co. at Vagabond House.** Ward Centre, 1200 Ala Moana Blvd. ☎ **808/593-0288.**

Home accessories, gift items, one-of-a-kind island crafts, and multicultural treasures are collected from the owners' travels and displayed in this attractive 1,700-square-foot space. Gleaming woods, fine porcelain and pottery, children's books, bath products, and Asian and Indonesian imports highlight this shop of wonders. Leave time to browse, because shopping here is more like a journey through an island-style kamaaina home, with unique photo gifts for all occasions.

✪ **Native Books & Beautiful Things.** Ward Warehouse, 1050 Ala Moana Blvd., ☎ **808/ 596-8885;** 222 Merchant St., downtown, ☎ 808/599-5511. Also at the Bishop Museum, 1525 Bernice St., ☎ 808/847-8288.

Come to any of the three locations of this *hui* (association) of artists and crafters and you'll be enveloped in a love of things Hawaiian, from musical instruments to calabashes, jewelry, leis, books, and items of woven fibers—beautiful things, indeed. You'll find contemporary Hawaiian clothing, handmade koa journals, Hawaii-themed home accessories, lauhala handbags and accessories, jams and jellies, photography, etched glass, hand-painted fabrics and clothing, stone poi pounders, and other wide-ranging, high-quality gift items. Some of Hawaii's finest artisans in all craft media have their works available here on a regular basis, and the Hawaiian-book selection is tops. The new 5,000-square-foot emporium at Ward Warehouse is a browser's paradise.

✪ **Nohea Gallery.** Ward Warehouse, 1050 Ala Moana Blvd. ☎ **808/596-0074.** Also at Kahala Mandarin Oriental Hawaii, 5000 Kahala Ave. ☎ 808/737-8688.

A fine showcase for contemporary Hawaii art and crafts, Nohea celebrates the islands with thoughtful, attractive selections in all media, from pit-fired raku and finely turned wood vessels to jewelry, handblown glass paintings, prints, fabrics (including Hawaiian-quilt cushions), and furniture. Ninety percent of the works are by Hawaii artists. Gleaming koa accessories, from hair sticks to jewelry boxes, are among the items that grace the pleasing showrooms.

Nui Mono. 2745 S. King St., Moiliili. ☎ **808/946-7407.**

We love the kimono clothing and accessories and the contemporary clothes made from ethnic fabrics, sold in this tiny shop in Moiliili. Handbags made of patchwork vintage fabrics and priceless kimono silks, drapey Asian shapes and ikat fabrics, richly textured vests and skirts, and warm, rich colors are the Nui Mono signature—and it's all moderately priced.

Quilts Hawaii. 2338 S. King St., Moiliili. ☎ **808/942-3195.**

Handmade Hawaiian quilts in traditional Hawaiian and contemporary patterns drape this shop from top to bottom. Hawaiian-quilt cushions (much more affordable than full-size quilts, which run, understandably, in the thousands of dollars) and quilt-sewing kits can also be found here, as well as a huge selection of quilt patterns. You can custom-order larger works.

Shop Pacifica. Bishop Museum, 1525 Bernice St. ☎ **808/848-4158.**

Local crafts, lauhala and Cook Island woven coconut, Hawaiian music tapes and CDs, pareus, and a vast selection of Hawaii-themed books anchor the museum's gift shop. Hawaiian quilt cushion kits, jewelry, glassware, seed and Niihau shell leis, cookbooks, and many other gift possibilities will keep you occupied between stargazing in the planetarium and pondering the shells and antiquities of the esteemed historical museum.

SHOPPING CENTERS

Ala Moana Center. 1450 Ala Moana Blvd. ☎ **808/946-2811.** Mon–Sat 9:30am–9pm; Sun 10am–5pm. Bus: 8, 19, or 20. The Ala Moana Shuttle Bus runs daily every 15 minutes from 8 spots in Waikiki; the Waikiki Trolley also stops at Ala Moana from various Waikiki locales (see "Getting Around," in chapter 4, "Getting to Know Oahu.").

The buzz, of course, is the three-story, super-luxe Neiman Marcus, which opened in September 1998—a bold move in Hawaii's troubled economy. Although plans call for 30 new shops and restaurants, a large entertainment and hospital complex, and a small hotel, the shopping center is for sale, so who knows? And of course, construction seems never-ending, with new stores and parking spots in the works. But there are practical touches, too, such as banks and airline ticket counters (in **Sears**), a foreign-exchange service (**Thomas Cook,** street level), a dry cleaners (**Al Phillips,** street level), a **U.S. Post Office** (street level), several optical companies (including 1-hour service by **LensCrafters**), the **Foodland Supermarket,** a pharmacy, and several services for quick photo processing.

Ala Moana's more than 200 shops and restaurants sprawl over several blocks, catering to every imaginable need, from over-the-top upscale (**Tiffany, Chanel, Versace**), to mainland chains such as **The Gap, The Body Shop,** and JCPenney. A perennial favorite, **Banana Republic** continues to weave its spell with huge reductions in its wonderfully minimalist clothing and accessories. Department stores such as **Liberty House** and the endlessly entertaining **Shirokiya** sell fashion and household items. And of course, for the bountiful pocketbooks, **Neiman Marcus** holds forth as queen of the fashionistas. One of the best stops for gifts is **Islands' Best,** a small, wonderful store that spills over with Hawaiian-made foodstuffs, ceramics, fragrances, and more. **Splash! Hawaii** is a good source for women's swimwear; for aloha shirts and men's swimwear, try **Liberty House, Town & Country Surf,** or the terminally hip **Hawaiian Island Creations.** Lovers of Polynesian wear and pareus shouldn't miss **Tahiti Imports.** Shoes? They're a kick at **Nordstrom** for men and women. The newly enlarged **food court,** first floor, makai section, is abuzz with dozens of stalls purveying Cajun food, ramen, pizza, Hawaiian plate lunches, vegetarian fare, green tea and fruit freezes (like frozen yogurt), panini (grilled sandwiches), and countless other treats.

Aloha Tower Marketplace. 1 Aloha Tower Dr., on the waterfront between piers 8 and 11, Honolulu Harbor. ☎ **808/528-5700.** Sun–Thurs 9am–9pm; Fri and Sat 9am–10pm. Various Honolulu trolleys stop at the Marketplace, but if you want a direct ride from Waikiki, take the $2 Aloha Tower Marketplace Express, which continues on to Hilo Hattie's in Iwilei.

Despite valet parking and trolley stops, parking is a discouraging aspect of shopping at Aloha Tower. Once you get to the new harborfront complex, however, a sense of nostalgia, of what it must have been like in the "Boat Days" of the 1920s to 1940s, inevitably takes over. Sleek ocean liners (as well as malodorous fishing boats) still tie up across the harbor, and the refurbished Aloha Tower stands high over the complex, as it did in the days when it was the tallest structure in Honolulu. Dining and shopping prospects include **Martin & MacArthur** gift shop, **Beyond the Beach** sportswear, and **Gordon Biersch Brewery** (see chapter 6, "Dining").

Kahala Mall. 4211 Waialae Ave., Kahala. ☎ **808/732-7736.** Mon–Sat 10am–9pm; Sun 10am–5pm. Bus: 1 and 58.

Chic, manageable, and unfrenzied, Kahala Mall is home to some of Honolulu's best shops. Located east of Waikiki in the posh neighborhood of Kahala, the mall has everything from a small **Liberty House** to chain stores such as **Banana Republic** and **The Gap,** and some 85 specialty shops (including 27 eateries and 8 movie theaters) in an enclosed, air-conditioned area. **Starbucks Coffee** is a java magnet, a stone's throw from **The Gourmet Express** and its fast, healthy salads, tortilla wraps, and fresh juices and smoothies. Our pick for the mall's best and brightest is **The Following Sea.** Other favorites include **Riches,** a tiny kiosk with a big, bold selection of jewelry; **The Compleat Kitchen,** for culinary needs; and **Eyewear Hawaii,** for sunglasses. Look also for the **Liberty House Men's Store** at the mauka corner of the mall, under a separate roof from the main store.

Royal Hawaiian Shopping Center. 2201 Kalakaua Ave. ☎ **808/922-0588.** Daily 9:30am–10pm. Bus: 2, 4, 8, 19, 20, or 47.

If you let it, this 3-block shopping complex in the heart of Waikiki could absorb your entire Hawaii budget. *Upscale* is the operative word here. Although there are drug-stores, lei stands, restaurants, and food kiosks, the most conspicuous stores are the European designer boutiques (**Chanel, Cartier, Hermès, Van Cleef & Arpels,** and more) that cater largely to visitors from Japan. One of our favorite stops is the **Little Hawaiian Craft Shop** (☎ 808/926-2662), which features a distinctive collection of Niihau shell leis, museum replicas of Hawaiian artifacts, and works by Hawaii artists as well as South Pacific crafts. **Beretania Florist,** located in the hut under the large banyan tree, will ship cut tropical flowers anywhere in the United States. A favorite fashion stop is **McInerny Galleria,** a cluster of boutiques under one roof, with such big names as **DKNY, Ralph Lauren, Coach,** and **Armani.**

Waikele Premium Outlets. 94–790 Lumiaina St., Waikele (about 20 miles from Waikiki). ☎ **808/676-5858.** Mon–Fri 9am–9pm; Sun 10am–6pm. Take H-1 west toward Waianae and turn off at exit 7. Bus: 2 from Waikiki, then transfer at King and Beretania sts. to no. 48, which drops you off directly in front of the center. Companies offering shopping tours with Waikiki pickups include Apple Tour (☎ 808/395-8557), E Noa Tours (☎ 808-591-2561), Da Shopping Shuttle (☎ 808/924-8882), and Polynesian Adventure Tours (☎ 808/833-3000).

Just say the word "Waikele" and my eyes glaze over. So many shops, so little time! And so much money to be saved while spending for what you don't need. There are two sections to this sprawling discount shopping mecca: the **Waikele Premium Outlets,** some 51 retailers offering designer and name-brand merchandise; and the **Waikele Value Center** across the street, with another 25 stores more practical than fashion-oriented, such as Eagle Hardware, Sports Authority, and Borders Books & Music. The 64-acre complex has made discount shopping a major activity and a travel pursuit in itself, with shopping tours for visitor groups and carloads of neighbor islanders and Oahu residents making virtual pilgrimages from all corners of the state. They come to hunt down bargains on everything from perfumes, luggage, and hardware to sporting goods, fashions, china, and footwear. Examples are Geoffrey Beene, Donna Karan, Saks Fifth Ave., Anne Klein, Max Studio, Levi's, Converse, Kenneth Cole, and dozens of other name brands at a fraction of retail. Newcomers Joan and David and the ultra-chic Barneys have added new cachet to this shopping haven.

Ward Centre. 1200 Ala Moana Blvd. ☎ **808/591-8411.** Mon–Sat 10am–9pm; Sun 10am–5pm. Bus: 19, 20, 47, 55, 56, or 57.

Although it has a high turnover and a changeable profile, Ward Centre is a standout for its concentration of restaurants and shops, including coffee bar and health-food haven **Mocha Java** (see chapter 6, "Dining"), **Ryan's Grill** (the happy-hour hangout), **Compadres,** and dining institution **A Pacific Cafe Oahu** (see chapter 6, "Dining"). The new industrial-chic **Brew Moon** microbrewery (see chapter 6, "Dining") has created some buzz next door to Ryan's; diners on the lanai can gaze out to the mountains and the sprawling **Pier 1 Imports,** the newcomer lifestyle store across the street. All these establishments are part of developer Victoria Ward's Kakaako development projects, which take up several blocks in this area: Ward Centre, Ward Farmers Market, Ward Village Shops, and Ward Warehouse. Ward Centre's gift shops and galleries include **Kamehameha Garment Company** (aloha shirts), **Tropical Clay** for island-themed ceramics, **Island Provision Co. at Vagabond House** (see "Hawaiiana/Gift Items," above) for unique home accessories; **Paper Roses** for wonderful paper products; **Honolulu Chocolate Company** (see "Edibles," above), and the very attractive **Art à la Carte.** Newcomer **Handblock** proffers wonderful table linens, clothing, and household accents; and **Borders Books & Music** bustles with browsers and music lovers.

Ward Warehouse. 1050 Ala Moana Blvd. ☎ **808/591-8411.** Mon–Sat 10am–9pm; Sun 10am–5pm. Bus: 19, 20, 47, 55, 56, or 57.

Older than its sister property, Ward Centre, and endowed with an endearing patina, Ward Warehouse remains a popular stop for dining and shopping. Recommended stops in the low-rise brown wooden structure include the ever-colorful **C. June Shoes,** with flamboyant designer women's shoes and handbags (tony, expensive, but oh-so-entertaining!); **Executive Chef,** for gourmet Hawaii food items and household accessories; **Out of Africa,** for pottery, beads, and interior accents; **East of Sun, West of Moon,** for its sensuous array of fragrances, linens, music, bath products, bedspreads, candles, and accessories for body, home, and spirit; **Kamuela Hat Company; Mamo Howell,** for distinctive aloha wear; and **Private World,** for delicate sachets, linens, and fragrances. Brilliant newcomers include **Paradise Walking Co.,** with Arche, Mephisto, and all manner of cloud-comfort footwear; and **Interior Flavors,** brimming with tasteful gifts and home accessories. For T-shirts and swimwear, check out the **Town & Country Surf Shop,** and for an excellent selection of sunglasses, knapsacks, and footwear to take you from the beach to the ridgetops, don't miss **Thongs 'N Things.** Favorite stops are **Native Books & Beautiful Things** and the **Nohea Gallery** (see "Hawaiiana/Gift Items," above), fine sources for quality Hawaii-made arts and crafts.

SURF & SPORTS

The surf-and-sports shops scattered throughout Honolulu are a highly competitive lot, with each trying to capture your interest (and dollars).

The Bike Shop. 1149 S. King St., near Piikoi St. ☎ **808/596-0588.**

Excellent for cycling and backpacking equipment for all levels, with major camping lines such as North Face, MSR, and Kelty.

Hawaiian Island Creations. Ala Moana Center. ☎ **808/941-4491.**

HIC is a super-cool surf shop offering sunglasses, sun lotions, surfwear, and accessories galore.

Local Motion. 1958 Kalakaua Ave. ☎ **808/979-7873.** Other locations, including Waikele.

Local Motion is the icon of surfers and skateboarders, both professionals and wannabes. The shop offers surfboards, T-shirts, aloha and casual wear, boogie boards, and countless accessories for life in the sun.

McCully Bicycle & Sporting Goods. 2124 S. King St. ☎ **808/955-6329.**

Find everything from bicycles and fishing gear to athletic shoes and accessories and a stunning selection of sunglasses.

The Sports Authority. 333 Ward Ave. ☎ **808/596-0166.** Also at Waikele Center, ☎ 808/677-9933.

A discount megaoutlet offering clothing, cycles, and equipment.

WINDWARD OAHU
KAILUA

Longs Drugs and **Liberty House** department store, located side-by-side on Kailua Road in the heart of this windward Oahu community, form the shopping nexus of the neighborhood.

Agnes Portuguese Bake Shop. 46 Hoolai St. ☎ **808/262-5367.**

This is the favorite, for more than 30 years, of Hawaii's malassada mavens. It is now in a new site a block from its previous location, with an abundance of free parking and an expanded menu of homemade soups, artisan breads, and unique pastries. The malassadas, sugary Portuguese dumplings—like doughnuts without holes—fly out of the bakery, along with a full variety of pastries, cookies, scones, Portuguese bean and other soups, and local- and European-style breads. The neighborhood is regularly infused with irresistible aromas from the bake shop, a Kailua staple.

✪ **Alii Antiques of Kailua II.** 9-A Maluniu Ave., Kailua. ☎ **808/261-1705.**

Abandon all restraint, particularly if you have a weakness for vintage Hawaiiana. Koa lamps and rattan furniture from the '30s and '40s, hula nodders, rare 1940s koa tables, Roseville vases, Don Blanding dinnerware, and a breathtaking array of vintage etched-glass vases and trays are some of the items in this unforgettable shop. Across the street, the owner's wife runs **Alii Antiques of Kailua,** chock-a-block with all those things that won't fit here: jewelry, clothing, Bauer and Fiesta ware, linens, Bakelite bracelets, and floor-to-ceiling collectibles.

BookEnds. 590 Kailua Road, Kailua. ☎ **808/261-1996.**

Bookstore veteran Pat Banning, buyer for the erstwhile Honolulu Book Shops for nearly 20 years, took over the location and much of the inventory when Honolulu Book Shops closed its Kailua store. BookEnds is the quintessential neighborhood bookstore, run by a pro who buys good books and knows how to find the ones she doesn't have. There are more than 60,000 titles in this cordial store.

Heritage Antiques & Gifts. 767 Kailua Rd. ☎ **808/261-8700.**

This Kailua landmark is known for its large selection of Tiffany-style lamps ($200 to $2,000), many of which are hand-carted back to the mainland. The mind-boggling selection includes European, Asian, American, local, and Pacific Island collectibles. It's engaging, the people are friendly, and the selection is diverse enough to appeal to the casual as well as the serious collector. Glassware, china, and estate, costume, and fine jewelry are among the items of note. Heritage has its own jeweler who custom-designs, repairs, and resurrects jewelry, and a stable of wood craftsmen turn out custom-made koa rockers and hutches to complement the antique furniture selection.

KANEOHE

Windward Mall. 46-056 Kamehameha Hwy. ☎ **808/235-1143.** Mon–Sat 9:30am–9pm; Sun 10am–5pm. Bus: 55 and 65.

The 91 stores and services spread out over windward Oahu's largest shopping complex include health stores, airline counters, surf shops, LensCrafters, and dozens of other retail businesses. A small food court serves pizza, Chinese food, tacos, and other morsels for the dine-and-dash set. Plans call for a 10-plex cinema in late 1999 and new retail tenants.

SHOPPING THE NORTH SHORE: HALEIWA

Like Hilo, Haleiwa means serious shopping for those who know that the unhurried pace of rural life can also conceal vast material treasures. Ask the legions of townies who drive an hour each way just to stock up on wine and clothes at Haleiwa stores. (Of course, a cooler is *de rigueur* for perishables.) Here are our Haleiwa highlights.

ART, GIFTS & CRAFTS

Haleiwa's shops and galleries display a combination of marine art, watercolors, sculptures, and a multitude of crafts trying to masquerade (unsuccessfully) as fine art. This is the town for gifts, fashions, and surf stuff—mostly casual, despite some price tags in the hundreds of thousands of dollars. The **Art Plantation,** 66–521 Kamehameha Hwy. (☎ **808/637-2343**), located in a historic wooden storefront, displays works by more than 150 local artists.

Global Creations Interiors, 66–079 Kamehameha Hwy. (☎ **808/637-1505**), offers international imports for the home, including high-quality Balinese bamboo furniture and lamps as well as colorful Yucatán hammocks and gifts and crafts by local potters, painters, and designers—in addition to its wonderful, casual clothes.

EDIBLES

Haleiwa is best known for its roadside shave-ice stands: the famous **M. Matsumoto,** with the perennial queue snaking along Kamehameha Highway, and nearby **Aoki's.** Shave ice is the popular island version of a snow cone, a heap of finely shaved ice topped with your choice of syrups, such as strawberry, rainbow, root beer, vanilla, or passion fruit. Aficionados order it with a scoop of ice cream and sweetened black azuki beans nestled in the middle.

For food-and-wine shopping, our mightiest accolade goes to **Fujioka Super Market,** 66–190 Kamehameha Hwy. (☎ **808/637-4520**). Oenophiles and tony wine clubs from town shop here for the best prices on California reds, coveted Italian reds, and a growing selection of cabernets, merlots, and French vintages that are thoughtfully selected and unbelievably priced. Fresh produce and no-cholesterol, vegetarian health foods, in addition to the standards, fill the aisles of this third-generation store.

Tiny, funky **Celestial Natural Foods,** 66–443 Kamehameha Hwy. (☎ **808/637-6729**), is the health foodies' Grand Central for everything from wooden spine-massagers to health supplements, produce, cosmetics, and bulk foods.

FASHION

Although Haleiwa used to be an incense-infused surfer outpost in which zoris and tank tops were the regional uniform and the Beach Boys and Ravi Shankar the music of the day, today it's one of the top shopping destinations for those with unconventional tastes. Specialty shops abound here. Top-drawer ✪ **Silver Moon Emporium,** North Shore Marketplace, 66–250 Kamehameha Hwy. (☎ **808/637-7710**), is an islandwide phenomenon with the terrific finds of buyer/owner Lucie Talbot-Holu. Exquisite clothing and handbags, reasonably priced footwear, hats straight out of *Vogue,* jewelry, scarves, and a full gamut of other treasures pepper the attractive boutique. Nearby **Oceania,** 66–218 Kamehameha Hwy. (☎ **808/637-4581**), has some treasures among its racks of casual and leisure wear. Foldable straw hats, diaphanous dresses, dressy T-shirts, friendly service, and good prices are what we've found at Oceania. **Oogenesis Boutique,** at 66–249 Kamehameha Hwy. (☎ **808/637-4580**), in the southern part of Haleiwa, features a storefront lined with vintage-looking dresses that flutter prettily in the North Shore breeze.

In addition to Silver Moon, other highlights of the prominent North Shore Marketplace include **Patagonia** (☎ **808/637-1245**) for high-quality surf, swim, hiking, kayaking, and all-around adventure wear; and **Jungle Gems** (☎ **808/637-6609**), the mother lode of gemstones, crystals, silver, and beadwork.

Among all these Haleiwa newcomers, the perennial favorite remains **H. Miura Store and Tailor Shop,** 66–057 Kamehameha Hwy. (☎ **808/637-4845**). You can custom-order swim trunks, an aloha shirt, or a muumuu from the bolts of Polynesian-printed fabrics that line the store, from tapa designs to two-color pareu prints. They will sew, ship, and remember you years later when you return. It's the most versatile tailor shop we've ever seen, with coconut-shell bikini tops, fake hula skirts, aloha shirts, and heaps of cheap and glorious knickknacks lining the aisles.

SURF SHOPS

Surfers say Haleiwa's ubiquitous surf shops are the best on earth. At the top of the heap is **Northshore Boardriders Club,** North Shore Marketplace, 66–250 Kamehameha Hwy. (☎ 808/637-5026), the mecca of the board-riding elite, with sleek, fast, elegant, and top-of-the-line boards designed by North Shore legends such as longboard shapers Barry Kanaiaupuni, John Carper, Jeff Bushman, and Pat Rawson. This is a Quicksilver "concept store," which means that it's the testing grounds for the newest and hottest trends in surfwear put out by the retail giant. Kanaiaupuni's other store, **B K Ocean Sports,** in the old Haleiwa Post Office at 66–215 Kamehameha Hwy. (☎ 808/637-4966), is a more casual version, appealing to surfers and watersports enthusiasts of all levels. Across the street, **Hawaii Surf & Sail,** 66–214 Kamehameha Hwy. (☎ 808/637-5373), offers new and used surfboards and accessories for surfers, bodyboarders, and sailboarders.

Strong Current Surf Design, North Shore Marketplace (☎ 808/637-3406), is the North Shore's nexus for memorabilia and surf nostalgia because of the passion of its owners, Bonnie and John Moore. Moore, a lifetime collector and surfer since 1963, expanded the commercial surf-shop space to encompass the **North Shore Surf and Cultural Museum** (see chapter 8, "Seeing the Sights"). From head level down, Strong Current sells shorts, jewelry, and ocean sportswear; from head level up, the walls and ceilings are lined with vintage boards, posters, and pictures from the '50s and '60s. Strong Current is a longboard surf shop, and the current popularity of longboarding among all age groups makes it a popular stop. World-famous North Shore shapers Dick Brewer and Mike Diffenderfer are among the big names who design the fiberglass and balsa wood boards.

Also in the North Shore Marketplace, **Barnfield's Raging Isle Sports** (☎ 808/637-7707) is the surf-and-cycle center of the area, with everything from wet suits and surfboards to surf gear and clothing for men, women, and children. The adjoining surfboard factory puts out custom-built boards of high renown. Cyclists also hightail it here because of its large inventory of mountain bikes for rent and sale; Marin, Kona, and Electra are among the name brands in its mountain-bike inventory.

A longtime favorite among old-timers is the newly expanded **Surf & Sea Surf Sail & Dive Shop,** 62–595 Kamehameha Hwy. (☎ 808/637-9887), a flamboyant roadside structure just over the bridge, with old wood floors, fans blowing, and a tangle of surf and swim wear, T-shirts, surfboards, boogie boards, fins, watches, sunglasses, and countless other miscellany; you can also rent surf and snorkel equipment here. **Tropical Rush,** 62–620-A Kamehameha Hwy. (☎ 808/637-8886), is a surfer haven with its huge inventory of surf and swim gear, much of it for rent: longboards and Perfect Line surfboards, Reef Brazil shoes and slippers, swimwear for men and women, T-shirts, visors, sunglasses, and scads of cool gear. An added feature is the shop's **surf report line** for the up-to-the-minute lowdown on wave action (☎ 808/638-7874), updated daily and quite entertaining, covering surf and weather details for all of Oahu.

10 Oahu After Dark

by Jocelyn Fujii

One of my favorite occasions in life is sunset at Ke Iki Beach, in the thatched, open-sided *hale* of my friend Alice Tracy's vacation rental, Ke Iki Hale (see chapter 5, "Accommodations"). The entire day builds up to sunset—shopping for the mai tai ingredients, checking the angle of the sun, swimming with the knowledge that the big, salty thirst will soon be quenched with a tall, homemade mai tai on the beach I love most in the world. When the sun is low, we make our mix: fresh lime juice, fresh lemon juice, fresh orange juice, passion-orange-guava juice, and fresh grapefruit juice, if possible. We pour this mix on ice in tall, frosty glasses, then add Meyer's rum, in which Tahitian vanilla beans have been soaking for days. (Add cinnamon if desired, or soak a cinnamon stick with the rum and vanilla beans.) A dash of Angostura bitters, a few drops of Southern Comfort as a float, a sprig of mint, a garnish of fresh lime, and voilà! The homemade Ke Iki mai tai, a cross between planter's punch and the classic Trader Vic's mai tai. As the sun sets, we lift our glasses and savor the moment, the setting, and the first sip—not a bad way to end the day.

In Hawaii, the mai tai is more than a libation. It's a festive, happy ritual that signals holiday, vacation, or a time of play, not work. Computers and mai tais don't mix. Mai tais and hammocks do. Mai tais and sunsets go hand in hand.

1 It Begins with Sunset . . .

Nightlife in Hawaii begins at sunset, when all eyes turn westward to see how the day will end, and revelers begin planning their Technicolor venue to launch the evening's festivities. Like seeing the same pod of whales or school of spinner dolphins, sunset viewers seem to bond in the mutual enjoyment of a natural spectacle. People in Hawaii are fortunate to have a benign environment that encourages this cultural ritual.

On Fridays and Saturdays at 6:30pm, as the sun casts its golden glow on the beach and surfers and beachboys paddle in for the day, **Kuhio Beach,** where Kalakaua Avenue intersects with Kaiulani, eases into evening with a torch-lighting ceremony and hula dancing. This is a thoroughly delightful, free weekend offering. Start off earlier with a picnic basket and your favorite libations and walk along the oceanside path fronting Queen's Surf, near the Waikiki Aquarium. (You can park along Kapiolani Park or near the Honolulu Zoo.) There are few more pleasing spots in Waikiki than the benches at the water's edge at this

Diamond Head end of Kalakaua Avenue, where lovers and families of all ages stop to peruse the sinking sun. A short walk across the intersection of Kalakaua and Kapahulu avenues, where the seawall and daring boogie boarders attract hordes of spectators, takes you to the Duke Kahanamoku statue on Kuhio Beach and the nearby Wizard Stones. There you can view the **torch-lighting** and **hula** and gear up for the **strolling musicians** who amble down Kalakaua Avenue every Friday evening from 8 to 10pm. The musicians begin at Beachwalk Avenue at the Ewa end of Waikiki and end up at the statue.

BEACHFRONT BARS   Waikiki's beachfront bars offer many possibilities, from the Royal Hawaiian Hotel's ✪ **Mai Tai Bar** (☎ 808/923-7311) a few feet from the sand, to the unfailingly enchanting ✪ **House Without a Key** at the Halekulani (☎ 808/ 923-2311), where the breathtaking **Kanoelehua Miller** dances hula to the riffs of Hawaiian steel-pedal guitar under a century-old kiawe tree. With the sunset and ocean glowing behind her and Diamond Head visible in the distance, the scene is straight out of Somerset Maugham—romantic, evocative, nostalgic. It doesn't hurt, either, that the Halekulani happens to make the best mai tais in the world. Halekulani has the after-dinner hours covered, too, with light jazz by local artists from 10:15pm to mid-night nightly (see "Jazz," below).

ALOHA TOWER MARKETPLACE   The landmark Aloha Tower at Honolulu Harbor, once Oahu's tallest building, has always occupied Honolulu's prime down-town location—on the water, at a naturally sheltered bay, near the business and civic center of Honolulu. Since the Aloha Tower Marketplace (1 Aloha Tower Dr., on the waterfront between piers 8 and 11, Honolulu Harbor; ☎ **808/528-5700**) was con-structed, it's gained popularity as an entertainment and nightlife spot, with more than 100 shops and restaurants, including several venues for Honolulu's leading musical groups. (Parking, however, is still a challenge.)

Unlike Waikiki, there are no swaying palm trees at your fingertips at Aloha Tower Marketplace, but you'll see tugboats and cruise ships from the popular open-air **Pier Bar** (☎ **808/536-2166**) and various venues throughout the marketplace offering live music throughout the week. The frequent appearances of the Brothers Cazimero at **Don Ho's Island Grill** (☎ **808/528-0807**) has turned the waterfront into a thriving late-night spot that promises to revive old-style Waikiki entertainment in a big way. Also at Aloha Tower, there's live music from 8pm nightly, except Sunday and Monday, at the Pier Bar: contemporary Hawaiian, swing, alternative rock, jazz. The Pier Bar's main stage, **Gordon Biersch Brewery** (see chapter 6, "Dining"), and the **Atrium Center Court** feature ongoing programs of foot-stomping good times. At the Gordon Biersch Brewery Restaurant, diners swing to jazz, blues, and island riffs with a changing roster of entertainers. Live music, from 8:30pm to 1am or 1:30am Wednesday through Saturday, has included the popular Nueva Vida and Piranha Brothers, with special appearances (no cover) by icons Willie K., Hapa, Kapena, and Fiji—the cream of contemporary Island artists.

Across the street from Aloha Tower Marketplace, the bar and lounge of **Palomino** (☎ 808/528-2400) is a magnet for revelers, often two deep at the bar; great appe-tizers, pizzas, service, and drinks, and you can order from the full dinner menu there.

DOWNTOWN   The downtown scene is awakening from a long slumber, thanks to the Hawaii Theatre and some tenacious entrepreneurs who want everyone to love Nuuanu Avenue as much as they do. At this writing, there are efforts to turn the occa-sional block parties along Nuuanu Avenue, called "Nuuanu Nights," into a regular monthly event. **Hanks Café** between Hotel and King streets on Nuuanu (☎ 808/ 526-1410) is new and noteworthy, a tiny, kitschy, friendly pub that spells FUN with its live music, open-mike nights, and special events that attract great talent and a supportive crowd—and it's open for lunch, too. (Hanks's cilantro-laden chili is famous.) Across the street from Hanks, **Punani's** (☎ **808/526-9395**) is also popular, and down the street, **Havana Cabana** (☎ **808/524-4277**) is a clubby late-night cigar-smoker's paradise with live music ranging from jazz to rock and R&B. At the makai end of Nuuanu, toward the pier, **Murphy's Bar & Grill** (☎ **808/531-0422**) and **O'Toole's Pub** (☎ **808/536-6360**) are the downtown ale houses and media haunts that have kept Irish eyes smiling for years.

HAWAIIAN MUSIC

Oahu has several key spots for Hawaiian music. A delightful (and powerful) addition to the Waikiki music scene is Hawaii's queen of falsetto **Genoa Keawe,** who fills the lobby of the Hawaiian Regent Hotel (☎ **808/922-6611**) with her larger-than-life voice. You'll find her at the hotel's **Lobby Bar** from 5:30 to 8:30pm every Thursday; the rest of the week except Monday, other contemporary Hawaiian musicians fill in.

Brothers Cazimero remain one of Hawaii's most gifted duos (Robert on bass, Roland on 12-string guitar), appearing spontaneously at Kahala Moon (closed in Kahala and soon to reopen at the old Willows site) and special venues throughout the year, including the new Don Ho's Island Grill. Watch the dailies, or ask the hotel concierge if the Brothers Caz, as they're called, are giving a special concert (as they do every May 1 at the Waikiki Shell), or if they've made Don Ho's their new home for good.

Impromptu hula and spirited music from the family and friends of the performers are an island tradition at places such as the Hilton Hawaiian Village's ✪ **Paradise Lounge** (☎ **808/949-4321**), which (despite its pillars) serves as a large living room for the full-bodied music of **Olomana.** The group plays Friday and Saturday from 8pm to midnight, with no cover charge. At ✪ **Duke's Canoe Club** at the Outrigger Waikiki (☎ **808/923-0711**), it's always three deep at the beachside bar when the sun is setting and the fabulous **Moe Keale** is playing with his trio. **Del Beazley, Brother Noland, Ledward Kaapana, Henry Kapono,** and other top names in Hawaiian entertainment have appeared at Duke's, where extra-special entertainment is a given. Usually, the entertainment is from 4 to 6pm on Friday, Saturday, and Sunday, and nightly from 10pm to midnight. Nearby, the Sheraton Moana Surfrider offers a regular program of Hawaiian music (and Renee Paulo at the piano bar) in the **Banyan Veranda** (☎ **808/922-3111**), which surrounds an islet-sized canopy of banyan tree and roots where Robert Louis Stevenson loved to linger.

The buzz in the Polynesian revue world is the Sheraton Princess Kaiulani's new **"Creation—A Polynesian Odyssey"** in the hotel's second-floor Ainahau Showroom, produced by Tihati, Hawaii's king of revues (☎ **808/931-4660**). It's an extravaganza of fire dancing, special effects, illusions, hula, and Tahitian dancing, nightly at 5:15 and 8pm, Princess Kaiulani guests who attend the earlier show pay $37.50, non-guests $60, buffet dinner included. At the 8pm show, non-guests pay $53, guests $35.

Our best advice for lovers of Hawaiian music is to scan the local dailies or the *Honolulu Weekly* to see if and where the following Hawaiian entertainers are appearing: **Ho'okena,** a symphonic rich quintet featuring **Manu Boyd,** one of the most prolific songwriters and chanters in Hawaii; **Hapa,** an award-winning contemporary Hawaii duo; **Keali'i Reichel,** premier chanter, dancer, and award-winning recording artist, voted "Male Vocalist of the Year" in the 1996 Na Hoku Hanohano Awards; **Robbie Kahakalau,** "Female Vocalist of the Year" in the same awards; **Kapena,** contemporary Hawaiian music; **Na Leo Pilimehana,** a trio of angelic Hawaiian singers; the **Makaha Sons of Niihau,** pioneers in the Hawaiian cultural renaissance; **Fiji;** and slack-key guitar master **Raymond Kane.**

Consider the gods beneficent if you happen to be here when the hula halau of **Frank Kawaikapuokalani Hewett** is holding its annual fund-raiser in Windward Oahu. It's a rousing, inspired, family effort for a good cause, and it always features the best in ancient and contemporary Hawaiian music. For the best in ancient and modern hula, it's a good idea to check the dailies for halau fund-raisers, which are always authentic, enriching, and local to the core.

Showroom acts that have maintained a following are led by the tireless, disarming **Don Ho,** who still sings *Tiny Bubbles* and remains a fixture at the **Waikiki Beachcomber** supper club (☎ **800/923-3981**). He's corny, but attentive to fans as he accommodates their requests and sings nostalgic favorites. He's also very generous in sharing his stage, so patrons are often in for surprise guest appearances by leading Hawaii performers. Ho gives two shows an evening from Sunday through Thursday. Across Kalakaua Avenue in the **Outrigger Waikiki on the Beach** (☎ **808/923-0711**), the **Society of Seven's** nightclub act (a blend of skits, Broadway hits, popular music, and costumed musical acts) is into its 29th year—no small feat for performers.

BLUES

The best news for blues fans is the growing network of dyed-in-the-wool blues lovers here who have their own newsletter, blues festivals, club gigs, and the indomitable leadership of Louie Wolfenson of the **Maui Blues Association** (☎ **808/879-6123**), the primary source for information on blues activities throughout the state. The blues are alive and well in Hawaii, with quality acts—both local and from the mainland—drawing enthusiastic crowds in even the funkiest of surroundings. **Junior Wells, Willie & Lobo, War,** and surprise appearances by the likes of **Bonnie Raitt** are among the past successes of this genre of big-time licks. The best-loved Oahu venue is **Anna Bannanas,** 2440 S. Beretania St. (☎ **808/946-5190**), still rocking after 30 years in the business, with reggae, blues, and rock, and video games and darts.

THE CLASSICS

"Aloha shirt to Armani" is what we call the night scene in Honolulu—mostly casual, but with ample opportunity to dress up if you dare to part with your flip-flops.

Audiences have stomped to the big off-Broadway percussion hit, *Stomp,* and enjoyed the talent of *Tap Dogs, Momix,* the American Repertory Dance Company, barbershop quartets, and John Ka'imikaua's halau at the ✪ **Hawaii Theatre,** 1130 Bethel St., downtown (☎ **808/528-0506**), still basking in its renaissance following a 4-year, $22-million renovation. The neoclassical beaux arts landmark features a 1922 dome, 1,400 plush seats, a hydraulically elevated organ, a mezzanine lobby with two full bars, Corinthian columns, and gilt galore. Breathtaking murals, including a restored proscenium centerpiece lauded as Lionel Walden's "greatest creation," foster an atmosphere that's making the theatre a leading multipurpose center for the performing arts.

The **Honolulu Symphony Orchestra** has booked some of its performances at the new theatre, but it still performs at the Waikiki Shell and the **Neal Blaisdell Concert Hall** (☎ **808/591-2211**). Meanwhile, for opera lovers, the highly successful **Hawaii Opera Theatre,** in its 39th season (past hits have included *La Bohème, Carmen, Turandot, Romeo and Juliet, Rigoletto,* and *Aïda*), still draws fans to the Neal Blaisdell Concert Hall, as do many of the performances of Hawaii's four ballet companies: **Hawaii Ballet Theatre, Ballet Hawaii, Hawaii State Ballet,** and **Honolulu Dance Theatre.** Contemporary performances by **Dances We Dance** and the **Iona Pear Dance Company,** a strikingly creative Butoh group, are worth tracking down if you love the avant-garde.

JAZZ

Construction for a new restaurant-entertainment complex in downtown Honolulu is due to begin in mid 1999 and is expected to be completed, in two phases, by 2000. Watch for the opening of the **Galleria Shopping Center** in downtown Honolulu, where the historic U.S. Post Office now stands (across from Iolani Palace). In the works are a JazzArt Café, featuring jazz and art, and jazz festivals and benefits, including the Honolulu Downtown Jazz Festival, around this downtown post office complex. Plans call for four annual festivals sponsored by the Galleria: the Beatles Fest, Country Dance Festival, Motown Downtown, and the Honolulu Downtown Jazz Festival.

In other parts of town, jazz lovers should watch for the Great Hawaiian Jazz Blow-Out every March (in its third year) at Mid-Pacific Institute's Bakken Hall. At the south end of Honolulu, near Diamond Head, **David Paul's Diamond Head Grill** (☎ 808/922-3734), is Honolulu's newest hot spot, with live music by jazz queens Azure McCall, Anita Hall, and the Betty Loo Taylor trio, from 9:30 to 11:30pm Tuesday through Saturday. McCall's torchy vocals and extensive repertoire turn dinner into a banquet. With good food, chic surroundings, and the likes of McCall and Hall, DPDHG is after-hours nirvana. **Nick's Fishmarket,** Waikiki Gateway Hotel, 2070 Kalakaua Ave. (☎ 808/955-6333), keeps winning awards for its seafood, but it's also a sophisticated hot spot with live entertainment nightly in its cozy lounge—mild jazz or Top 40 contemporary hits.

Jazz Hawaii (☎ 808/737-6554) has an updated list of who's playing where, including the Jazz Hawaii Big Band that performs at selected venues around town. This wonderful organization has brought together Hawaii's best musicians in jazz, blues, Latin, calypso, and Brazilian music, contributing to a much higher level of entertainment in Honolulu since it emerged in 1993.

Tops in taste and ambience is the perennially alluring **Lewers Lounge** in the Halekulani, 2199 Kalia Rd. (☎ 808/923-2311). Too bad Loretta Ables isn't there anymore; new licks are by **Bruce Hamada** and other local artists in soft jazz. Watch for **Sandy Tsukiyama,** a gifted singer (Brazilian, Latin, jazz) and one of Honolulu's great assets, and jazz singers **Rachel Gonzales** and **Loretta Ables.** Other groups in jazz, blues, and R&B include **Blue Budda, Bongo Tribe, Secondhand Smoke, Bluzilla, Piranha Brothers,** and the **Greg Pai Trio.**

ALTERNATIVE CLUBS

Anna Bannanas (see "Blues," above) is the granddaddy of them all, still packing them in, with bands known to generate the most perspiration on the most enthusiastic dance floor in Honolulu. This indomitable club is a venue for groups with roots in reggae, blues, world music, and alternative music. Most shows start at 9:30pm, and the cover charge depends on the show. The under-30s also flock to the **Wave Waikiki** (☎ 808/941-0424), a small, dark, and edgy room that shakes with the rock and R&B groups that play there. Another hot spot is **Beach Hall,** formerly The Source (☎ 808/951-5336), in Puck's Alley (the University area)—booty music to the max, with hip hop, punk, R&B, and raves.

Near the new convention center and down the street from the Wave is the terminally hip **Hard Rock Cafe,** 1837 Kapiolani Blvd. (☎ 808/955-7383), the bastion of decibels run amok, offering live entertainment on many, but not all, Friday and Saturday nights. These no-cover events bring out a hip crowd for the local alternative, reggae, and classic-rock bands.

TOP 40S

Nicholas Nickolas, Ala Moana Hotel, 410 Atkinson Dr. (☎ 808/955-4466), has the best view: From the 36th floor of the hotel (take the express elevator), watch the

Honolulu city lights wrap around the room and cha-cha-cha to the vertigo! It has live music and dancing nightly, and an appetizer menu nightly from 5pm (see chapter 6, "Dining").

DISCOS

Downstairs in the lobby of the Ala Moana Hotel, **Rumours Nightclub** (☎ 808/955-4811) is the disco of choice for those who remember that Paul McCartney was a Beatle before Wings. The theme changes by the month, but generally, it's the "Big Chill" '60s, '70s, and '80s music on Fridays; the "Little Chill" on Saturdays; ballroom dancing from 5 to 9pm on Sundays; ballroom dancing on Tuesdays; karaoke on Wednesdays; and an "after-work office party" on Thursday until midnight. A spacious dance floor, good sound system, and Top 40s music draw a mix of generations. Across town in Waikiki, the Hawaiian Regent Hotel's **Eurasia** (☎ 808/921-5335), open nightly from 9pm to 4am, is big with swing fans, with a live swing band on Wednesday nights and Latin music on Thursdays. The rest of the nights, you're in the hands of hip Honolulu deejays, occasionally for live radio broadcasts. At Restaurant Row, **Ocean Club,** 500 Ala Moana Blvd. (☎ 808/526-9888; see chapter 6, "Dining"), is the Row's hottest, hippest, and coolest spot. Good seafood appetizers, attractive happy-hour prices, a fabulous quirky interior, and passionate deejays in alternative garb make up a dizzyingly successful formula. The minimum age is 23, and the dress code calls for "smart-casual"—no T-shirts, slippers, or beachwear.

2 . . . And More

It's true that Elvis and Marilyn didn't die. They're still wowing fans through their imper-sonators, having achieved entertainment immortality with skillful makeup and voice coaches. Watch Madonna, Michael Jackson, Roy Orbison, Diana Ross, Janet Jackson, Prince, Whitney Houston, Marilyn Monroe, Elvis, and other entertainment icons at the **Legends in Concert** show at the Aloha Showroom of the Royal Hawaiian Shopping Center (☎ 808/971-1400). The recently revamped dinner show has added a magic act, new china and menu items (steak and scampi), and a finely tuned cast of impersonators in a $10-million showroom with laser lights, smoke effects, and high-tech stage and sound systems. At least five personalities are featured at each performance, with Elvis, performed by uncanny look-alike Jonathan Von Brana, and Madonna, performed by Von Brana's real-life wife, Eileen Fairbanks, among the show's staples. Two shows (6:25 and 9pm) are featured 7 nights a week at $29 for cocktails, $65 for dinner show, and $99 for deluxe dinner show, with reduced children's rates available.

Finally, for late-night schmoozing, with a theater complex nearby, the Restaurant Row's **Row Bar,** 500 Ala Moana Blvd. (☎ 808/528-2345), always seems to be full, smoky, and somewhat, if impersonally, convivial, except after the theaters have emp-tied from an Oliver Stone movie.

FILM

A quick check in both dailies and the *Honolulu Weekly* will tell you what's playing where in the world of feature films. For film buffs and esoteric movie lovers, **The Movie Museum,** 3566 Harding Ave. (☎ 808/735-8771), has special screenings of vintage films and rents a collection of hard-to-find, esoteric, and classic films. The **Honolulu Academy of Arts Theatre,** 900 S. Beretania St. (☎ 808/532-8768), is the film-as-art center of Honolulu, offering special screenings, guest appearances, and cul-tural performances, as well as noteworthy programs in the visual arts.

Additionally, major movie theater complexes throughout Oahu bring celluloid to the masses more conveniently. In the heart of Waikiki, on Kalakaua Avenue and on

Seaside Avenue, three **Waikiki Theatres** are among the largest and most luxurious in multiplex-plagued Honolulu, showing major, mainstream feature films. In the university area of Moliili, the **Varsity Twins,** at University Avenue near Beretania Street, specializes in the more avant-garde, artistically acclaimed releases. Not far away, at King Street near Kalakaua, the **Cinerama Theatre** is the big-screen lover's delight. The Kahala Mall's **Kahala 8-Plex** and **Kapolei Megaplex** (a 16-theater complex), in west Oahu near the Ko Olina Resort, are the biggest movie theater complexes on the island.

At the nine **Wallace Theatres** on Restaurant Row near downtown Honolulu, free parking in the evenings, discount matinees, and special discounted midnight shows take a big step toward making movies friendlier and more affordable.

DINNER CRUISES

The best news in the dinner cruise world is the brilliant move by *Navatek I* (Pier 6; ☎ **808/848-6360**) to introduce Hawaii regional cuisine on its cruises. Noted chef George Mavrothalassitis, formerly of Halekulani's La Mer and now the chef-owner of his own place called Chef Mavro Restaurant (see chapter 6, "Dining"), has developed the menu for the *Navatek*'s nightly dinner cruises off the coast of Waikiki. This means that not only does the 140-foot-long, ultra-stable SWATH (Small Waterplane Area Twin Hull) vessel promise spill-proof mai tais and a bob-free, seasick-less ride, but it's now in the gourmet dinner arena.

There are several structures to the *Navatek* cruises, involving number of courses, upper-deck or lower-deck seating, and time of cruise, but generally the offerings are Sunset Dinner Cruise, daily from 5 to 7:30pm; Moonlight Dinner Cruise, called La Lumiere, daily 8:15 to 10:15pm; and Skyline Dinner Cruise on the main deck, 8:15 to 10:15pm. The food, views of the sunset and the Waikiki skyline, and occasional dolphin and turtle sightings are infinitely more enjoyable on a stable, state-of-the-art craft like *Navatek*.

For a less expensive alternative, many choose the **Windjammer Cruises** (Pier 7; ☎ **808/537-1122**), the prominently lit tall ship that's visible from Waikiki nightly. It looks like a sailboat but is motorized, with one sail daily from 5:15 to 7:30pm. The evening includes Polynesian entertainment and dancing.

LUAU!

Regrettably, there's no commercial luau on this island that comes close to Maui's Old Lahaina Luau, or the Big Island's legendary Kona Village luau. The two major luaus on Oahu are **Germaine's** (☎ **808/941-3338**) and **Paradise Cove Luau** (☎ **808/ 973-LUAU**), both about a 40-minute drive away from Waikiki on the leeward coast. Bus pickups and drop-offs in Waikiki are part of the deal. Athough Germaine's tries awfully hard and is a much smaller and more intimate affair, Paradise Cove (itself a mixed bag, with 600 to 800 guests a night) is a more complete experience. The small thatched village makes it more of a Hawaiian theme park, with Hawaiian games, hukilau net throwing and gathering, craft demonstrations, and a beautiful shoreline looking out over what's usually a storybook sunset.

O'Brian Eselu's hula halau has been entertaining luau goers here for years. Tahitian dance, ancient and modern hula, white-knuckle fire dancing, and robust entertainment make it a fun-filled evening for those who don't expect an intimate gathering and are spirited enough to join in with the corny audience participation. The food is safe, though not breathtaking. Hawaiian kalua pig, lomi salmon, poi, and coconut pudding and cake are provided, but for the less adventurous, there is always a spread of teriyaki chicken, mahi-mahi, pasta salad, potato salad, and banana bread. Paradise Cove costs $49.50 for adults and $29.50 for children 6 to 12 years old. For

$10 more, the Royal Alii Service ensures table service instead of the usual buffet, pitchers of mai tais and Blue Hawaii cocktails on the table, and seating close to the stage. To attend Germaine's, the cost is $46 per adult, $25 for children. Although these luaus can be crowded, commercial affairs, everyone seems to have fun.

Visitors who attend a Polynesian revue in a dinner-showroom setting often find it a reasonable alternative to a luau and a lot of fun, too, minus the palm-tree silhouettes and picture-perfect sunsets. **Kalo's South Seas Revue** at the Hawaiian Hut Theater Restaurant (410 Atkinson Dr.; ☎ **808/941-5205**) lights up the 500-seat room with flames, fast-beating drums, and swaying hips in a wide-ranging program of Polynesian entertainment. Hula, fire dance, Tahitian dance, and Hawaiian, Maori, Tongan, and other Pacific traditions make it a fast-paced show. It's a commercial show, however, not an intimate backyard affair, so expect more entertainment than cultural enlightenment. The show includes a prime rib buffet dinner; $49 covers the show, dinner, and a double standard or a single exotic drink, and the show costs only $27. Dinner show at 5:30pm daily; show only at 6:30pm.

Appendix: Honolulu & Oahu in Depth

by Jeanette Foster & Jocelyn Fujii

A wise Hawaiian *kupuna* once told me that the islands are like children—that each is special yet different, that each is to be loved for its individual qualities. Known as the "gathering place," Oahu is the commercial and population center of Hawaii.

It's an astounding experience to spend hours flying across the expansive blue of the Pacific, and then to see suddenly below you the whites and pastels of Honolulu, the most remote large urban area on earth, a 26-mile-long city of some 875,000 souls living in the middle of nowhere. Once on its streets, you'll find bright city lights, five-star restaurants, hopping nightclubs, world-class shopping, great art and architecture, and grand old hotels.

Nine of ten visitors to Hawaii—some 5 million a year—stop on Oahu, and most of them end up along the busy streets of Waikiki, Honolulu's famous hotel district and its most densely populated neighborhood. On some days, it seems like the entire world is sunning itself on Waikiki's famous beach.

Beyond Waikiki, Honolulu is clean and easy to enjoy. Founded by King Kamehameha, "reformed" by Boston missionaries, and once dominated by the "Big Five" cartels, Honolulu has come of age just in time for the 21st century. The old port town has reshaped its waterfront, altered its skyline, and built a convention center—all the while trying to preserve its historic roots and revive its Polynesian heritage.

Out in the country, Oahu can be as down-home as the music of a slack-key guitarist. That's where you'll find a big blue sky, perfect waves, empty beaches, rainbows and waterfalls, sweet tropical flowers, and fiery Pacific sunsets. In fact, nowhere else within 60 minutes of a major American city can you snorkel in a crystal-clear lagoon, climb an old volcano, surf monster waves, fish for record-sized marlin, kayak to a desert isle, picnic on a sandbar, soar in a glider over tide pools, skin dive over a sunken airplane, bicycle through a rainforest, golf a championship course, or sail into the setting sun. Visitors also have more opportunities to learn about the traditions of Hawaii: Learn to dance the hula from a real *kumu hula* (hula teachers), visit a *heiau* (Hawaiian temple) with a kupuna, or try native Hawaiian medicine from the rainforest.

And weather?: No other Hawaiian island has it as nice as Oahu. The Big Island is hotter, Kauai is wetter, Maui has more wind, and Molokai and Lanai are drier. But Oahu enjoys a kind of perpetual late spring, with light trade winds and 82°F days almost year-round. In fact, the climate is supposed to be the best on the planet. Once you have that, the rest is easy.

1 Honolulu & Oahu Today

Not just another pretty place in the sun, America's only island state has positioned itself as one of the cultural centers and meeting places of the Pacific Rim, with an international cast of characters playing key roles.

Even busy Waikiki has cleaned up its act: Timeshare vendors have been replaced with flower lei stands, and authentic chant and hula in traditional dress are offered nightly at sunset. Waikiki is no longer a place of tacky T-shirts and souvenir stands; it's evolved into one of the shopping capitals of the Pacific, where people fly in to browse European designer boutiques like Cartier, Dunhill, Ferragamo, and Ettore Bugatti. The new four-story, 1.1 million-square-foot Hawaii Convention Center now rises at the gateway to Waikiki, enhancing the state's position as a crossroad between East and West.

Hawaii has some of the world's newest and finest world-class beach resorts, contemporary palaces that would astound even the islands' hedonistic kings. Here you can dine on the freshest seafood and island-grown fruits and vegetables, receive the attention of your very own butler, and while away lazy days in secret gardens and private pools.

The old and new are combining to create a level of style and service that only enhances Oahu's aloha spirit. Oahu is not just a place where East meets West, but where the tropical past is carried forward into the future. "Our goal is to teach and share our culture," says Gloriann Akau, who is an island manager for the Aloha Festivals. "In 1946, after the war, Hawaiians needed an identity. We were lost and needed to regroup. When we started to celebrate our culture, we began to feel proud. We have a wonderful culture that had been buried for a number of years. This brought it out again. Self-esteem is more important than making a lot of money."

In 1985, as glitzy mega-resorts with borrowed cultures began to appear in the islands, native Hawaiian educator, author, and *kupuna* George Kanahele started infusing Hawaiian values into hotels. (A *kupuna* is an elder with leadership qualities who commands great respect; Kanahele is a *kupuna* with a Ph.D. from Cornell University.) "You have the responsibility to preserve and enhance the Hawaiian culture, not because it's going to make money for you but because it's the right thing to do," Kanahele told the Hawaii Hotel Association. "Ultimately, the only thing unique about Hawaii is its Hawaiianess. Hawaiianess is our competitive edge."

From general managers to maids, employees at two major resorts took 16 hours of Hawaiian cultural training. They held focus groups to discuss the meaning of *aloha*—the Hawaiian concept of unremitting love. They applied aloha to their work and their lives. Kaanapali Beach Hotel on Maui was the first to give their staff Hawaiian cultural training; they were followed by the Outrigger Hotel chain, one of the biggest in Hawaii. Many others have joined the movement.

Impressions

If paradise consists solely of beauty, then these islands were the fairest that man ever invaded, for the land and sea were beautiful and the climate was congenial.

—James A. Michener, *Hawaii*

THE QUESTION OF SOVEREIGNTY

The cultural renaissance has made its way into politics, so don't be surprised if you read about Hawaiians calling for independence for their homeland. Under the banner of sovereignty, many *kanaka maoli*—or native people, as they call themselves—are demanding the restoration of rights taken away more than a century ago when the United States overthrew the Hawaiian monarchy and claimed the islands. Their demands for sovereignty were not lost on President Bill Clinton, who was picketed at a Democratic political fund-raiser at Waikiki Beach in July 1993. Four months later, Clinton signed a law that stated the U.S. Congress "apologizes to native Hawaiians on behalf of the people of the United States for the overthrow of the Kingdom of Hawaii on January 17, 1893, with the participation of agents and citizens of the United States, and deprivation of the rights of native Hawaiians to self-determination."

While this could be construed to mean a return to the way things were in Hawaii a century ago with kings and queens and a royal court, not even neo-nationalists are convinced that's possible. First, the Hawaiians themselves must decide if they want sovereignty, since each of the 30 identifiable sovereignty organizations, and more than 100 splinter groups, has a different view of self-determination. They range from total independence from the United States to a nation-within-a-nation, which is similar to the status of Native American Indians.

2 History 101

Paddling outrigger canoes, the first ancestors of today's Hawaiians followed the stars and birds across a trackless sea to Hawaii, which they called "the land of raging fire." Those first settlers were part of the great **Polynesian migration** that settled the vast triangle of islands stretching from New Zealand in the southwest, Easter Island in the east, and Hawaii in the north. No one is sure when they arrived in Hawaii from Tahiti and the Marquesas Islands, some 2,500 miles to the south, but a dog-bone fish hook found at the southernmost tip of the Big Island has been carbon-dated to A.D. 700.

An entire Hawaiian culture arose over the next 1,500 years. The settlers built temples, fishponds, and aqueducts to irrigate taro plantations. Sailors became farmers and fishermen. Each island was a separate kingdom. The *alii* (high-ranking chiefs) created a caste system and established taboos. Violators were strangled. High priests asked the gods Lono and Ku for divine guidance, and ritual human sacrifices were common.

THE "FATAL CATASTROPHE"

No ancient Hawaiian ever imagined a *haole* (a person with "no breath") would ever appear on "a floating island." But one day in 1779 just such a white-skinned person sailed into Waimea Bay on Kauai, where he was welcomed as the god Lono.

The man was 50-year-old **Capt. James Cook,** already famous in Britain for "discovering" much of the southern Pacific. Now on his third great voyage of exploration, Cook had set sail from Tahiti northward across uncharted waters to find the mythical Northwest Passage linking the Pacific and Atlantic oceans. On his way, Cook stumbled upon the Hawaiian Islands quite by chance. He named them the Sandwich Islands, for the Earl of Sandwich, First Lord of the Admiralty, who had bankrolled his expedition.

Overnight, Stone Age Hawaii entered the age of iron. Gifts were presented and trade established: nails for fresh water, pigs, and the affections of Hawaiian women. The sailors brought syphilis, measles, and other diseases to which the

Hawaiians had no natural immunity, thereby unwittingly wreaking havoc on the native population. (While on a trip to Europe in 1825, King Kamehameha II and his queen Kamamalu died of measles in London.)

After an unsuccessful attempt to find the Northwest Passage, Cook returned to Kealakekua on the Big Island, where a fight broke out. The great navigator was killed by a blow to the head. After this "fatal catastrophe," the British survivors sailed home. Hawaii was now on the sea navigation charts. French, Russian, and American traders on the fur route between Canada's Hudson's Bay Company and China anchored in Hawaii to get fresh water. More trade and more disastrous liaisons ensued.

Two more sea captains left indelible marks on the islands: The first was American **John Kendrick,** who in 1791 filled his ship with sandalwood and sailed to China. By 1825, Hawaii's sandalwood forests were gone, enabling invasive plants to run amok on the islands. The second was Englishman **George Vancouver,** who in 1793 left cows and sheep, which nibbled the islands to the high-tide line. The king sent to Mexico and Spain for cowboys to round up the wild cattle, thus beginning the islands' *paniolo* (cowboy) tradition.

The tightly woven fabric of Hawaiian society, kept in check by royal and religious edicts, began to unravel after the death of **King Kamehameha I** in 1819. The king had used guns seized from a British ship to unite the islands under his rule. His successor, **Queen Kaahumanu,** abolished the old taboos, thus opening the door for a religion of another form.

STAYING TO DO WELL

In April of 1820, God-fearing missionaries arrived from New England bent on converting the pagans. "Can these be human beings?" exclaimed their leader, the **Rev. Hiram Bingham,** upon first glance at "the almost naked savages" whose "appearance of destitution, degradation, and barbarism" he found "appalling."

Intent on instilling their brand of rock-ribbed Christianity in the islands, the missionaries covered the natives in clothing from head to toe, banned them from dancing the hula, and nearly dismantled their ancient culture. They tried to keep the whalers and sailors out of the bawdy houses, where a flood of whiskey quenched fleet-size thirsts and where the virtue of native women was never safe. The missionaries also taught reading and writing, created the 12-letter Hawaiian alphabet, started a letter press, and began writing the islands' history, which was until then only an oral account in half-remembered chants.

Children of the missionaries became the islands' business leaders and politicians. They married Hawaiians and stayed on in the islands, causing one wag to remark that the missionaries "came to do good and stayed to do well."

In 1848, **King Kamehameha III** proclaimed the Great Mahele (division), which enabled commoners and eventually foreigners to own crown land. In two generations, more than 80% of all private land was in haole hands. Sugar planters imported waves of immigrants to work the fields as contract laborers. The first Chinese came in 1852, followed by 7,000 Japanese in 1885, and the Portuguese in 1878.

King David Kalakaua was elected to the throne in 1874. This popular "Merrie Monarch" built Iolani Place in 1882, threw extravagant parties, and restored the hula and other native arts to grace. For this he was much loved. He also gave Pearl Harbor to the United States; it became the westernmost bastion of the U.S. Navy—and the bull's-eye of the infamous Japanese air raid on the sleepy Sunday of December 7, 1941. In 1891, King Kalakaua visited chilly San Francisco, caught a cold, and died in the royal suite of the Sheraton Palace. His sister, **Queen Liliuokalani,** assumed the throne.

A SAD FAREWELL

On January 17, 1893, a group of American sugar planters and missionary descendants, with the support of gun-toting marines, imprisoned Queen Liliuokalani in her own palace. With this single act the Hawaiian monarchy was dead, and a new republic was established, controlled by **Sanford Dole,** a powerful sugarcane planter. In 1898, Hawaii became an American territory ruled by Dole and his fellow sugarcane planters and the Big Five, a cartel that controlled banking, shipping, hardware, and every other facet of economic life in the islands.

Oahu's central Ewa Plain soon filled with row crops. The Dole family planted pineapple on their vast acreage. Planters imported more contract laborers from Puerto Rico (1900), Korea (1903), and the Philippines (1907–31). Most of the new immigrants stayed on, established families, and integrated into island life. At the same time, native Hawaiians became a landless minority in their own homeland.

For a half century, sugarcane was king in Hawaii (it was generously subsidized by the U.S. government). The sugar planters dominated the territory's economy, shaped its social fabric, and kept the islands in a colonial-plantation state with bosses and field hands. The workers eventually went on strike for higher wages and improved working conditions. Subsequently, planters found it increasingly difficult to compete with third-world countries that had access to cheaper labor costs, and they saw their market share start to shrink. Hawaii's lush fields of sugar and pineapple gradually went to seed, and the plantation era ended.

THE TOURISTS ARRIVE

Tourism proper started in Hawaii in the 1860s. Kilauea, on the Big Island of Hawaii, became the world's prime attraction. Adventure travelers, who rode on horseback 29 miles from Hilo, came to Hawaii to peer into the boiling hellfire of Halemaumau. The journal of missionary William Ellis, the first American to see the Kilauea volcano in 1823, inspired many to visit it. "Astonishment and awe for some moments rendered us mute and like statues we stood," he wrote. "Our eyes riveted on the abyss below . . . one vast flood of burning matter . . . rolling to and fro its fiery surge and flaming billows." In 1865, a grass version of Volcano House was built on the Halemaumau Crater rim to shelter them. It was Hawaii's first tourist hotel. But Hawaii's tourism industry really got off the ground with the demise of the plantation era, and it has shaped the islands' history in ways that sugarcane and pineapples never did.

In 1901, W. C. Peacock built the elegant beaux arts **Moana Hotel** on Waikiki Beach, and W. C. Weedon convinced Honolulu businessmen to bankroll his plan to advertise Hawaii in San Francisco. Travelers were going to California, and Weedon meant to persuade them to see Hawaii, too. Armed with a stereopticon and tinted photos of Waikiki, Weedon sailed off in 1902 for 6 months of lecture tours to introduce "those remarkable people and the beautiful lands of Hawaii." He drew packed houses. A tourism promotion bureau was formed in 1903, financed by the port's rat-control plague tax. About 2,000 visitors came to Hawaii that year.

Steamships were Hawaii's tourism lifeline. It took 4½ days to sail from San Francisco to Honolulu. Streamers, leis, pomp, and a warm **"Boat Day"** welcomed each Matson Liner at downtown's Aloha Tower. Well-heeled visitors brought trunks, servants, even their Rolls-Royces, and stayed for months. Hawaii amused the idle rich with personal tours, floral parades, and shows spotlighting that naughty dance, the hula.

Beginning in 1935 and running for the next 40 years, Webley Edwards's weekly live radio show, **"Hawaii Calls,"** infused the sounds of Waikiki—surf, slide steel guitar, sweet Hawaiian harmonies, drumbeats—into the hearts of millions of listeners in America, Australia, and Canada.

In 1936, visitors could fly to Honolulu on the *Hawaii Clipper,* a seven-passenger Pan American Martin M-130 flying boat, for $360 one-way. The flight took 21 hours and 33 minutes. Modern tourism was born, with five flying boats providing daily service between San Francisco and Honolulu. The 1941 visitor count was a brisk 31,846 through December 6.

REMEMBER PEARL HARBOR

On December 7, 1941, Japanese Zeros came out of the rising sun to bomb American warships based at Pearl Harbor. It was the "day of infamy" that plunged the United States into World War II and gave the nation its revenge-laced battle cry, "Remember Pearl Harbor!"

The aftermath of the attack brought immediate changes to the islands. Martial law was declared, thus stripping the Big Five cartels of their absolute power in a single day. Feared to be spies, Japanese-Americans from Hawaii and California were sent to internment camps. Hawaii was "blacked out" at night, Waikiki Beach was strung with barbed wire, and Aloha Tower was painted in camouflage. Only young men bound for the Pacific came to Hawaii during the war years. Tens of thousands returned to graves in a Honolulu cemetery called The Punchbowl.

The postwar years saw the beginnings of Hawaii's faux culture. Harry Yee invented the Blue Hawaii cocktail and dropped in a tiny Japanese parasol. Vic Bergeron created the mai tai, a rum-and-fresh-lime-juice drink, and opened **Trader Vic's,** America's first theme restaurant that featured the art, decor, and food of Polynesia. Arthur Godfrey picked up a ukulele and began singing hapa-haole tunes on early television shows. Burt Lancaster and Deborah Kerr made love in the surf near Hanauma Bay in the 1954 movie *From Here to Eternity.* In 1955, Henry J. Kaiser built the Hilton Hawaiian Village, and the 11-story high-rise Princess Kaiulani Hotel opened on a site where the real princess once played. Hawaii greeted 109,000 visitors that year.

STATEHOOD

In 1959, Hawaii became the last star on the Stars and Stripes, the 50th state of the union. In that same year Hawaii saw the arrival of the first jet airliners, which brought 250,000 tourists to the fledgling state. The personal touch that had defined the aloha spirit gave way to the sheer force of numbers. Waikiki's room count virtually doubled in 2 years, from 16,000 in 1969 to 31,000 units in 1971, and more followed before city administrators finally put a cap on the growth of the world's most famous resort area. By 1980, the number of annual arrivals reached 4 million.

In the early 1980s, the Japanese government decided its citizens should travel overseas, and out they went. Waikiki was one of their favorite destinations, and they brought lots of spending money. The effect on sales in Hawaii was phenomenal: European boutiques opened stores in Honolulu, and duty-free shoppers became the main supporter of Honolulu International Airport. Japanese investors competed for the chance to own or build part of Hawaii. Hotels sold so quickly and at such unbelievable prices that heads began to spin with dollar signs.

In 1986, Hawaii's visitor count surpassed 5 million. Two years later, it went over 6 million. Expensive fantasy mega-resorts blossomed on the neighbor islands like giant artificial flowers, swelling the luxury market with ever swankier accommodations. The highest visitor count ever recorded hit 6.9 million in 1990, but the bubble burst in early 1991 with the Gulf War and worldwide recessions. In 1992, Hurricane Iniki devastated Kauai, and airfare wars sent Americans to Mexico. Overbuilt with luxury hotels, Hawaii slashed its room rates, enabling visitors to stay in luxury digs at affordable prices—a trend that continues today.

3 Life & Language

Plantation work brought so many different people to Hawaii that the state is now a rainbow of ethnic groups. No one group is a majority; everyone's a minority. Living here are Hawaiians, Caucasians, African-Americans, American Indians, Eskimos, Aleuts, Japanese, Chinese, Filipinos, Koreans, Tahitians, Asian Indians, Vietnamese, Guamanians, Samoans, Tongans, and other Asian and Pacific islanders. Add a few Canadians, Dutch, English, French, German, Irish, Italians, Portuguese, Scottish, Puerto Ricans, and Spanish.

More than a century ago, W. Somerset Maugham noted that "All these strange people live close to each other, with different languages and different thoughts; they believe in different gods and they have different values; two passions alone they share: love and hunger." More recently, noted travel journalist Jan Morris said of Hawaii's population: "Half the world's races seem to be represented and interbred here, and between them they have created an improbable microcosm of human society as a whole."

It's indeed a remarkable potpourri. Most retain an element of the traditions of their homeland. Some Japanese-Americans in Hawaii, even after three and four generations removed from the homeland, are more traditional than the Japanese of Tokyo. And the same is true of many Chinese, Korean, Filipinos, and the rest of the 25 or so ethnic groups that make Hawaii a kind of living museum of Asian and Pacific cultures.

WHAT *HAOLE* MEANS

When Hawaiians first saw Western visitors, they called the pale-skinned, frail men *haole* because they looked so out of breath. In Hawaiian, *ha* means breath, and *ole* means an absence of what precedes it. In other words, a lifeless-looking person.

Today, the term *haole* is generally a synonym for Caucasian or foreigner and is used casually without intending to cause any disrespect. However, if uttered by an angry stranger who adds certain adjectives like stupid or dumb, the term haole can be construed as a mild racial slur.

THE HAWAIIAN LANGUAGE

Almost everyone here speaks English, so except for pronouncing place names, you should have no trouble communicating in Hawaii. Many folks in Hawaii now speak Hawaiian, for the ancient language is making a comeback. Everybody who visits Hawaii, in fact, will soon hear the words *aloha, mahalo, wahine,* and *kane.* If you've just arrived, you're a *malihini.* Someone who's been here a long time is a *kamaaina.*

When you finish a job or your meal, you are *pau* (over). On Friday it's *pau hana,* work over. You put *pupus* (that's Hawaii's version of hors d'oeuvres) in your mouth when you go *pau hana.* Pupus are easier to spell—and eat.

The Hawaiian alphabet, created by the New England missionaries, has only 12 letters—the five regular vowels (a, e, i, o, and u) and seven consonants (h, k, l, m, n, p, and w). The vowels are pronounced in the Roman fashion—

Real Hawaiian Style

With 25 different ethnic groups, including the largest Asian mix in the United States, Hawaii has a real diffusion of styles and cultures. Yet out of this rich melange there emerges a distinct Hawaiian style. Sooner or later everyone, even the visitor, picks up on it and puts it into practice. It's speech, body language, local habits, and a way of life that distinguishes those who live in the islands from those who visit.

It's a mix of surfer, Hawaii hang-loose, traditional Chinese, and coastal haole. There's Aloha Friday (every Friday), pidgin ('Eh fo' real, brah), and the shaka greeting (stick out your pinky and thumb, pull in your three middle fingers, and shake—hang loose, brah).

People from Hawaii stand in line at noon to order plate lunches, ask for "two scoops rice," like to eat Spam, and drink Budweiser beer. They seldom honk their car horns (it's considered rude). They're all comfortable eating with chopsticks. They barbecue in public beach parks, and hold baby luaus for kids when they turn 1 year old.

They vote Democrat, check the surf report on "Good Morning Hawaii," listen to Hawaiian music on KCCN, and register their opinion on The Hawaii Poll. They worry about the high cost of housing and the loss of jobs. They wear shower sandals known as *zoris* outdoors but never indoors, and they often go barefoot. They specify "aloha attire" at the funeral when their *tutu* (grandmother) dies.

Some young men wear queues—the long plait of hair hanging down their backs that their Asian grandfathers gladly shed—as a sign of ethnic pride. Some now wear the traditional Polynesian zigzag tattoos that English sailors first saw in Tahiti in 1767.

Although women in old Hawaii went topless, young women today wear the long muumuu dresses introduced by the missionaries. Today, the only bare breasts you'll see are on nude beaches, which technically are illegal, but never mind that.

Everyone wears flowers, in their hair or around their neck. Men and women often tuck a single blossom over their ear. It's very Polynesian, and a clue to your current status with the opposite sex: Over the right ear means available, over the left means spoken for.

Make eye contact and say hello by raising your eyebrows with a smile. That's Hawaiian-style. Try it—it works.

that is, *ah, ay, ee, oh,* and *oo* (as in "too")—not *ay, ee, eye, oh,* and *you,* as in English. For example, *huhu* is pronounced "who-who." Almost all vowels are sounded separately, although some are pronounced together, as in Kalakaua: *Kah-lah-cow-ah.*

PIDGIN 'EH FO' REAL, BRAH

As you get to know Hawaii, you'll reach beyond "aloha" and "mahalo" and discover words like *da kine,* a ubiquitous multipurpose term that can mean "that thing over there," or the "whatchamacallit," or "the very best," as in "when you care enough to send da kine card." *Da kine* is a word from Hawaii's other native tongue: pidgin English.

Pidgin developed as a means for sugar planters to communicate with their Chinese laborers in the 1800s. Today pidgin is spoken by those who grew up in Hawaii to communicate with their peers. It's a manner of speaking that

A Hawaiian Primer

Here are basic Hawaiian words, with their English meanings, which you will hear often in Hawaii and see throughout this book:

ali'i Hawaiian royalty

aloha Greeting or farewell

Ewa In the direction of Ewa, an Oahu town; generally meaning west ("Drive Ewa 5 miles")

hala The pandanus tree, the leaves of which are used for weaving

halau School

hale House or building

haole Foreigner, Caucasian

heiau Hawaiian temple or place of worship

holoholo To have fun, relax

hoolaulea Celebration

hui A club, assembly

hula Native dance

imu Underground oven lined with hot rocks, used for cooking the luau pig

kahili Royal standard of red and yellow feathers

kahuna Priest or expert

kalua To bake underground in the imu (as in kalua pig)

kamaaina Old-timer

kanaka maoli Native Hawaiians

kane Man

kapa Tapa, bark cloth

kapu Taboo, forbidden

keiki Child

kokua Help, cooperate

kumu hula Teacher of Hawaiian dance

kupuna An elder with leadership qualities who commands great respect; grandparent

lanai Porch or veranda

lei Garland

lomilomi Massage

luau Feast

mahalo Thank you

makai A direction, toward the sea

malihini Stranger, newcomer

malo Loincloth

mana Spirit power

mauka Direction, toward the mountains

mele Song or chant

muumuu Loose-fitting gown or dress

nene Official state bird, a goose

ohana Family

ono Delicious

pahu Drum

pali Cliff

pau Finished, done

poi Crushed taro root, made into a starchy paste

pupu Hors d'oeuvre

wahine Woman

---

seems to endure despite efforts to suppress it. At a local ball game, fans may shout **"Geevum!"** (Give 'em). A ruffled clerk may tell her friend someone gave her **"stink eye"** (a dirty look). **"No huhu"** (don't get mad), soothes the friend. You could be invited to hear an elder **"talk story"** (relating memories) or to enjoy local treats like **"shave ice"** (tropical snow cone) and **"crack seed"** (highly seasoned preserved fruit). Local residents also punctuate their speech by inserting a word like "yeah" into sentences for emphasis, or as a segue meaning "do you know what I mean?" For example: "Got to be there 6am, you know. Junk, yeah? Maybe humbug, but, boss's speech, 'ats why." This translates into: "I've got to be there by 6am. It's too bad, isn't it? It's an inconvenience, but the boss is giving a speech."

Action words undergo a kind of poetic squeeze, so that each has a lot of different meanings. Take the word **"broke."** It's immortalized in the most famous pidgin phrase of all—the motto of the 442nd Infantry Battalion, World War II's fearless band of Japanese-American heroes from Hawaii and California who risked their lives to prove their loyalty: "Go For Broke." Then there's **"wen' go broke"** (something got busted or torn, or simply stopped). **"Broke da mouth"** (tastes really good) is the favorite pidgin phrase of Dr. Derek Bickerton, professor of linguistics at University of Hawaii, who teaches a course on Creole languages. He says Hawaiian pidgin is more than a makeshift list of sing-song terms used to bridge a language gap. Over decades, a real Creole language developed with its own order and syntax, relying not only on English and Hawaiian but borrowing words and some grammar from several languages—Japanese, Chinese, Filipino, Portuguese, and the tongues of all the other ethnic groups who came to work the sugarcane fields a century ago.

Today, although the plantations are gone, the next generations and the new immigrants continue the pidgin tradition in their own way. However, modern pressures may be driving pidgin underground. Pure pidgin speakers these days tend to be older people in remote areas. Visitors to Waikiki will be lucky to hear the real thing at all.

A FEW MORE PIDGIN WORDS & PHRASES

'owzit!   How's it?
laters   See you later
chance em   Go for it
moah bettah   The best
cheeken skeen   Goosebumps
Eh, fo' real, brah   It's true, brother.

4 A Taste of Hawaii

by Jocelyn Fujii

TRIED & TRUE: HAWAII REGIONAL CUISINE

There's talk that Indian food is the next wave, and fusion is a been-there-done-that. Not so—not yet in Hawaii. Hawaii's leading chefs may be tempering their zeal for east-meets-west flavorings and techniques, but the regional style of using fresh ingredients from land and sea remains firmly rooted and is growing.

Chefs predict seafood bars, red meat, vegetarian and health-conscious food, and Indian cookery as some of the new directions of the year. *Simplify* is the word of the season. But Hawaii's tried-and-true baseline remains Hawaii regional cuisine (HRC), established in the mid-1980s as a culinary revolution that catapulted Hawaii into the global epicurean arena. The international training, creative vigor, fresh ingredients, and cross-cultural menus of the 12 original HRC chefs have made the islands a culinary destination applauded and emulated nationwide. (In a tip of the toque to island tradition, "ahi"—a word ubiquitous in Hawaii—has replaced "tuna" on many chic New York menus.) And options have proliferated at all levels of the local dining spectrum: Waves of new Asian residents have planted the food traditions of their homelands in the fertile soil of Hawaii, resulting in unforgettable taste treats true to their Thai, Vietnamese, Japanese, Chinese, and Indo-Pacific roots. Like the peoples of Hawaii, traditions are mixed and matched as well—and when combined with the bountiful, fresh harvests from sea and land for which Hawaii is known, these ethnic and culinary traditions take on renewed vigor and a cross-cultural, uniquely Hawaiian quality.

A decade ago, visitors could expect to find frozen mahi-mahi beurre blanc with frozen or canned vegetables as the premium dish on a fine-dining menu in Hawaii. But not anymore. It's a whole new world in Hawaii's restaurant kitchens.

Today, you can expect to encounter Indonesian sates, Chinese stir-frys, Polynesian imu-baked foods, and guava-smoked meats in sophisticated presentations in the state's finest dining rooms. If there's pasta or risotto or rack of lamb on the menu, it could be *nori* (seaweed) linguine with *opihi* (limpet sauce), or risotto with local seafood served in taro cups, or a rack of lamb in Cabernet and hoisin sauce (fermented soybean, garlic, and spices), or with macadamia nuts and coconut.

It has been called many things: Euro-Asian, Pacific Rim, Pacific Edge, Euro-Pacific, Fusion cuisine, Hapa cuisine. By whatever name, Hawaii regional cuisine has evolved as Hawaii's singular cooking style, what some say is the last American regional cuisine, this country's final gastronomic, as well as geographic, frontier. This style of cooking highlights the fresh seafood and produce of Hawaii's rich waters and volcanic soil, the cultural traditions of Hawaii's ethnic groups, and the skills of well-trained chefs—such as Roy Yamaguchi (Roy's on Oahu, Big Island, Maui, and Kauai), Peter Merriman (Merriman's on the Big Island), and Jean-Marie Josselin (A Pacific Cafe on Kauai, Maui, and Oahu)—who broke ranks with their European predecessors to forge new ground in the 50th state.

Fresh ingredients are foremost, and farmers, ranchers and fishermen work together to provide steady supplies of just-harvested seafood, seaweed, fern shoots, vine-ripened tomatoes, goat cheese, lamb, herbs, taro, gourmet lettuces, and countless harvests from land and sea that wind up in myriad forms on ever-changing menus, prepared in Asian and Western culinary styles.

Fresh fruit salsas and sauces (mango, lychee, papaya, pineapple, guava), ginger-sesame-wasabi flavorings, corn cakes with sake sauces, tamarind and fish sauces, coconut-chili accents, tropical-fruit vinaigrettes, and other local and newly arrived seasonings from Southeast Asia and the Pacific impart unique qualities to the preparations.

Here's a sampling of what you can expect to find on a Hawaii regional menu: seared Hawaiian fish with lilikoi shrimp butter; tiger shrimp in *sake-uni* (sea urchin) beurre blanc; taro cakes and Pahoa corn cakes; Molokai sweet-potato vichychoisse; Ka'u orange sauce and Kahua Ranch lamb; pot stickers with ginger sauce; fern shoots from Waipio Valley; Maui onion soup and Hawaiian bouillabaisse, with fresh snapper, Kona crab, and fresh aquacultured shrimp; and gourmet Waimanalo greens, picked that day. With menus that often change daily and the unquenchable appetites that the leading chefs have for cooking on the edge, the possibilities for once-in-a-lifetime dining adventures are more available than ever in Hawaii.

PLATE LUNCHES & MORE LOCAL FOOD

Although Hawaii regional cuisine has put Hawaii on the epicurean map, at the other end of the spectrum is the cuisine of the hoi polloi, the vast and endearing world of "local food." By that we mean plate lunches and poke, shave ice and saimin, bento lunches and manapua, cultural hybrids all.

Reflecting a polyglot population of many styles and ethnicities, Hawaii's idiosyncratic dining scene is eminently inclusive. Consider Surfer Chic: barefoot in the sand, in swimsuit, chowing down on a plate lunch ordered from a lunch wagon, consisting of fried mahi-mahi, "two scoops rice," macaroni salad, and a few leaves of green, typically julienned cabbage. (Generally, teriyaki beef or shoyu chicken are options.) Greasy gravy is often the condiment of choice, accompanied by a soft drink in a paper cup. Like saimin—the local version of noodles in broth topped with scrambled egg, green onions, and sometimes pork—the plate lunch is Hawaii's version of high camp.

Because this is Hawaii, at least a few licks of *poi,* the Hawaiian staple of cooked, pounded taro, and the other examples of indigenous cuisine are de rigeuer, if not at a corny luau, then at least in a Hawaiian plate lunch. The native samplers include foods from before and after Western contact, such as *lau-lau* (pork, chicken, or fish steamed in ti leaves), *kalua* pork (pork cooked in a Polynesian underground oven known here as an *imu*), *lomi* salmon (salted salmon with onions, tomatoes, and green onions), chicken long rice, squid *luau* (octopus cooked in coconut milk and taro tops), *poke* (cubed raw fish seasoned with onions and seaweed and the occasional sprinkling of roasted *kukui* nuts), *haupia* (creamy coconut pudding), and *kulolo* (steamed pudding of coconut, brown sugar, and taro).

Bento, another popular choice for the dine-and-dash set, is also available throughout Hawaii. The compact, boxed assortment of picnic fare usually consists of neatly arranged sections of rice, pickled vegetables, and fried chicken, beef, or pork. The bento is a derivative of the "kau kau tin" that served as the modest lunch box for Japanese immigrants who labored in the sugar and pineapple fields. Today you'll find bentos dispensed ubiquitously throughout Hawaii, from department stores like Daiei and Shirokiya (bento bonanzas) to corner delis and supermarkets.

Also from the plantations come *manapua,* a bready, doughy round with tasty fillings of sweetened pork or sweet beans. In the old days, the Chinese "manapua man" would make his rounds in the camps and villages with bamboo containers balanced on a rod over his shoulders. Today you'll find white or whole-wheat manapua containing chicken, vegetables, curry, and other savory fillings.

The daintier Chinese delicacy, dim sum, is made of translucent wrappers filled with fresh seafood, pork hash, and vegetables, served for breakfast and lunch in Chinatown restaurants. The Hong Kong–style dumplings are ordered fresh and hot from bamboo steamers from invariably brusque servers who move their carts from table to table. Much like hailing a taxi in Manhattan, you have to be quick and loud for dim sum.

TASTY TREATS: SHAVE ICE & MALASSADAS

For dessert or a snack, particularly in Haleiwa, the prevailing choice is shave ice, the island version of a snow cone. At places like Matsumoto Store in Haleiwa, particularly on hot, humid days, long lines of shave ice lovers gather for their cones of rainbow-colored, finely shaved ice topped with sweet tropical syrups. The fast-melting mounds require prompt, efficient consumption and are quite the local summer ritual for sweet tooths. Aficionados order shave ice with ice cream and sweetened azuki beans plopped in the middle.

You may also encounter malassadas, the Portuguese version of a doughnut, and if you do, it's best to eat them immediately. A left-over malassada has all the appeal of a heavy, lumpy, cold doughnut. When fresh and hot, however, as at school carnivals (where they attract the longest lines), or at bakeries and roadside stands (such as Agnes Portuguese Bake Shop in Kailua), the sugary, yeasty doughnut-without-a-hole is enjoyed by many as one of the enduring legacies of the Portuguese in Hawaii.

Ahi, Ono & Opakapaka:
A Hawaiian Seafood Primer

The fresh seafood in Hawaii has been described as the best in the world. In the pivotal book, *The New Cuisine of Hawaii* by Janice Wald Henderson, acclaimed chef Nobuyuki Matsuhisa (chef-owner of Matsuhisa in Beverly Hills and Nobu in Manhattan) wrote, "As a chef who specializes in fresh seafood, I am in awe of the quality of Hawaii's fish; it is unparalleled anywhere else in the world." Without doubt, the surrounding waters, the waters of the Northwestern Hawaiian Islands, and a growing aquaculture industry are fertile grounds for this most important of Hawaii's food resources.

The reputable restaurants in Hawaii buy fresh fish daily at predawn auctions or from local fishermen. Some chefs even spearfish their ingredients themselves. "Still wiggling" is the ultimate term for freshness in Hawaii. The fish can then be grilled over *kiawe* (mesquite) or prepared in innumerable ways.

Although most menus include the western description for the fresh fish used, most often the local nomenclature is listed, turning dinner for the uninitiated into a confusing, quasi-foreign experience. To help familiarize you with the menu language of Hawaii, here's a basic glossary of island fish:

Ahi: Yellowfin or bigeye tuna, important for its use in sashimi and poke, at sushi bars, and in Hawaii regional cuisine.

Aku: Skipjack tuna, frequently used by local families in home cooking and poke.

Ehu: Red snapper, delicate and sumptuous, yet lesser known than opakapaka (see below).

Hapuupuu: Grouper, a sea bass whose use is expanding from ethnic to nonethnic restaurants.

Hebi: Spearfish, mildly flavored and frequently featured as the "catch of the day" in upscale restaurants.

PINEAPPLES, PAPAYAS & OTHER FRESH ISLAND FRUITS

Lanai isn't growing pineapples commercially anymore, but low-acid, white-fleshed, wondrously sweet Hawaiian Sugarloaf pineapples are being commercially grown, on a small scale, on Kauai as well as the Big Island.

That is just one of the developments in a rapidly changing agricultural scene in Hawaii, where the lychee-like Southeast Asian rambutan; longan (Chinese dragon's-eye lychees); 80-pound Indian jackfruits; starfruit; luscious, custardy mangosteen; and the usual mangoes, papayas, guava, and *lilikoi* (passion fruit) make up the dazzling array of fresh island fruit that come and go with the seasons.

Papayas, bananas, and pineapples grow year-round, but pineapples are always sweetest, juiciest, and yellowest in the summer. While new papaya hybrids are making their way into the marketplace, the classic bests include the fleshy, firm-textured Kahuku papayas, the queen of them all; the Big Island's sweet Kapoho and Puna papayas; and the fragile, juicy, and red Sunrise papayas from Kauai. Apple bananas are smaller, firmer, and tarter than the

Kajiki: Pacific blue marlin, also called *au*, with firm flesh and high fat content that make it a plausible substitute for tuna in some raw fish dishes and as a grilled item on menus.

Kumu: Goatfish, a luxury item on Chinese and upscale menus, served en papillote or steamed whole, Oriental-style, with sesame oil, scallions, ginger, and garlic.

Mahi-mahi: Dolphinfish (the gamefish, not the mammal) or dorado, a classic sweet, white-fleshed fish requiring vigilance among purists because it is often disguised as fresh when it's actually "fresh-frozen"—a big difference.

Monchong: Bigscale or sickle pomfret, an exotic, tasty fish, scarce but gaining a higher profile on island menus.

Nairagi: Striped marlin, also called *au;* good as sashimi and in poke, and often substituted for ahi in raw fish products.

Onaga: Ruby snapper, a luxury fish, versatile, moist, and flaky; top-of-the-line.

Ono: Wahoo, firmer and drier than the snappers, often served grilled and in sandwiches.

Opah: Moonfish, rich and fatty, versatile; used cooked, raw, smoked, and broiled.

Opakapaka: Pink snapper, light, flaky, and luxurious, suited for sashimi, poaching, sautéeing, and baking; the best-known upscale fish.

Papio: Jack trevally, light, firm, and flavorful, and favored in island cookery.

Shutome: Broadbill swordfish, of beeflike texture and rich flavor.

Tombo: Albacore tuna, with a high fat content, suitable for grilling and sautéeing.

Uhu: Parrotfish, most often encountered steamed, Chinese style.

Uku: Gray snapper of clear, pale-pink flesh, delicately flavored and moist.

Ulua: Large jack trevally, firm-fleshed and versatile.

standard and are a local specialty among the dozens of varieties (20 types grow wild) that flourish throughout the Islands.

Lychees and mangoes are long-awaited summer fruit. Mangoes begin appearing in late spring or early summer and can be found at roadside fruit stands in windward Oahu, at Chinatown markets, and at health food stores, where the high prices may shock you. A favorite is the white pirie, rare and resiny, fiberless, and so sweet and juicy it makes the high-profile Hayden seem prosaic. White piries are difficult to find but occasionally appear, along with lychees and other coveted seasonal fruit, at the Maunakea Marketplace in Chinatown or at Paradise Produce Company nearby.

Molokai watermelons are a summer hit and the best watermelons in the state. But Kahuku watermelons, available from stands along Oahu's North Shore roadside in the summer months, give them a run for their money; they're juicy and sweet, and the season is woefully short-lived.

In the competitive world of oranges, the Kau Gold navel oranges from southern Big island put Sunkist to shame. Grown in the volcanic soil and sunny conditions of the South Point region (the southernmost point in the United States), the oranges, a winter crop, are brown, rough, and anything but pretty. But the browner and uglier they are, the sweeter and juicier. Because the thin-skinned oranges are tree-ripened, they're fleshy and heavy with liquid, and will spoil you for life.

If you're eager to sample the newly developed crops of South American and Southeast Asian fruit with unpronounceable names that are appearing in island cuisine, check out Frankie's Nursery in Waimanalo. It's the hot spot of exotic fruit, *the* place to sate your curiosity and your palate.

5 The Natural World: An Environmental Guide to the Islands

by Jeanette Foster

The Oahu of today—with its crescent-shaped coves gently encircling azure water, thundering waterfalls exploding into cavernous pools, and vibrant rainbows arching through the early morning mist—differs dramatically from the island that came into being at the dawn of time.

Born of violent volcanic eruptions from deep beneath the ocean's surface, the first Hawaiian islands emerged about 70 million years ago—more than 200 million years after the major continental land masses had been formed. Two thousand miles from the nearest continent, Mother Nature's fury began to carve beauty from barren rock. Untiring volcanoes spewed forth curtains of fire that cooled into stone. Severe tropical storms, some with hurricane-force winds, battered and blasted the cooling lava rock into a series of shapes. Ferocious earthquakes flattened, shattered, and reshaped the islands into precipitous valleys, jagged cliffs, and recumbent flatlands. Monstrous surf and gigantic tidal waves rearranged and polished the lands above and below the reaches of the tide.

A geological youngster, Oahu itself was formed only 3 to 5 million years ago, when the Waianae volcano spewed lava above the ocean's surface. It continued to erupt until 2½ million years ago; erosion and other climatic forces then went to task on it until only a crescent-shaped piece on its eastern rim, now known as the Waianae Range, remained. Nearby, between 1 and 3 million years later, the Koolau volcano erupted. The series of new eruptions created the plateau between the two volcanoes, which eventually became the flat central part of Oahu. Finally, about 1.1 million years ago, several cone-building eruptions began on the southeast end of the young island. The cones remaining after the eruptions (which ended around 31,000 years ago) can be seen today: **Diamond Head, Koko Head, Koko Crater,** and **Hanauma Bay.**

It took many more years to chisel the dramatic cliffs of the west and east ends of the island, to form the majestic peak of **Mt. Kaala,** to cut the deep ridges through which waterfalls flow on the north side of the island, to form the reefs of Hanauma Bay, and to shape the coral-sand beaches that ring Oahu. The result is an island like no other on the planet—a tropical dream rich in unique flora and fauna, surrounded by a vibrant underwater world, and covered with a landscape that will stay in your memory forever.

THE LANDSCAPE

Oahu, the island where the major metropolis of Honolulu is located, is the third largest island in the Hawaiian archipelago (after the Big Island and Maui). It's also the most urban, with a resident population of nearly 850,000; in fact, nearly half the population of the entire state of Hawaii resides in just one quarter of Oahu—in Honolulu and Waikiki. Pearl Harbor, with its naturally deep waters, is the key to Oahu's dominant position in the state. Ancient Hawaiians using outrigger canoes could maneuver easily in fairly shallow waters, but European ships, with deep keels, needed a deep-draft harbor. Pearl Harbor was perfect: It has three deep lochs, which are actually river valleys gouged out during the ice age when the sea level was lower.

The island, which is 40 miles long by 26 miles wide, is ringed by more than 130 sandy beaches and defined by two mountain ranges: the **Waianae Ridge** (Mt. Kaala, at 4,050 feet, is the highest point on the island) in the west, and in the east, the jagged **Koolaus,** which form a backdrop for the city of Honolulu. These two ranges divide the island into three different environments. The Koolaus, with their spectacular peaks, fluted columns, lone spires, and steep verdant valleys, keep the naturally rainy windward side of the island lush and beautiful with tropical vegetation and flowing waterfalls. Mist frequently forms around the peaks like an ethereal lei, rainbows sprout from the sky, and continuous but gentle rain blesses the land. On the other side of the island, the area between the Waianae Range and the ocean (known as the leeward side) is drier; it has an arid landscape with little rainfall and sparse vegetation. Powdery sand beaches, one after another, line the shoreline. Perpetually sunny days and big, thundering surf mark the Waianae coastline.

In between the two mountain ranges lies the **central valley,** moderate in temperature and vibrant with tropical plants and verdant agricultural fields. Because this area was formerly used for agricultural and military purposes, widespread residential development is relatively new. With the demise of the sugarcane and pineapple industries, the skyrocketing real estate prices, and the overall shortage of space on Oahu, the central plain has become an attractive suburban alternative, and this part of Oahu is now burgeoning with homes.

Not only is Oahu surrounded by water, but water permeates the landscape. Natural lakes and man-made reservoirs supply water to sustain life, but also to provide recreational opportunities, especially for fishing enthusiasts. Streams abound on the island, and many have waterfalls, from Sacred Falls' spectacular cascades to the gentle, meandering Nuuanu Stream, which feeds into the "Jackass Ginger" swimming hole.

Hawaii's most well-known area, **Waikiki,** which lies along the western end of the island's southern coast, hasn't always been home to the soft sand and swaying palms that are its trademarks. In fact, its name, which means "spouting water," came from the gushing springwaters that kept the area a perpetual swamp. Until the 1920s, Waikiki was populated by noisy ducks, enormous toads, and other water creatures that inhabited the area's fishponds; damp taro patches; and waterlogged rice paddies. But in 1922, the swamps were drained to make way for the Waikiki reclamation project. Sand was imported to create the "Waikiki Beach" we see today. Anchoring one end of Waikiki Beach is Oahu's world-famous symbol, Diamond Head. The Hawaiians called this crater *lae'ahi,* which means brow (*lea*) of the *ahi* fish. Some years later, mapmakers shortened this name to *Leahi.* Today, we call the crater Diamond Head because some British sailors in 1825, who had perhaps overindulged in liquid libations during shore leave, mistakenly thought that the glittering—but worthless—calcite crystals they found in the crater were diamonds. Despite their error, the name stuck.

THE FLORA OF OAHU

The Oahu of today radiates with sweet-smelling flowers, lush vegetation, and exotic plant life. To help you identify some of the plants you'll see on the island, consult *Flowers of Hawaii* (World Wide Distributors) by Amy

Hamaishi; *Hawaii's Flowering Trees* (Island Heritage Press); *Hawaiian Flowers and Flowering Trees* (Tuttle Publishing) by Lorraine Kuck and Richard Togg; and *Plants and Flowers of Hawaii* (University of Hawaii Press) by S.H. Sohmer and R. Gustafson.

Some of the more memorable trees, plants, and flowers on the islands include:

AFRICAN TULIP TREES   Even at a long distance, you can see the flaming red flowers on these large trees, which can grow over 50 feet tall. Children love the trees because the buds hold water—they use them as water pistols.

ANGEL'S TRUMPET   This is a small tree that can grow up to 20 feet tall, with an abundance of large pendants (up to 10 inches in diameter)—white or pink flowers that resemble, well, trumpets. The Hawaiians call this *nana-honua,* which means "earth gazing." The flowers, which bloom continually from early spring to late fall, have a musky scent. However, beware: All parts of the plant are poisonous, and all parts contain a strong narcotic.

ANTHURIUMS   One of Hawaii's most popular cut flowers, anthuriums originally came from the tropical Americas and the Caribbean islands. There are more than 550 species, but the most popular are the heart-shaped flowers (red, orange, pink, white, even purple) with a tail-like spath (green, orange, pink, red, white, purple, and in combinations thereof). Look for the heart-shaped green leaves in shaded areas. These exotic plants have no scent, but will last several weeks in a vase.

BANYANS   Among the world's largest trees, banyans have branches that grow out and away from the main trunk. These branches form descending roots that grow down to the ground to form and feed additional trunks, making the tree very stable during tropical storms.

BIRD OF PARADISE   This native of Africa has become something of a trademark of Hawaii. It is easily recognizable by the orange and blue flowers nestled in gray-green bracts, looking somewhat like birds in flight.

BOUGAINVILLEA   Originally from Brazil and named for the French navigator Louis A. de Bougainville, these colorful, tissue-thin bracts (ranging in color from majestic purple to fiery orange) hide tiny white flowers.

BROMELIADS   The pineapple plant is the best known bromeliad. Native to tropical South America and the Caribbean islands, there are more than 1,400 species. "Bromes," as they are affectionately called, are generally spiky plants ranging in size from a few inches to several feet in diameter. They're popular not only for their unusual foliage but also for their strange and wonderful flowers. The flowers range from colorful spikes to delicate blossoms resembling orchids. Bromeliads are widely used in landscaping and as interior decoration, particularly in resort areas like Waikiki.

GINGERS   Some of Hawaii's most fragrant flowers are white and yellow gingers (which the Hawaiians call *'awapuhi-ke'oke'o* and *'awapuhi-melemele*). Usually found in clumps, growing 4- to 7-feet tall, in the areas blessed by rain, these sweet-smelling, 3-inch wide flowers are composed of three dainty petal-like stamen and three long, thin petals. White and yellow gingers are so prolific that many people assume they are native to Hawaii; actually, they were introduced in the 19th century from the Indo-Malaysia area. Look for yellow and white gingers from late spring to fall. If you see them on the side of the road, stop and pick a few blossoms—your car will be filled with a divine fragrance for the rest of the day. The only downside of white and yellow gingers is that, once picked, they stay fresh for only a short time.

Other members of the ginger family frequently seen on Oahu (there are some 700 species) include red ginger, shell ginger, and torch ginger. Red ginger consists of tall, green stalks with foot-long red "flower heads." The red "petals" are actually bracts; inch-long white flowers are protected by the bracts and can be seen if you look down into the red head. Red ginger ('awapuhi-'ula'ula in Hawaiian), which unfortunately does not share the heavenly smell of white ginger, lasts a week or longer when cut. Look for red ginger from spring through late fall. Cool, wet mountain forests provide ideal conditions for shell ginger; Hawaiians called it 'awapuhi-luheluhe, which means "drooping" ginger. Natives of India and Burma, these plants, with their pearly white, clam shell–like blossoms, bloom from spring to fall.

Perhaps the most exotic gingers are the red or pink torch gingers. Cultivated in Malaysia as seasoning (the young flower shoots are used in curries), torch ginger rises directly out of the ground; the flower stalks (which are about 5 to 8 inches in length) resemble the fire of a lighted torch. One of the few gingers that can bloom year-round, the Hawaiians call this plant 'awapuhi-ko'oko'o, or "walking-stick" ginger.

HELICONIAS   Some 80 species of the colorful heliconia family came to Hawaii from the Caribbean and Central and South America. The brightly colored bracts (yellow, red, green, orange, etc.) overlap and appear to unfold like origami birds as they climb up (or down, as heliconias have both erect and pendant bracts). The most obvious heliconia to spot is the lobster claw, which resembles a string of boiled crustacean pincers—the brilliant crimson bracts alternate on the stem. Another prolific heliconia is the parrot's beak. Growing to about hip height, the parrot's beak is composed of bright-orange flower bracts with black tips, not unlike the beak of a parrot. Look for parrot's beak in the spring and summer, when it blooms in profusion.

HIBISCUS   One variety of this year-round blossom is the official state flower: the yellow hibiscus. The 4- to 6-inch hibiscus flowers come in a range of colors, from lily-white to lipstick-red. The flowers resemble crepe paper, with stamens and pistils protruding spirelike from the center. Hibiscus hedges can grow up to 15 feet tall. Once plucked, the flowers wither quickly.

JACARANDA   Beginning about March and sometimes lasting until early May, these huge, lacy-leaved trees metamorphose into large clusters of spectacular lavender-blue sprays. The bell-shaped flowers drop quickly, leaving a majestic purple carpet beneath the tree.

MARIJUANA   Also known as *pakalolo* ("crazy weed" in Hawaiian), this plant is illegally cultivated throughout the islands. You probably won't see it as you drive along the roads, but if you go hiking, you may glimpse the feathery green leaves with tight clusters of buds. Despite years of police effort to eradicate the plant, the illegal industry continues. Don't be tempted to pick a few buds, as the purveyors of this nefarious industry don't take kindly to poaching.

MONKEYPOD TREES   One of Hawaii's most majestic trees, they grow more than 80 feet tall and 100 feet across and are often seen near older homes and in parks. The leaves of the monkeypod drop in February and March. The wood from the tree is a favorite of woodworking artisans.

NIGHT-BLOOMING CEREUS   Look along rock walls for this spectacular night-blooming cactus flower. Originally from Central America, this vinelike member of the cactus family has green scalloped edges and produces foot-long white flowers that open as darkness falls and wither as the sun rises. The plant also bears a red fruit that is edible.

ORCHIDS   In many minds, nothing says Hawaii more than orchids, yet the orchid family is the largest in the entire plant kingdom, and orchids are found in most parts of the world. There are some species native to Hawaii, but they're inconspicuous in most places, so people often overlook them. The most widely grown orchid—and the major source of flowers for leis and garnish for tropical libations—is the vanda orchid. The vandas used in Hawaii's commercial flower industry are generally lavender or white, but they grow in a rainbow of colors, shapes, and sizes. The orchids used for corsages are the large, delicate cattleya; the ones used in floral arrangements—you'll probably see them in your hotel lobby—are usually dendrobiums.

PLUMERIA   Also known as frangipani, this sweet-smelling, five-petal flower, found in clusters on trees, is the most popular choice of lei makers. The Singapore plumeria has five creamy-white petals, with a touch of yellow in the center. Another popular variety, ruba—with flowers from soft pink to flaming red—is also used in making leis. When picking plumeria, be careful of the sap from the flower, as it is poisonous and can stain clothes.

PROTEAS   Originally from South Africa, this unusual plant comes in more than 40 different varieties. Proteas are shrubs that bloom into a range of flower types. Different species of proteas range from those resembling pincushions to a species that looks just like a bouquet of feathers. Proteas are long-lasting as cut flowers, and once dried, they last for years.

TARO   Around pools, streams, and in neatly planted fields, you'll see the green heart-shaped leaves of taro. Taro was a staple for ancient Hawaiians, who pounded the root into poi. Originally from Sri Lanka, taro is grown not only as a food crop, but also as an ornamental.

FRUIT TREES

BANANA   Edible bananas are among the oldest of the world's food crops. By the time Europeans arrived in the islands, the Hawaiians had more than 40 different types of bananas planted. Most banana plants have long green leaves hanging from the tree, with the flower giving way to fruit in clusters.

BREADFRUIT   A large tree—over 60 feet tall—with broad, sculpted, dark-green leaves. The fruit is round and about 6 inches or more in diameter. The ripe fruit, a staple in the Hawaiian diet, is whitish-yellow.

LYCHEE   This evergreen tree, which can grow to well over 30 feet across, originated in China. Small flowers grow into panicles about a foot long in June and July. The round, red-skinned fruit appears shortly afterward.

MANGO   From the Indo-Malaysian area comes the delicious mango, a fruit with peachlike flesh. Mango season usually begins in the spring and lasts through the summer, depending on the variety. The trees can grow to more than 100 feet tall. The tiny reddish flowers give way to a green fruit that turns red-yellow when ripe. Some people enjoy unripe mangoes, sliced thin or in chutney as a traditional Indian preparation. Be careful, because the mango sap can cause a skin rash on some people.

PAPAYA   Yellow pear-shaped fruit (when ripe) found at the base of the large, scalloped-shaped leaves on a pedestal-like, nonbranched tree. Papayas ripen year-round.

THE FAUNA OF OAHU

When the Polynesians from the Society Islands arrived in Hawaii, around A.D. 1000, they found only two endemic mammals: the **hoary bat** and the **monk seal.** The Hawaiian monk seal, a relative of warm-water seals previously found in the Caribbean and Mediterranean, was nearly slaughtered into extinction for its skin and oil during the 19th century. Recently, these seals have experienced a minor population explosion in a few of their haunts, forcing relocation of some males from their protected homes in the inlets north of the main Hawaiian Islands. Periodically, these endangered marine mammals turn up at beaches throughout the state. They are protected under federal law by the Marine Mammals Protection Act. If you're fortunate enough to see a monk seal, just look; don't disturb one of Hawaii's living treasures.

What's perhaps even more astonishing is what the first Polynesians didn't find—there were no reptiles, amphibians, mosquitoes, lice, fleas, not even a cockroach. They did bring a few creatures from home: dogs, pigs, and chickens (all were for eating). A stowaway on board the Polynesian sailing canoes was the rat. Oahu still has feral goats and wild pigs, which generally make a nuisance of themselves by destroying the rainforest and eating native plants. Non-native game birds (ring-neck pheasants, green pheasants, Erkel's francolins, Japanese quail, spotted doves, and zebra doves) are also found on Oahu.

The Hawaiian islands have only one tiny earthworm-like snake. Strict measures are taken to keep other snakes out of Hawaii. On the island of Guam, the brown tree snake has obliterated most of the bird population. Officials in Hawaii are well aware of this danger to Hawaii and are vigilant to prevent snakes from entering the state.

Two non-native creatures that visitors to Oahu are likely to see are the following:

GECKOS These harmless, soft-skinned, insect-eating lizards come equipped with suction pads on their feet, enabling them to climb walls and windows so they can reach tasty insects like mosquitoes and cockroaches. You'll see them on windows outside a lighted room at night or hear their cheerful chirp.

MONGOOSES The mongoose is a mistake. It was brought here in the 19th century to counteract the ever-growing rat problem. But rats are nocturnal creatures, sleeping during the day and wandering at night. Mongooses are day creatures. Instead of getting rid of the rat problem, the mongooses eat bird eggs, contributing to the deterioration of the native bird population in Hawaii.

BIRDS

The inspiration for the first Polynesian voyages to Hawaii may have come from the **Kolea,** or Pacific golden plover—a homely speckled bird that migrates from Siberia and Alaska every year, traveling through Hawaii and down to the Marquesas, Tahiti, and New Zealand. Historians wonder if the Marquesans, watching the birds arrive and depart, speculated where they came from and what that place was like. When the first Marquesans arrived in Hawaii between A.D. 500 and 800, scientists say they found 67 varieties of endemic Hawaiian birds, a third of which are now believed to be extinct, including the *koloa* (the Hawaiian duck).

In the past 200 years, more native species of birds have become extinct in the Hawaiian Islands than anywhere else on the planet. Of the 67 native Hawaiian species, 23 are extinct, 29 are endangered, and one is threatened (*'alala,* the Hawaiian crow). Two native birds that have managed to survive are the nene and the pueo.

NENE Endemic to Hawaii, the nene is Hawaii's state bird. It is being brought back from the brink of extinction through captive breeding and the implementation of strenuous protection laws. A relative of the Canada goose, the nene stands about 2 feet high and has a black head and yellow cheeks, a buff neck with deep furrows, a grayish-brown body, and clawed feet. It gets its name from its two-syllable, high nasal call: "nay-nay." Although they're not found on Oahu, the approximately 500 nenes alive today can be seen at Haleakala National Park on Maui, at Mauna Kea State Park bird sanctuary, and on the slopes of Mauna Kea on the Big Island.

PUEO The Hawaiian short-eared owl, which grows to about 12 to 17 inches, can be seen at dawn and dusk on Kauai, Maui, and the Big Island. The brown-and-white bird with a black bill goes hunting for rodents at night. Pueos are highly regarded by Hawaiians: According to legend, spotting a pueo is a good omen.

SEABIRDS On the east coast of Oahu, from Kahuku to Makapuu Point, are numerous small islands, islets, and rocks that are nesting areas for seabirds native to the region. Once part of the island of Oahu, these small land masses, some just a few hundred yards offshore, are environmentally necessary for the survival of these birds. The seabird population has suffered since the arrival of people to the Hawaiian Islands, as coastal areas have been altered for human use. Many seabirds are ground nesters, making them easy prey for non-indigenous animals like dogs, cats, rats, and mongooses. Non-indigenous plants, such as sea grape and lantana, have encroached on the nesting grounds as well.

Because of their ecological importance, the offshore islands dotting Oahu's windward coast have been made part of the Hawaii State Seabird Sanctuary. Shearwaters, noddies, and petrels are among the birds that use the protected islands for roosting and nesting, and migratory birds such as ruddy turnstones, wandering tattlers, and golden plovers forage along the shore. The islands also provide protected environments for native coastal vegetation. Because the nesting grounds are fragile environments, access to the offshore islands is limited; visitors should observe all posted signs. Many seabirds build their nests under dense vegetation or in shallow, sandy burrows that cannot be seen by unwary hikers and sight-seers. Human disturbance can cause birds to abandon their nests, leaving eggs and chicks exposed.

The seabirds found on these offshore islands include the following:

Great Frigate Bird (*'Iwa*) The Hawaiian name *iwa,* meaning "thief," refers to the frigate birds' habit of snatching food from other birds in midair. Frigate birds are superb flyers and so well adapted to life in the air that they can barely walk on land. They are often seen soaring above Waimanalo Bay on the island's windward side.

Wandering Tattler (*'Ulili*) Wandering tattlers are migrants who travel annually over 2,000 miles from Alaska to Canada to Hawaii, where they spend their winters foraging for insects and fish. They're usually solitary and can be seen hunting for food along rocky shorelines and tidal flats. Their Hawaiian name, *'ulili,* mimics their unique call.

Sooty Tern (*'Ewa'ewa*) These seabirds nest in large numbers on the offshore islands of Manana and Moku Manu. They lay single, camouflaged eggs directly on the ground, and are easily disturbed by curious humans.

Ruddy Turnstones (*'Akekeke*) These winter visitors, who fly from their Arctic nesting grounds to Hawaii in August and September, can be seen probing with their bills in search of insects and tiny crustaceans along Oahu's shorelines.

Bristle-thighed Curlew (*Kioea*) In early August, the *kioea* leave their nesting grounds in the Alaskan tundra and fly to Hawaii (as well as to other islands in the Pacific). They prefer undisturbed sandy shorelines and secluded grassy meadows.

Wedge-tailed Shearwater (*'Ua'u kani*)   The most common birds found on the offshore islands, these birds get their Hawaiian name from their eerie, drawn-out call.

Red-footed Booby (*'A*)   These large white birds are often seen flying low over the water, far out to sea, in search of fish and squid. Fishermen love to spot these birds because 'a often circle and feed directly over schools of tuna or mahi-mahi.

Red-tailed Tropicbird (*Koa'e'ula*)   Distinguished by their white plumage and long red tailfeathers, these birds nest not only on the offshore islands, but also on Oahu's cliffs.

Brown Noddy (*Nolo koha*)   These common birds nest in small colonies on the open ground and raise their single offspring on a diet of small fish and crustaceans.

Bulwer's Petrel (*'Ou*)   These birds spend most of their life at sea, returning to land—usually back to the island where they were born—only to mate. They're nocturnal feeders, spending nights hunting for small surface-water fish.

SEALIFE

Oahu has an extraordinarily unique world to explore offshore, beneath the sea. Approximately 680 species of fish are known to inhabit the underwater world around the Hawaiian islands. Of those, approximately 450 species stay close to the reef and inshore areas.

CORAL   The reefs surrounding Hawaii are made up of various coral and algae. The living coral grow through sunlight that feeds a specialized algae, called zooxanthellae, which in turn allows the development of the coral's calcareous skeleton. It takes thousands of years for reefs to develop. The reef attracts and supports fish and crustaceans, which use the reef for food, habitat, mating, and raising their young. Mother Nature can cause the destruction of the reef with a strong storm or large waves, but humans—through a seemingly unimportant act such as touching the coral or allowing surface runoff of dirt, silt, or chemicals to blanket the reef and cut off the life-giving light—have proved even more destructive to the fragile reefs.

The coral most frequently seen in Hawaii are hard, rocklike formations named for their familiar shapes: antler, cauliflower, finger, plate, and razor coral. Wire coral looks just like its name—a randomly bent wire growing straight out of the reef. Some coral appear soft, such as tube coral; it can be found in the ceilings of caves. Black coral, which resembles winter-bare trees or shrubs, is found at depths of over 100 feet.

REEF FISH   Of the approximately 450 reef fish, about 27% are native to Hawaii and found nowhere else on the planet. This may seem surprising for a string of isolated islands, 2,000 miles from the nearest land mass. But over the millions of years of gestation of the Hawaiian islands, as they were born from the erupting volcanoes, ocean currents—mainly from the Indo-Malay Pacific region—carried the larvae of thousands of marine animals and plants to Hawaii's reef. Of those, approximately 100 species not only adapted, but thrived. Some species are much bigger and more plentiful than their Pacific cousins; many developed unique characteristics. Some, like the lemon or milletseed butterfly fish, are not only particular to Hawaii but also unique within their larger, worldwide family in their specialized schooling and feeding behaviors.

Another surprising thing about Hawaii endemics is how common some of the native fish are. You can see the saddleback wrasse on practically any snorkeling excursion or dive in Hawaiian waters. Here are some of the reef fish you might encounter in the waters off Oahu:

Angel Fish Often mistaken for butterfly fish, angel fish can be distinguished by looking for the spine, located low on the gill plate. Angel fish are very shy; several species live in colonies close to coral for protection.

Blennys Small, elongated fish, blennys range from 2 to 10 inches long, with the majority in the 3-to-4-inch range. Blennys are so small that they can live in tide pools. Because of their size, you might have a hard time spotting one.

Butterfly Fish Some of the most colorful of the reef fish, butterfly fish are usually seen in pairs (scientists believe they mate for life) and appear to spend most of their day feeding. There are 22 species of butterfly fish, of which three (bluestripe, lemon or milletseed, and multiband or pebbled butterfly fish) are endemic. Most butterfly fish have a dark band through the eye and a spot near the tail resembling an eye to confuse their predators (the moray eel loves to lunch on butterfly fish).

Eels Moray and conger eels are the common eels seen in Hawaii. Morays are usually docile unless provoked or if there is food or an injured fish around. Unfortunately, some morays have been fed by divers and—being intelligent creatures—associate divers with food; thus, they can become aggressive. But most morays like to keep to themselves, hidden in a hole or crevice. Morays might look menacing, but conger eels look downright happy, with big lips and pectoral fins (situated so that they look like big ears) that give them a perpetually smiling face. Conger eels have crushing teeth so they can feed on crustaceans; in fact, because they're sloppy eaters, they usually live with shrimp and crabs, who feed off the crumbs they leave.

Parrotfish One of the largest and most colorful of the reef fish, parrotfish can grow as large as 40 inches long. Parrotfish are easy to spot—their front teeth are fused together, protruding like buck teeth and resembling a parrot's beak. These unique teeth allow the parrotfish to feed by scraping algae from rocks and coral. The rocks and coral pass through the parrotfish's system, resulting in fine sand. In fact, most of the sand found in Hawaii is parrotfish waste; one large parrotfish can produce a ton of sand a year. Hawaiian native parrotfish species include yellowbar, regal, and spectacled.

Scorpion Fish This is a family of what scientists call "ambush predators." These fish hide under camouflaged exteriors and ambush their prey when they come along. Several sport a venomous dorsal spine. These fish don't have a gas bladder, so when they stop swimming, they sink—that's why you usually find them "resting" on ledges and on the ocean's bottom. Although they are not aggressive, an inattentive snorkeler or diver could inadvertently touch one and feel the effects of those venomous spines—so be very careful where you put your hands and feet while you're in the water.

Surgeon Fish Sometimes called tang, the surgeon fish get their name from the scalpel-like spines located on each side of their bodies near the base of their tails. Some surgeon fish have a rigid spine; others have the ability to fold their spine against their body until it's needed for defense purposes. Some surgeon fish, like the brightly colored yellow tang, are boldly colored. Others are adorned in more conservative shades of gray, brown, or black. The only endemic surgeon fish—and the most abundant in Hawaiian waters—is the convict tang (*manini* in Hawaiian), a pale white fish with vertical black stripes (like a convict's uniform).

Wrasses   This is a very diverse family of fish, ranging in size from 2 to 15 inches. Several wrasses are brilliantly colored and change their colors through aging and sexual dimorphism (sex changing). Wrasses have the unique ability to change gender from female (when young) to male with maturation. There are several wrasses that are endemic to Hawaii: the Hawaiian cleaner, short-nose, belted, gray (or old woman), psychedelic, pearl, flame, and the most common Hawaiian reef fish, the saddleback.

GAME FISH   Fishers have a huge variety to choose from in the waters off Oahu, from pan-sized snapper to nearly 1-ton marlin. Hawaii is known around the globe as *the* place for big game fish—marlin, swordfish, and tuna—but its waters are also great for catching other offshore fish (like mahi-mahi, rainbow runner, and wahoo), coastal fish (barracuda, scad), bottom fish (snappers, sea bass, and amberjack), and inshore fish (trevally, bonefish, and others), as well as freshwater fish (bass, catfish, trout, bluegill, and oscar).

Billfish are caught year-round. Six different kinds are found in the offshore waters around the islands: Pacific blue marlin, black marlin, sailfish, broadbill swordfish, striped marlin, and shortbill spearfish. Hawaii billfish range in size from the 20-pound shortbill spearfish and striped marlin to an 1,805-pound Pacific blue marlin, the largest marlin ever caught on rod and reel anywhere in the world. **Tuna** ranges in size from small (a pound or less) mackerel tuna used as bait (Hawaiians call them *oioi*), to 250-pound yellowfin ahi tuna. Other species of tuna found in Hawaii are bigeye, albacore, kawakawa, and skipjack.

Some of the best eating fish are also found in offshore waters: **mahi-mahi** (also known as dolphin fish or dorado) in the 20- to 70-pound range, **rainbow runner** (*kamanu*) from 15 to 30 pounds, and **wahoo** (*ono*) from 15 to 80 pounds. Shoreline fishers are always on the lookout for **trevally** (the state record for giant trevally is 191 pounds), **bonefish, ladyfish, threadfin, leatherfish,** and **goatfish.** Bottom fishermen pursue a range of **snappers**—red, pink, gray, and others—as well as **sea bass** (the state record is a whopping 563 pounds) and **amberjack,** which weigh up to 100 pounds.

Reservoirs on Oahu are home to Hawaii's many freshwater fish: **bass** (large, smallmouth, and peacock), **catfish** (channel and Chinese), **rainbow trout, bluegill sunfish, pungee,** and **oscar.** The state record for freshwater fish is the 43-pound, 13-ounce channel catfish caught in Oahu's Lake Wilson.

WHALES   Humpbacks   The most popular visitors to Hawaii come every year in the winter, around November, and stay until the springtime (April or so) when they return to their summer home in Alaska. Humpback whales—some as big as a city bus and weighing many tons—migrate to the warm, protected Hawaiian waters in the winter to mate and calve. You can take whale-watching cruises that let you observe these magnificent leviathans close up on every island, or you can spot their signature spouts of water from shore as they expel water in the distance. Humpbacks grow up to 45 feet long, so when they breach (propel their entire body out of the water) or even wave a fluke, you can see it for miles.

Other Whales   Humpbacks are among the biggest whales found in Hawaiian waters, but other whales—like pilot, sperm, false killer, melon-headed, pygmy killer, and beaked whales—can be seen year-round. These whales usually travel in pods of 20 to 40 animals and are very social, interacting with each other on the surface.

The Green Flash

The Green Flash is a common sight in Hawaii at sunset (and, no, we don't mean you have to drink a couple of mai tais to see it). As the last sliver of sun sinks into the ocean, the atmosphere works like a prism and bends the last rays of light, scattering the blue end of the spectrum, so just for a second you see an emerald green "flash." If you're up early enough, and looking out over the ocean, you can see the flash at sunrise, too.

SHARKS   Yes, Virginia, there are sharks in Hawaii. But chances are you won't see a shark unless you specifically go looking for one. The ancient Hawaiians had great respect for sharks and believed that some sharks were reincarnated relatives who had returned to assist them.

About 40 different species of shark inhabit the waters surrounding Hawaii; they range from the totally harmless whale shark—at 60 feet, the world's largest fish—that has no teeth and is so docile that it frequently lets divers ride on its back, to the not-so-docile, infamous—and extremely uncommon—great white shark. The most common sharks seen in Hawaii are white-tip reef sharks, gray reef sharks (about 5 feet long), and blacktip reef sharks (about 6 feet long). Since records have been kept, starting in 1779, there have been only about 100 shark attacks in Hawaii, of which 40% have been fatal. The largest number of attacks has occurred after someone fell into the ocean from the shore or from a boat. In these cases, the sharks probably attacked after the person was dead.

General rules for avoiding sharks are: Don't swim at sunrise, sunset, or where the water is murky because of stream runoff—sharks might mistake you for one of their usual meals. And don't swim where there are bloody fish in the water (sharks become aggressive around blood).

OAHU'S ECOSYSTEM PROBLEMS

Oahu may be paradise, but even paradise has its problems. The biggest threat Oahu's natural environment faces is human intrusion—simply put, too many people want to experience paradise firsthand. From the magnificent underwater world to the breathtaking rainforest, the presence of people isn't always benign, no matter how cautious or environmentally aware they might be.

MARINE LIFE   Hawaii's beautiful and abundant marine life has attracted so many visitors that they threaten to overwhelm it. A great example of this over-enthusiasm is Oahu's Hanauma Bay, a marine preserve. Thousands of people flock to this beautiful bay, which features calm, protected waters for swimming and snorkeling areas loaded with tropical reef fish. An overabundance of visitors forced government officials to limit the number of people entering the bay at any one time. Commercial tour operators have been restricted entirely in an effort to balance the people-to-fish ratio.

People who fall in love with the colorful tropical fish and want to take live memories back home with them are also thought to be affecting the health of Hawaii's reefs. The growth in home, office, and decorative aquariums has risen dramatically in the past 20 years. As a result, more and more reef fish collectors are taking a growing number of reef fish from Hawaiian waters.

The reefs surrounding the islands have faced increasing ecological problems over the years. Runoff of soil and chemicals from construction, agriculture, erosion, and even heavy storms can blanket and choke a reef, which needs sunlight to survive. In addition, the intrusion of foreign elements—like breaks in sewage lines—can cause problems for Hawaii's reefs. Human contact with the reef can upset the ecosystem, too. Coral, the basis of the reef system, is very fragile; snorkelers and divers grabbing onto coral can break off pieces that have taken decades to form. Feeding fish can upset the balance of the ecosystem (not to mention upsetting the digestive system of the fish). One glass-bottomed–boat operator on the Big Island reported that they fed an eel for years, considering it their "pet" eel. One day the eel decided that he wanted more than just the food being offered and bit the diver's fingers. Divers and snorkelers report that in areas where the fish are routinely fed, the fish have become more aggressive; schools of certain reef fish—normally shy—surround divers, demanding to be fed.

FLORA   One of Hawaii's most fragile environments is the rainforest. Any intrusion—from hikers carrying seeds on their shoes to the rooting of wild boars—can upset the delicate balance in these complete ecosystems. In recent years, development has moved closer and closer to the rainforest.

FAUNA   The biggest impact on the fauna in Hawaii is the decimation of native birds by feral animals, which have destroyed the birds' habitats, and by mongooses that have eaten the birds' eggs and young. Government officials are vigilant about snakes because of the potential damage tree snakes can do to the remaining birdlife.

VOG   When the trade winds stop blowing for a few days, Oahu feels the effects of the volcanic haze—caused by gases released by the continuous eruption of the volcano on the flank of Kilauea, on the Big Island, and the smoke from the fires set by the flowing lava—that has been dubbed "vog." The hazy air, which looks like smog from urban pollution, limits viewing from scenic vistas and wreaks havoc on photographers trying to get clear panoramic photographs. Some people claim that the vog has even caused bronchial ailments.

CULTURE   Almost since the arrival of the first Europeans, there has been a controversy over balancing the preservation of history and indigenous cultures and lifestyles with economic development. The question of what should be preserved—and in what fashion—is continually debated in Hawaii's rapidly growing economy. Some factions argue that the continuously developing tourism industry will one day destroy the very thing that visitors come to Hawaii to see; another sector argues that Hawaii's cost of living is so high that new development and industries are needed so residents can earn a living.

Index

See also separate Accommodations and Restaurant indexes, below.

ACCOMMODATIONS

Restaurant Index

FROMMER'S® DOLLAR-A-DAY GUIDES

Australia from $50 a Day
California from $60 a Day
Caribbean from $70 a Day
England from $70 a Day
Europe from $60 a Day
Florida from $60 a Day

Hawaii from $70 a Day
Ireland from $50 a Day
Israel from $45 a Day
Italy from $70 a Day
London from $85 a Day
New York from $80 a Day

New Zealand from $50 a Day
Paris from $85 a Day
San Francisco from $60 a Day
Washington, D.C.,
   from $60 a Day

FROMMER'S® PORTABLE GUIDES

Acapulco, Ixtapa &
   Zihuatanejo
Alaska Cruises & Ports of Call
Bahamas
Baja & Los Cabos
Berlin
California Wine Country
Charleston & Savannah
Chicago

Dublin
Hawaii: The Big Island
Las Vegas
London
Maine Coast
Maui
New Orleans
New York City
Paris

Puerto Vallarta, Manzanillo
   & Guadalajara
San Diego
San Francisco
Sydney
Tampa & St. Petersburg
Venice
Washington, D.C.

FROMMER'S® NATIONAL PARK GUIDES

Family Vacations in the
   National Parks
Grand Canyon

National Parks of the
   American West
Rocky Mountain

Yellowstone & Grand Teton
Yosemite & Sequoia/
   Kings Canyon
Zion & Bryce Canyon

FROMMER'S® GREAT OUTDOOR GUIDES

New England
Northern California

Southern California & Baja
Washington & Oregon

FROMMER'S® MEMORABLE WALKS

Chicago
London

New York
Paris

San Francisco
Washington D.C.

FROMMER'S® IRREVERENT GUIDES

Amsterdam
Boston
Chicago
Las Vegas

London
Los Angeles
Manhattan

New Orleans
Paris
San Francisco

Seattle & Portland
Vancouver
Walt Disney World
Washington, D.C.

FROMMER'S® BEST-LOVED DRIVING TOURS

America
Britain
California

Florida
France
Germany

Ireland
Italy
New England

Scotland
Spain
Western Europe

THE UNOFFICIAL GUIDES®

Bed & Breakfast in
New England
Bed & Breakfast in
the Northwest
Beyond Disney
Branson, Missouri
California with Kids
Chicago

Cruises
Disneyland
Florida with Kids
The Great Smoky &
Blue Ridge
Mountains
Inside Disney
Las Vegas

London
Miami & the Keys
Mini Las Vegas
Mini-Mickey
New Orleans
New York City
Paris
San Francisco

Skiing in the West
Walt Disney World
Walt Disney World
for Grown-ups
Walt Disney World
for Kids
Washington, D.C.

SPECIAL-INTEREST TITLES

Born to Shop: France
Born to Shop: Hong Kong
Born to Shop: Italy
Born to Shop: New York
Born to Shop: Paris
Frommer's Britain's Best Bike Rides
The Civil War Trust's Official Guide
to the Civil War Discovery Trail
Frommer's Caribbean Hideaways
Frommer's Europe's Greatest Driving Tours
Frommer's Food Lover's Companion to France
Frommer's Food Lover's Companion to Italy
Frommer's Gay & Lesbian Europe
Israel Past & Present
Monks' Guide to California

Monks' Guide to New York City
The Moon
New York City with Kids
Unforgettable Weekends
Outside Magazine's Guide
to Family Vacations
Places Rated Almanac
Retirement Places Rated
Road Atlas Britain
Road Atlas Europe
Washington, D.C., with Kids
Wonderful Weekends from Boston
Wonderful Weekends from New York City
Wonderful Weekends from San Francisco
Wonderful Weekends from Los Angeles

WHEREVER YOU TRAVEL, *H*ELP IS NEVER FAR AWAY.

From planning your trip to providing travel assistance along the way, American Express® Travel Service Offices are always there to help you do more.

Honolulu, Waikiki & Oahu

American Express Travel Service
Commerce Tower, Ste. 104
1440 Kapiolani Blvd.
(808) 946-7741

American Express Travel Service
Hilton Hawaiian Village
Tapa Tower, 2005 Kalia Rd.
(808) 951-0644

American Express Travel Service
Hyatt Regency Waikiki
2424 Kalakaua Ave.
(808) 926-5441

Travel

www.americanexpress.com/travel

American Express Travel Service Offices
are located throughout the United States.
For the office nearest you, call 1-800-AXP-3429.